BECOMING CATHOLIC

BECOMING
CATHOLIC

FINDING ROME IN THE AMERICAN
RELIGIOUS LANDSCAPE

DAVID YAMANE

OXFORD
UNIVERSITY PRESS

OXFORD
UNIVERSITY PRESS

Oxford University Press is a department of the University of Oxford.
It furthers the University's objective of excellence in research, scholarship,
and education by publishing worldwide.

Oxford   New York

Auckland   Cape Town   Dar es Salaam   Hong Kong   Karachi
Kuala Lumpur   Madrid   Melbourne   Mexico City   Nairobi
New Delhi   Shanghai   Taipei   Toronto

With offices in

Argentina   Austria   Brazil   Chile   Czech Republic   France   Greece
Guatemala   Hungary   Italy   Japan   Poland   Portugal   Singapore
South Korea   Switzerland   Thailand   Turkey   Ukraine   Vietnam

Oxford is a registered trade mark of Oxford University Press
in the UK and certain other countries.

Published in the United States of America by
Oxford University Press
198 Madison Avenue, New York, NY 10016

© Oxford University Press 2014

Library of Congress Cataloging-in-Publication Data
Yamane, David.
Becoming Catholic : finding Rome in the American religious
landscape / David A. Yamane.
    p.   cm.
Includes bibliographical references and index.
ISBN 978-0-19-996498-7 (hardcover : alk. paper) — ISBN 978-0-19-996499-4
(ebook) — ISBN 978-0-19-936470-1 (ebook) 1. Catholic Church—United States.
2. Catholic converts—United States. 3. Initiation rites—Religious aspects—Catholic
Church. I. Title.
BX1406.3.Y36 2014
282'.73—dc23

2013031205

1   3   5   7   9   8   6   4   2

Printed in the United States of America on acid-free paper

CONTENTS

ACKNOWLEDGMENTS

My fellow sociologist Jerome Baggett compared his excellent recent book on American Catholics to that of "the art lover who earnestly tries to describe a beautiful painting to a friend." He explains, "I know that this book on American Catholicism does not capture its totality," because it of necessity represents "a limited range of vision presented through a finite set of analytical categories."[1] As I was completing this book, Baggett's words were humbling: "limited range of vision . . . finite set of analytical categories." In working on this research project for over a decade, I have been staking a claim—and dedicating a significant portion of my life—to both the importance of the subject and the significance of this particular analysis. And it is true that *Becoming Catholic* is the only book-length sociological analysis of the Rite of Christian Initiation of Adults (RCIA), a process that has brought over two million people into the Catholic church over the past 25 years and has become a model of initiation in other Christian traditions. I want to go further and call it a *comprehensive* study, but Baggett's words will not allow me. Poring over the thousand pages of field notes, the hundreds of pages of interview transcripts, and the mountain of survey responses that constitute the empirical basis of this book, I realize that I have collected enough data for several books on the RCIA process. This is a humbling realization. But Baggett's words were also liberating. They helped me see that I do not have to tell the complete story of "the RCIA." This is one story, and I wish I had time to write others. I hope this book will inspire the telling of other stories of initiation in the Catholic church and other religious traditions. There is much more to tell.

As long as I have been working on this project, I have been incurring debts. Small grants from the Society for the Scientific Study of Religion, the Religious Research Association, and the University of Notre Dame's Institute for Scholarship in the Liberal Arts allowed me to conduct surveys of and interviews with individuals going through the RCIA process, as well as those responsible for leading RCIA processes, in the Diocese of Fort Wayne–South Bend, Indiana. In this part of the data collection, which took place from 2000 to 2002, I was greatly assisted by a number of Notre Dame students who served as interviewers and transcriptionists, data entry clerks, and library researchers: Greg Boughton, Zach Decker, Sharon Dowdell, Ashley Heinz, Salvadora Hernandez, Jamie McClintock, Sarah MacMillen, Kirk Miller, Jeremy Montemarano, and Rachel Turk. I apologize to any student I have left out.

These initial efforts led to a larger grant from the Louisville Institute for the Study of American Religion for yearlong ethnographies of six parishes in 2001–2002. I am grateful to the Louisville Institute, and especially to its recently retired Executive Director James Lewis, for entrusting this grant to me. The grant allowed me to hire Kelly Culver as part of my research team. It also supplemented support from the University of Notre Dame, which paid for sociology graduate student Sarah MacMillen to serve as my research assistant and allowed me to take a leave from teaching. Together, Sarah, Kelly, and I formed an ethnography team, each of us observing two of the six parishes for nearly a year. During that time, we met almost weekly to exchange and discuss our field notes, observations, ideas, and the challenges we faced as ethnographers. Although I was their supervisor, the effort was collaborative. The fruits of this collaboration can be seen in a pastoral/theological book we co-authored based on our fieldwork, *Real Stories of Christian Initiation: Lessons for and from the RCIA* (Collegeville, MN: Liturgical Press, 2006).

Becoming Catholic is a sociological companion to the more descriptive and practical *Real Stories*. The two books share some of the same data, but the empirical base and concepts employed in this book are much broader. Still, my debts to Sarah and Kelly are evident throughout this work, so much so that I often found it more natural to write "we" than "I." Because I am the sole author named on this book, I do end up writing "I" most of the time, but I can truly say that I could not have written this book without their earlier efforts. I note in the introductory chapter, but it bears repeating, that all accounts of events taking place at "St. Innocent" and "St. John Bosco" are based on observations made by Sarah MacMillen, which I have taken from her field notes and partially rewritten. Kelly Culver made and recorded the observations at "Queen of Peace" and "St. Peter's," and the same caveat applies. I conducted the fieldwork at "St. Mark's" and "St. Mary's." (Quotation marks denote that these are pseudonyms.) Neither Sarah nor Kelly has read any part of this book in advance of its publication, so I bear complete responsibility for any shortcomings related to the analysis of the fieldwork data.

After moving from Notre Dame to Wake Forest University in 2005, I received a university-supported research leave, which helped me to keep alive the hope of completing this book. The encouragement of my colleague Robin Simon and the support of sociology department administrator Joan Habib also kept me on track. I am also very grateful to Theo Calderara of Oxford University Press who for many years e-mailed me annually to ask how my project was going. Like a spring rain that is both bracing and rejuvenating, his continuing interest in this project kept me motivated and moving forward.

This book would not be possible without the aforementioned data—surveys, interviews, and fieldwork. Thanks are due to all those willing to have their lives subjected to scrutiny for the sake of scholarship. I commend especially those who completed surveys with questions that probably seemed odd and response categories that often did not fit their realities, and those interviewees who were asked difficult questions they could not easily answer. In the fieldwork parishes, everyone involved—the clerical and lay pastoral staffs, volunteer catechists and sponsors, and the individuals going through the process—graciously opened themselves up to us with no expectation that they would receive anything in return other than our sociological gaze. Although they expected (and received) no compensation, I hope that I repay their generosity in part by accurately conveying their beliefs, practices, and experiences.

The great sociologist of religion Robert Bellah passed away in the summer of 2013. Although I took just one class with him, as an undergraduate at UC–Berkeley in 1989, those who know his work well will see his intellectual influence throughout this book. But more fundamentally, I would not have even become a sociologist of religion if I had not studied with this master a quarter century ago. That small opportunity continues to be a blessing.

The critical input I received from the OUP reviewers helped me to clarify my purpose and tighten my focus from prospectus to final manuscript. Charlotte Steinhardt, assistant editor for religion at OUP and Michelle Dellinger, senior project manager at Integra, were similarly helpful in turning my manuscript into a published book. Thanks also to Dorothy Bauhoff, who meticulously copyedited the final manuscript.

In the end, I surely would not have finished this book without my writing accountability partner and fellow Wake Forest professor, Lynn Neal, and my love and light, Sandy Stroud. Words cannot express my heartfelt gratitude to these two cherished friends.

NOTES ON TERMINOLOGY
AND SOURCES

Ordo is short for *Ordo Initiationis Christianae Adultorum*, the Latin text (*editio typica*) promulgated in 1972 and translated into the English (vernacular typical edition) as *Rite of Christian Initiation of Adults*. The translation of the title is somewhat confusing because the *Ordo* is actually a *collection of liturgical rites* that together constitute the *order* of initiation. I, therefore, sometimes use the term *Ordo* to refer to the RCIA process as a whole as distinct from the various specific rites (e.g., Rite of Acceptance, Rite of Election).

Catechumenate originally referred to the extended period of instruction that individuals (called "catechumens," that is, "hearers of the word") entered into as preparation for baptism in the church in the fourth and fifth centuries. Since the promulgation of the new *Ordo*, "catechumenate" specifically refers to the second major period of the adult initiation process (see Table 1.1 in Chapter 1).

***Rite of Christian Initiation of Adults,* or *RCIA* (in italics),** refers to the officially approved English translation (the vernacular typical edition) of *Ordo Initiationis Christianae Adultorum*. This ritual text was mandated for use in the United States by the National Conference of Catholic Bishops from September 1, 1988, forward. It also contains material not included in the Latin typical edition, such as combined rites for situations in which both unbaptized and baptized individuals are present (Appendix I) and the *National Statutes for the Catechumenate* (Appendix III).

Rite of Christian Initiation of Adults, or RCIA (not italicized), refers to any process of adult initiation that attempts to follow to some degree the steps and stages given in the ritual text. Some organizations, like the National Pastoral Life Center, discourage the use of the acronym because they believe it conveys a sense of the RCIA as a "program" rather than a process. I do not share that fear and find repeated use of alternatives like "the adult initiation process" linguistically cumbersome, though I do use that phrase occasionally for the sake of variety.

National Statutes **(abbreviated as *NS*)** refers to the *National Statutes for the Catechumenate*, approved by the United States bishops on November 11, 1986, and confirmed by the Vatican Congregation for Divine Worship on June 26, 1988. Published as Appendix III to the *Rite of Christian Initiation of Adults*, they have the status of a complementary norm in accord with Canon 788§3 of the Code of Canon Law on the catechumenate. The *National Statutes* govern the adult initiation process in the United States.

Normative vision of the RCIA process refers to the Catholic church's officially sanctioned understanding of the structure and purpose of the RCIA process as reflected in the ritual text (*Rite of Christian Initiation of Adults*) and the United States bishops' *National Statutes for the Catechumenate*. I do not assume that this is the correct vision or that this vision is mechanically reproduced in every parish. In fact, this sociological study of the RCIA highlights the many variations in the implementation of this normative vision.

BECOMING CATHOLIC

INTRODUCTION: BECOMING CATHOLIC IN AMERICA

Travels with Charley in Search of America recounts an epic 10,000-mile road trip that John Steinbeck took in 1960 from Sag Harbor, New York, to the West Coast and back in his truck, Rocinante. Early in his travelogue, Steinbeck tells of an encounter with a liquor store salesman in Connecticut from whom he has just purchased "bourbon, scotch, gin, vermouth, vodka, a medium good brandy, aged applejack, and a case of beer." Steinbeck's conversation with the "young-old man" went like this:

> "Must be quite a party."
> "No—it's just traveling supplies."
> He helped me to carry the cartons out and I opened Rocinante's door.
> "You going in that?"
> "Sure"
> "Where?"
> "All over."
> And then I saw what I was to see so many times on the journey—a look of longing. "Lord! I wish I could go."
> "Don't you like it here?"
> "Sure. It's all right, but I wish I could go."
> "You don't even know where I'm going."
> "I don't care. I'd like to go anywhere."[1]

It is perhaps not surprising that a land peopled by nomadic native tribes, global explorers, pilgrims, and refugees is restless in its very spirit. Indeed, some argue that restlessness is definitive of American character, that Americans "live now (and always have) in the future tense," rather than dwelling in the past.[2] The centrifugal forces that produce this restlessness cannot help but affect religious life in America.

The formal disestablishment of religion in the First Amendment to the Constitution of the United States encoded openness to religious diversity into the DNA of the country. That openness allowed for—and perhaps even promoted—considerable religious vigor in the early decades of the new republic, including revivalism and the birth of new, distinctively American religions like Mormonism. Still, American *culture* remained steadfastly Protestant during this time. It was not for another century that cultural disestablishment of American (Protestant) religion took place, aided in particular by internal divisions between fundamentalists and modernists within Protestantism and by waves of Catholic immigrants who challenged Protestant hegemony in politics, education, and elsewhere. Sociologist Phillip Hammond calls this the "second disestablishment" of American religion. It resulted in a moderate pluralism in mid-twentieth century America that allowed Protestants, Catholics, and Jews to be seen as equal contributors to the "American Way of Life."[3]

In the decades following World War II, the moderate denominational pluralism of *Protestant-Catholic-Jew* would give way to the seemingly unlimited diversity of religious options in present-day America. Religion as a source of social integration and collective identity gave way to a more individualized approach to faith, which centered on *personal autonomy*, "meaning both an enlarged arena of voluntary choice and an enhanced freedom from structural restraint." This "third disestablishment" of American religion is driven by structural and cultural changes in American society. Increasing geographic mobility (especially suburbanization), social mobility (driven by rapidly expanding higher education), and familial mobility (rising rates of divorce and blended families) all loosen the connection between place, family, and inherited faith.[4]

Alongside and related to these structural changes was a profound cultural change that significantly increased the centrality of individualism and individual choice. According to Robert Bellah, in earlier times, religious life was a "one possibility thing"; in modern society, it becomes an "infinite possibility thing." Bellah and his co-authors in *Habits of the Heart* present an exemplar of the final disestablishment of American religion in the person of Sheila Larson. "I believe in God. I'm not a religious fanatic. I can't remember the last time I went to church. My faith has carried me a long way. It's Sheilaism. Just my own little voice." Recognizing the voice of religious individualism in a highly transient society, the authors conclude that "'Sheilaism' somehow seems a perfectly natural expression of current American religious life."[5]

This shift from *ascribed* (inherited) to *achieved* (chosen) religious identity highlights the connection between the religious sphere and developments taking place in modern society generally. Modernity creates a situation of unprecedented choice. Indeed, according to Peter Berger, modernity universalizes *heresy* (choice) by creating "a new situation in which picking and choosing becomes an imperative."[6] Not only is religious identity increasingly chosen, but so are family, ethnic, and other identities. In societies based on tradition, individuals have relatively clearly defined roles; in societies in which modernity has taken root, individuals must establish their roles for themselves. "Modernity," writes Anthony Giddens, "is essentially a post-traditional order. The transformation of time and space, coupled with the disembedding mechanisms, propel social life away from the hold of preestablished precepts or practices." Or, as Karl Marx put it, somewhat more poetically, "All fixed, fast-frozen relationships, with their train of ancient and venerable prejudices and opinions, are swept away, all new-formed ones become antiquated before they can ossify. All that is solid melts into air." This sense of "change [as] a constant of modern life," of nomadically exploring new worlds, of wanting to go somewhere, *anywhere*, is central to the experience of modernity for many people.[7]

Tradition in Modernity

Although Jasper claims that religion does not succeed at "calming the inner restlessness of American[s],"[8] I argue that the centrifugal forces in American society do produce counterbalancing centripetal *desires*—a search for some grounding, continuity, stability—at root, a desire to be home. Steinbeck's *Travels with Charley* again provides a telling commentary. Having traveled from his home in New York up to Maine, across the country to Washington State, down the West Coast, through the Southwest and across Texas to New Orleans, Steinbeck directed Rocinante back north, toward New York. Toward the end, he writes:

> My own journey started long before I left, and was over before I returned. I know exactly where and when it was over. Near Abingdon, in the dog-leg of Virginia, at four o'clock of a windy afternoon, without warning or good-by or kiss my foot, my journey went away and left me stranded far from home. . . . The road became an endless stone ribbon, the hills obstructions, the trees green blurs, the people simply moving figures with heads but no faces. . . . After Abingdon—nothing. The way was a gray, timeless, eventless tunnel, but at the end of it was the one shining reality—my own wife, my own house in my own street, my own bed. It was all there, and I lumbered my way toward it.[9]

I do not—indeed, cannot—deny the profound dislocations and fragmentation created by modernity. Still, it seems premature to declare, as sociologist Wade Clark Roof did at the end of the twentieth century, that when it comes to American religion "Whirl is King."[10] Americans do have to deal with the centrifugal forces of modern society, but they still frequently do so by looking to religious traditions to provide some stability in the face of constant change.[11]

At the same time that Americans have nearly unlimited discretion to choose and an unprecedented number of options from which to choose, they frequently opt for *convention*. Indeed, Roof himself finds that 59% of American baby boomers are "born-again Christians" or "mainstream believers" and only 14% are "metaphysical believers" or "spiritual seekers." More recently, Christian Smith's studies of American youth reveal that "the vast majority of American teenagers are *exceedingly conventional* in their religious identities and practices. Very few are restless, alienated, or rebellious; rather, the majority of teenagers seems basically content to follow the faith of their families with little questioning."[12]

The persistence of tradition in modern society has become an important object of inquiry among scholars of American religion. It contrasts sharply with early interpretations of the emerging modern social order, which held that the "acids of modernity" were destructive of traditional religion, especially the supernatural beliefs that undergird it.[13] As one astute observer puts it, recalling Marx, "One wonders whether all things traditional truly melt into air" in modern society. Particularly in the United States, tradition survives. Of course, this does not mean that Giddens is wrong in characterizing modernity as post-traditional; modern social institutions in fact do not operate on the basis of traditional norms.[14] So, the question now is: How is tradition brought into modernity and transformed by modern social forces, including the centrifugal forces embodied in the triple disestablishment of religion, as well as the centripetal forces that arise in response?

Becoming Catholic approaches this broad question through an examination of the process by which individuals become Catholic in a late-modern society: the Rite of Christian Initiation of Adults (RCIA). In focusing attention on the parishes that implement this process of adult initiation and the individuals who go through it, the story of the RCIA provides a window onto the Catholic tradition as it is carried by these individuals and organizations through the flux of modernity. As Jerome Baggett has observed in his book *Sense of the Faithful*—about how American Catholics *live* their faith—Catholicism is not simply transmitted mechanically from the Vatican to dioceses to parishes to individuals, but is actively produced and negotiated in parishes and by individuals.[15]

Vatican II, Catholic Revolution, and the RCIA

As one of the most central institutions in the history of the West, the Roman Catholic church has not been immune to the developments that we call modernity. The most significant set of changes in the recent history of the church, those introduced by the Second Vatican Council (1962–1965), are seen by most observers as an accommodation to the forces of modernization.[16] Vatican II marked an unprecedented openness to modernity, and the changes it introduced have been nothing short of revolutionary. In promoting the opening up of the church to the world and its internal updating (a process captured by the Italian term *aggiornamento*), "the Council fathers had gleefully poured new wine into old wineskins and the wineskins had burst."[17]

Three Council documents were particularly crucial to establishing a new understanding of the Roman Catholic church itself and its role in the modern world. *Dignitatis Humanae* (the Declaration on Religious Freedom) recognized the fundamental human right to freedom of conscience and, in doing so, accepted the disestablishment of religion and the separation of church and state. *Gaudium et Spes* (the Pastoral Constitution on the Church in the Modern World) accepted the legitimacy of the modern secular state and advocated participation in and critical dialogue with it.[18] And *Lumen Gentium* (the Dogmatic Constitution on the Church), while not ignoring the church hierarchy, promoted a radically new vision of the church as the "People of God," assisted by the ordained priesthood in realizing the "universal call to holiness." The promulgation of these documents during the Council created a moment of effervescence that led to profound changes in the church and whose effects continue to be felt today.[19]

As significant as these changes are, the revolution that has most directly affected the average Catholic in the pews has been liturgical—in the style and substance of worship.[20] Because initiation in the Catholic church is sacramental—involving the sacraments of baptism, confirmation, and Eucharist—it also falls under the umbrella of liturgy. Thus, among the liturgical changes called for in the Second Vatican

Council document *Sacrosanctum Concilium* (the Constitution on the Sacred Liturgy, discussed further in Chapter 1) was a new book of rites for adult initiation. This mandate was fulfilled in 1972 when the Latin *editio typica*—typical edition, the official source text—of the *Ordo Initiationis Christianae Adultorum* was published. This new "order of initiation" was introduced into the Catholic church in the United States with a provisional English translation made available in 1974. It was not until 1988, however, that the National Conference of Catholic Bishops published the official American English translation (the vernacular typical edition) of the *Rite of Christian Initiation of Adults* and issued *National Statutes for the Catechumenate*, establishing norms for and mandating the use of the new process. Although it is not yet fully implemented in every parish, the Rite of Christian Initiation of Adults is the officially recognized process by which adults "become Catholic" in America today.[21]

Since 1988, well over two million individuals in the United States have entered the church through the RCIA process. The *Official Catholic Directory* reports that, on average over the past ten years, 67,298 adults annually have been baptized Catholic and 83,050 baptized Christians annually have been "Received into Full Communion" with the Roman Catholic church in the United States. These 150,000-plus people becoming Catholic *annually* over the past decade in themselves would compose one of the 50 largest religious bodies in America. Catholic converts collectively are 11% of all Catholics today, and 2.6% of the entire adult population in the United States; together, these 5.85 million individuals are the fifth largest religious body in America, just behind the Mormon church and ahead of the Evangelical Lutheran Church in America.[22] A group this large clearly warrants attention.

But the importance of understanding conversion to Roman Catholicism today is not merely numerical. This book is not just about the individuals who are becoming Catholic, but about the process they go through. The process of initiating new members, as theologian Aidan Kavanagh has written, "defines simultaneously both the Christian and the Church, and the definition is unsubordinated to any other except the gospel itself."[23] Thus, the implementation of the RCIA has the potential to tell us a great deal about both American Catholics and American Catholicism today. It also requires us to recover for the sociological study of religion the concept of *initiation* and allows us to understand how initiation works in modern (Western, industrial) society.

BRINGING INITIATION BACK IN

One place where we can see clearly the dynamics of tradition and modernity is in the area of initiation. In his 1956 Haskell Lectures on the History of Religions at the University of Chicago, Mircea Eliade commented, "It has often been said that one of the characteristics of the modern world is the disappearance of any meaningful rites of initiation."[24] The qualifier *meaningful* in Eliade's statement is significant, because something as fundamental to human societies across cultures and over time as rites of initiation does not simply melt into air, modernity notwithstanding. Thus, Ronald Grimes highlights a unique and contradictory aspect of Western industrialized societies, one perhaps implied by Eliade: "Initiation goes on all the time," but we lack "explicit or compelling initiation ceremonies." The centrifugal forces of modernity have rendered the initiation that does take place in Western industrial societies more diffuse, haphazard, individualized, and even sometimes only imaginary. In the face of this, some communities are attempting to create or re-create rites of passage that are mindful and intentional. As Grimes observes, "the past two decades have witnessed a resurgence of interest in the construction of rites of passage."[25]

There was no study of rites of passage per se prior to the publication in 1909 of the foundational work *Les Rites de Passage* by ethnographer and folklorist Arnold van Gennep.[26] Van Gennep observed that changes in status—existential or social—are part and parcel of the human experience. Birth, puberty, marriage, childbirth, and death are experienced and commemorated (to varying degrees) in virtually all human societies. These transitions are accomplished through rites of passage that carry individuals into new statuses or states of being such as life, adolescence, adulthood, parenthood, and the afterlife. When a rite of passage marks an entry into membership in a group, the specific focus is on initiation rites. Whether considering broader life course passages or more focused group initiations, van Gennep sees these transitions not as binary—from old to new, outsider to insider—but as entailing three phases. The main dynamics of rites of passage, in terms of their order and content, are *separation*, *transition*, and *incorporation*.

The first phase in this process is formal separation from the group. Most examples of separation are geographic or physical. Van Gennep gives the example of the novice seeking to become a *peai* among the Caribs (Amerindians of the Lesser Antilles after whom the Caribbean was named), who must leave to live with an elder for a period of many years. According to anthropologist Victor Turner, as part of the installation rites of the Kanongesha (chieftain) of the Ndembu tribe of Zambia, a small "death" shelter is built out of leaves a mile away from the village, in which the chief-to-be must reside for a period, physically separated from the rest of the tribe. Similarly, in the Lakota vision quest rite of passage from boyhood to manhood, the 16-year-old is put "in a vision pit" for four days.

Separation creates a transitional phase, during which individuals are without status, on the margins, boundary, or threshold of the group. Here Turner builds on van Gennep with his famous concept of "liminality"—an intermediate ritual stage "betwixt and between" different states of being or social statuses.[27] This is a period of learning, cleansing, testing, trial, and so on. For example, Carib *peais* "seclude themselves in a hut, where they whip the novice and make him dance till he falls faint; he is 'bled' by black ants and made to 'go mad' by being forced to drink tobacco juice," among other trials. In Turner's study of Ndembu chieftain initiation rites, the chief-to-be, having been separated to his "death" shelter, is portrayed as a slave, reviled and made fun of by his people. In the Lakota vision pit, the statusless individual goes "without food or water for four days and nights."

The third and final phase in van Gennep's model is incorporation—literally being made part of the body (*corpus*) of the group. The individual takes on a new status and is entitled and empowered to act in ways that accord with the new state of being in the group. For example, having been exhausted to the point of sleep, the Carib novice "awakens and revives as a *peai*." From the trial of the death shelter, the Ndembu chief-to-be rejoins his tribe, eats with his people, and is granted his chieftainship. Emerging from the vision pit, Lame Deer reflects, "When it was all over, I would no longer be a boy, but a man. I would have my vision. I would be given a man's name."[28]

These examples of initiation rites will be foreign to the direct experience of most readers of this book. Although individuals in modern societies may be fascinated by the "fantastic, elaborate masks, costumes, or other body decoration" described by van Gennep, Turner, and others, most are also thankful that they personally "do not have to endure tooth filing, circumcision, subincision, cicatrization, tattooing, and the like" as part of communal initiation ceremonies.[29] Indeed, because the clearest examples of van Gennep's model come from small-scale, often non-Western, societies, the question of its applicability to modern, Western, industrial societies is raised. The complex, fragmentary, individualized character of these societies is a challenging context within which to practice sustained, rigorous, communal rites of passage.

A contemporary exception that proves this rule is initiation into the United States Marine Corps (USMC), which follows van Gennep's tripartite model of rites of passage very closely. *Separation:* Marie Corps recruits are geographically isolated from their friends, family, and community by being taken to the USMC Recruit Depot on Parris Island or in San Diego. Upon arrival, they are immediately stripped of status indictors such as their hair, clothing, and name. *Transition:*

Over the course of their training, they are subjected to intensive and extensive physical and psychological challenges, intended to "break them down" so that they can later be built back up to be proper Marines. This includes a 54-hour final test called "the Crucible." *Incorporation:* The recruit who successfully completes the Crucible participates in the "Eagle, Globe and Anchor Ceremony," in which these elements of the USMC emblem are given to signify that the individual is incorporated—part of the Corps, an always faithful (*Semper Fidelis*) and proud "Marine."[30]

It is telling that the clearest example of a contemporary initiation rite comes from what Erving Goffman called a "total institution." Such an institution allows those in charge to physically isolate individuals and control their everyday lives in ways that modern, voluntary institutions cannot.[31] How then are we to understand the utility of van Gennep's model to our study of contemporary rites of initiation in an ever more voluntary institution like the Catholic church in America? I argue that we should treat the model as what Max Weber called an "ideal type." Understood as ideal types, conceptual schemas are not mirrors of reality, but are analytical constructs that reduce the complexity of social realities by accentuating certain common elements of a phenomenon.[32] Although he did not use the language of ideal types, van Gennep himself recognized that his basic three-stage model was a simplification, and that if applied too bluntly could easily lead to oversimplification. He observed that the category of "rites of passage" could be further subdivided into rites of separation, transition rites, and rites of incorporation. "These three subcategories are not developed to the same extent by all peoples or in every ceremonial pattern." Some ceremonies will place a greater emphasis on separation rites (e.g., funerals), some on incorporation rites (e.g., marriage), and some on transition rites (e.g., fertility). In some cases—for example, adoption, birth of additional children, or remarriage—the importance of these ceremonies may be reduced. "Thus, although a complete scheme of rites of passage theoretically includes preliminary rites (rites of separation), liminal rights (rites of transition), and postliminal rites (rites of incorporation), in specific instances these three types are not always equally important or equally elaborated." Therefore, van Gennep concludes, "I am trying to group all these rites as clearly as possible, but since I am dealing with activities I do not expect to achieve as rigid a classification as the botanists have, for example."[33] Ideal types in the social sciences help organize the infinitely complex reality of the world by focusing our attention on key elements of social reality and giving us a basis for comparison of our models and that reality. As an ideal type, we should judge van Gennep's tripartite model not as right or wrong, but as more or less useful. Though published over 100 years ago, the schema continues to provide a useful benchmark against which to compare contemporary rites of passage.[34]

In his work on the modern reinvention of rites of passage, Grimes does not mention the Rite of Christian Initiation of Adults, but he could have. In "returning to the sources" for an earlier model of initiation (what French theologians called *ressourcement*; see Chapter 1), the creators of the contemporary RCIA in the 1960s engaged in the very process of reinvention that Grimes calls for. Indeed, as noted, it is part of a broader-scale reinvention of the church itself during and following the Second Vatican Council. In developing the RCIA process, theologians and liturgists looked to the ancient church for a model of initiation that could be adapted to the modern context; they found it in the pattern of initiation used in the Mediterranean churches of the fourth and fifth centuries. As theologian Mark Searle explains, "It was in this world and at this time (mainly between AD 350 and 450) that the rites of Christian initiation reached their fullest development and attained the classical forms which Christians of subsequent generations were content to reproduce."[35]

In the ancient church, the initiation process maps nicely onto van Gennep's tripartite structure of separation-transition-incorporation. *Separation:* As described by Searle, during the period of preparation (called "the catechumenate"), individuals (called "catechumens"—ones undergoing instruction) actually lived apart from the rest of the Christian community. Searle observes that the purpose of separation is "to draw a line of clear demarcation between before and after, outside and inside, the old self and the new that is coming to birth." *Transition:* The period of the catechumenate itself was seen as "not merely a time for instruction," but "above all a time for facing and doing battle with the 'dragon of the sea,' as Cyril [of Jerusalem] also puts it." The "forty days" (*quadrageima*) prior to Easter were a time of more intensive preparation for the sacraments of initiation, including ascetic practices of prayer and fasting, as well as confessions and exorcisms. *Incorporation:* At the conclusion of this process of apprenticeship in the Christian life, the "awe-inspiring rites of initiation" marked the aggregation of the catechumen into the mystical body of Christ.[36] Thus, van Gennep's ideal type and the ancient church's model of initiation provide a solid benchmark against which to compare the contemporary RCIA, allowing us to explore the various ways in which tradition is transformed when it is recovered and brought into modern society.

There is also an analytical advantage of bringing the concept of initiation back into the sociology of religion. A comprehensive review of the research literature in three major journals (*Journal for the Scientific Study of Religion, Review of Religious Research*, and *Sociology of Religion*) over the past 20 years yields no published studies of the process of initiation. This is unfortunate. Focusing on initiation as a social process that unfolds in stages over time offers an advance over dueling conceptions of "conversion" and "reaffiliation" (or "switching") in the study of individual religious change. Rodney Stark and Roger Finke have attempted to bring more precision and clarity to this area by defining conversion as "shifts across religious traditions" and reaffiliation as "shifts within religious traditions."[37] But this distinction is operationally untenable. The change from being a nominal Lutheran to being an active Catholic is more than (mere) reaffiliation, and the change from being an active Catholic to being a nominal Jew is less than (radical) conversion.

Rather than seeing conversion and switching as mutually exclusive alternatives, I agree with the idea that membership change (switching) and conversion are "two related but not identical phenomena."[38] For example, conversion may precede membership change or follow it. Today, some people become members of new religious organizations for various pragmatic reasons without experiencing any fundamental change in beliefs or practices—that is, reaffiliation before conversion. Other people experience fundamental changes in their beliefs or practices before they ever officially join a new organization—that is, conversion before reaffiliation. The concept of initiation helps us to bring these two lines of thinking together. If we define *switching* as changing religious affiliation without (necessarily) experiencing any other religious change, and *conversion* as experiencing change in the direction of greater religiosity (as understood by the tradition to which the individual affiliates), then *initiation* can be defined as a process of reaffiliation that seeks to foster conversion to the faith. What is unique about the RCIA as a rite of passage is precisely that it seeks to tie the process of conversion to the process of reaffiliation by offering an extended period of formation (transition) leading up to the rites of initiation and full membership (incorporation) in the Catholic church. At the same time, there is no guarantee that an individual in the RCIA process will either reaffiliate or experience conversion. That is an empirical question, one of many that the concept of initiation itself raises and that I seek to address sociologically in this study.

APPROACHING THE RCIA SOCIOLOGICALLY

Although the Rite of Christian Initiation of Adults is "the most mature fruit of all the liturgical reforms mandated by the Second Vatican Council,"[39] very little is known empirically about it. For at least a decade after the publication of the *Ordo* in 1972 and the provisional English translation of the *Rite* in 1974, the RCIA process was not widely implemented in American parishes. For example, when Dean Hoge published *Converts, Dropouts, Returnees* in 1981, an RCIA process had not been implemented in any of the parishes he studied.[40] After 1988, when the United States bishops issued *National Statutes* for and mandated use of the RCIA process, its adoption expanded rapidly. By the turn of the twenty-first century, more than 80% of American parishes were using some version of the RCIA process. Forty years after the publication of the *Ordo* and 25 years since use of the *Rite* was mandated, the RCIA process is well enough established that some assessment can be made of its contribution to the life of individual Catholics and Catholic parishes. At the same time, it remains new enough that any empirical assessment contributes immensely to our knowledge and understanding.[41]

This book examines the process of becoming Catholic in the United States today through a comprehensive case study of the RCIA process in the Roman Catholic Diocese of Fort Wayne–South Bend in Indiana. At the heart of this research is fieldwork conducted in six parishes from August 2001 through June 2002. During that time, two associates—Sarah MacMillen and Kelly Culver—and I attended hundreds of meetings and dozens of rites, met scores of individuals who were considering becoming Catholic, and recorded more than a thousand typed, single-spaced pages of observational notes.[42] In the pages that follow, I have changed the names and potentially identifying characteristics of the people and places observed in our fieldwork to preserve their anonymity. All accounts of events taking place at "St. Innocent" or "St. John Bosco" are based on observations made by MacMillen, which I have taken from her field notes and partially rewritten. Kelly Culver is responsible for observations made and recorded at "Queen of Peace" and "St. Peter's," and the same caveat applies. I conducted the fieldwork in "St. Mark's" and "St. Mary's" parishes.

This ethnographic data is complemented by closed-ended surveys and open-ended interviews with individuals in the RCIA process. In fall 2000 and again in fall 2001, I collected baseline quantitative data on 224 individuals who were in the early stages of the RCIA process in 32 different parishes in the diocese. In the summer of 2001 and 2002, I collected a complete second wave of quantitative data on 167 of these individuals. Of the 167 individuals for whom I have two complete waves of data, 159 had completed the RCIA process. During the first wave of data collection, I also conducted qualitative interviews with 56 of the original 224 respondents. In the second wave, I was able to complete follow-up interviews with 39 of these individuals. During the open-ended interviews, individuals were given the opportunity to choose their own pseudonyms, by which they are called in this book. For individuals who did not choose a pseudonym, I provided one. I also changed some inconsequential identifying information about respondents as necessary to preserve their anonymity.

Finally, I collected organizational-level data on parishes through closed-ended surveys and open-ended interviews with individuals responsible for the RCIA process in this same time period. I have data on 53 of the 78 parishes in the diocese, including all 32 parishes from which I have individual respondents. As a quantitative complement to the qualitative fieldwork data, having survey data on individuals and their parishes allows me to explain individuals' different levels of religious change over the course of the initiation process in terms of the specific characteristics of the RCIA in the parishes in which they were initiated.

I use these data to address several specific questions. First, concerning *motivation*—of the innumerable options available in the American religious landscape today, why do some people choose Roman Catholicism (Chapter 2)? Second, concerning *catechesis* and *formation*—once individuals enter the RCIA process, what do they learn about Catholicism and how do they learn to be Catholic (Chapters 3 and 4)? Third, concerning *incorporation*—does the initiation process actually do what it claims it does, namely, make those becoming Catholic a part of the body of the church (Chapter 5)? Finally, concerning *outcomes*—how do the individuals who become Catholic change over the course of the RCIA process, and does the initiation process itself explain that change (Chapter 6)? In answering these questions, I take the reader on a journey through the RCIA process.

This book is organized according to the temporal sequence of adult initiation in the Catholic church today, as specified in the *Rite of*

Christian Initiation of Adults and the United States bishops' *National Statutes for the Catechumenate* (see Table 1.1 in Chapter 1). Chapter 1 gives some historical context for and an overview of the contemporary RCIA process. Chapter 2 focuses on what motivates people to enter the RCIA process in the first place. Chapter 3 examines the instruction that takes place in the first two periods of the RCIA process, inquiry and the catechumenate. Chapter 4 centers on the third stage of the process, the Period of Purification and Enlightenment, which immediately precedes the reception of the sacraments of initiation at the Easter Vigil. Chapter 5 differs slightly from the previous two chapters in that it addresses not a period of the RCIA process but a ritual transition—the climax of the adult initiation process in the reception of the Easter sacraments, a moment that merits its own discussion. Chapter 6 takes as its point of departure the fourth and final period of the RCIA process, the Period of Mystagogy. Chapters 2 through 6 are each preceded by descriptive accounts (i.e., "stories") drawn from the fieldwork I conducted with MacMillen and Culver. These "preludes" are meant to give readers, especially those unfamiliar with the Rite of Christian Initiation of Adults or those who have a profound interest in it, a better "feel" for what the process looks like on the ground. Each story also sets the stage for the sociological analysis in the chapter that follows it.

Chapter Summaries

Chapter 2: The Circumstantial Convert as Moral Actor. In a world of religious choice, why do some people become Catholic? How do people find Rome in the American religious landscape? Catholic apologists sometimes suggest that people are overwhelmed by the "Splendor of Truth" embodied by the one, true church. To be sure, some of the most high-profile converts to Catholicism historically (and today) come to the tradition due to an intellectual conversion. One thinks of John Henry Newman, Jacques Maritain, G. K. Chesterton,

Thomas Merton, Cardinal Avery Dulles, Scott Hahn, and Richard John Neuhaus. But most of the individuals we studied in common Midwestern parishes found their way to the Roman Catholic church through mundane mechanisms like family and co-workers.[43] This is not surprising because, according to Rodney Stark's well-established network theory of conversion, most people are recruited to religious groups by someone they know, most frequently a spouse.[44] This theory does an excellent job of explaining the mechanisms by which people are recruited to the Catholic church. In this sense, most converts to Roman Catholicism in America today are products of their circumstances, not religious seekers or even consumers shopping for faith.

Although Stark's network theory accounts for the *mechanisms* of recruitment, it neglects the *motivations* for change. After all, some people become Catholic prior to marriage and some after decades of marriage. What explains the difference? This chapter explains why people become Catholic by looking at the decision to convert not as a rational choice by individuals seeking to maximize their religious utility or to conserve their household religious capital, but as a moral action by individuals seeking to align their actions with broader moral worldviews and belief systems. In developing this alternative to rational choice theories of conversion, I draw on the work of Christian Smith in his book *Moral, Believing Animals*.[45]

Chapter 3: Visions of Catholicism in RCIA Catechesis. In their aptly titled book *Transforming Catholicism*, David Maines and Michael McCallion take as their point of departure the Vatican II Constitution on the Sacred Liturgy (*Sacrosanctum Concilium*). Looking at liturgical change since the Second Vatican Council, many transformations of Catholicism are obvious, most notably in the Mass. But Maines and McCallion bring a sociological perspective to this issue, which allows them to see a second level of transformation in the Vatican II church: the transformation of liturgical ideals into concrete liturgical practices at the local level. Liturgical changes suggested in *Sacrosanctum Concilium* are not simply transmitted from Rome to Detroit or South Bend or elsewhere, but are implemented in different ways in different countries, dioceses, and parishes.[46] This idea of transformation through implementation recurs in this book as well. Although there is a single, universal normative order of initiation for the entire Catholic church worldwide—found in the *Ordo Initiationis Christianae Adultorum*—its implementation in different contexts varies considerably. The way that the RCIA process is implemented at the local level has the potential to tell us something about different understandings of the Catholic tradition, what the Catholic church is, and what it means to be Catholic.

This chapter focuses on the different visions of Catholicism that are expressed in the formal catechesis (instruction) that takes place in the first two periods of the RCIA process, inquiry and the catechumenate. Recognizing that religious education is often modeled on other secular forms of schooling, I approach catechesis from the perspective of the sociology of education, in particular the sociology of the curriculum. Like educational curricula in general, RCIA curricula in different parishes can be "read" for the beliefs, values, and understandings that they explicitly espouse or implicitly convey. Here it is important to distinguish between what education scholars call the *explicit* curriculum and the *hidden* curriculum. The explicit curriculum is the substantive content to be taught, and this can be seen most clearly in the syllabus of topics to be covered in the course of study. The explicit curriculum is important because it is an index of what parishes think is important for those becoming Catholic to know. But the explicit curriculum is just one part of what is taught in the schooling process.

The hidden curriculum teaches not content but more general orientations, especially orientations to authority. The hidden curriculum is best examined through the *pedagogy* employed—how instruction is organized and how content is delivered to students. For example, the great Brazilian philosopher of education, Paulo Freire, distinguishes between traditional, hierarchical pedagogies and critical, democratic pedagogies. Understanding catechesis in the RCIA process, therefore, requires attention to both the explicit and hidden dimensions of the curriculum, both what those becoming Catholic are taught to believe explicitly and what implicit lessons they are taught about how they should believe. This distinction between *what to believe* about Catholicism and *how to believe* as a Catholic is essential to grasping the similarities and differences between parishes in their visions of Catholicism. Although there are some interesting similarities in visions of Catholicism in the explicit curriculum that cut across parishes, there are also important differences between parishes in the hidden curriculum. In an effort to bring class back into the sociology of religion, I tie these pedagogical differences to social class differences between parishes.

Chapter 4: Liturgy, Experience, and Formation. Like many rites of passage, the periods and ritual transitions of the Rite of Christian Initiation of Adults are designed to lead people gradually into a deeper understanding of faith and higher levels of practice in the church, culminating in crossing a final threshold of initiation into skillful membership. To facilitate this movement among those becoming Catholic, the centrality of catechetical instruction seen in the inquiry period and the catechumenate gives way—to some extent, imperfectly—to a greater emphasis on liturgical practices, personal experience, and interior reflection in the Period of Purification and Enlightenment. In a word, emphasis shifts from instruction (learning about Catholicism) to formation (learning to be Catholic). Although formation can take place throughout the entire RCIA process, it is especially prominent in this final period of preparation for the rites of initiation to be celebrated at the Easter Vigil.

The understanding of formation on which I draw in this chapter comes from those who have written on professional education, especially on the formation of medical professionals like doctors and nurses. Doctors do not learn how to be doctors and nurses do not learn how to be nurses simply by reading books, any more than someone becomes a bike rider just by reading *Peter Learns to Ride His Bicycle* (a book actually published in 2011)—or any more than someone becomes Catholic just by reading the *Catechism of the Catholic Church*. According to religion scholar and medical educator

Margaret Mohrmann, formation requires individuals to bring with them or to develop an embodied, experiential base of understanding, and requires mentors or teachers to build on this base, giving shape and adding to it.[47] In examining whether formation takes place in this period of the RCIA process, I pay attention to both necessary aspects of this formational equation: experience *and* what it is made into. I find that formation takes place unevenly. There are moments when significant experiences are generated in liturgical rites, but many times no effort is made to give shape to those experiences. And there are moments, albeit rarer, when teachers attempt to shape understandings but without any experiential basis to form. But sometimes the RCIA process does bring together individual experience and the Catholic tradition in a formational way. When this happens, teacher-mentors help to initiate their apprentices into Catholicism as a set of practices and a way of living. They teach their students how to dance the Catholic dance, or, as Jerome Baggett has put it, to have "a feel for the [Catholic] game."[48]

Chapter 5: Objective and Subjective Incorporation through the Sacraments of Initiation. The Rite of Christian Initiation of Adults as a rite of passage should culminate, according to van Gennep's model, in the incorporation of new Catholics into the body of the church. In being incorporated, these individuals take on a new status ("Catholic") and are entitled and empowered to act in ways that accord with this new state of being. In contemporary practice, this should take place during Easter Vigil Masses, during which individuals receive the sacraments of initiation and thereby become Catholic. Or do they? Among ritual studies scholars, there is some disagreement about the "effectiveness" of rituals, especially initiation rituals. Ronald Grimes, for example, argues that some who analyze rituals tend to view them from afar and idealize them. This creates "the problem of dissonance": initiations do *not* do what people claim they do. Similarly, examining Victor Turner's analysis of rites of passage specifically, Vincent Crapanzano criticizes Turner's "ritual illusion," accepting at face value "that ritual actually does what it says it does."[49]

Do initiation rituals do what they say they do? Specifically, are individuals who are initiated into the Catholic church through the RCIA actually *incorporated*, as van Gennep would argue? In this chapter—the only chapter of this book that centers on a ritual transition rather than one of the periods in the RCIA process—I answer the question, "Yes and sometimes." The emphatic "yes" refers to what I call the *objective* dimension of incorporation. From an objective perspective, receiving the sacraments of initiation is a significant threshold for the individual becoming Catholic, after which the individual has a new status: full membership in the church, with its attendant rights and responsibilities. The individual now can receive the Eucharist, check the "Catholic" box, join a parish, get married in the church, and so on. So, in this sense I agree with British social anthropologist Jean La Fontaine, who argues that initiation rituals do in fact do what they say they do. The second part of my answer, the hedging "sometimes," refers to the *subjective* dimension of incorporation. As the language suggests, here things are less clear. In some cases, the sacraments of initiation inspire a feeling of family, home, and community reflective of incorporation. In other cases, people receive the Easter sacraments and simply drift off into the night unattached. Thus, examining the subjective dimension calls our attention not to the universal outcome of initiation, but to the diversity of incorporation outcomes. In the end, the critics are half-right (or half-wrong). Understanding both the objective and subjective dimensions is necessary to a full understanding of incorporation through the Rite of Christian Initiation of Adults.

Chapter 6: The Difference It Makes. As Chapter 5 makes clear, reception of the sacraments of initiation in the Catholic church completes the RCIA process as a rite of passage by objectively incorporating individuals into the church body. But the process does not end at Easter. It actually concludes with a period of "post-baptismal catechesis" called "mystagogy." Because the Period of Mystagogy is the most haphazardly implemented of the four periods of the RCIA process, this chapter departs from it, in both senses of the term. It takes this period as its starting point, but it also leaves it behind. I do not analyze what happens during mystagogy per se, but step back from the process after the initiation of new Catholics to answer the question, What difference does the RCIA process make? If we compare what individuals look like after they are initiated to what they looked like when they begin the initiation process, do they look different?

A complete answer to this broad question would require a book in itself. To confine this analysis to a single chapter, I focus my attention on two outcomes in particular. First, I consider how individuals' understandings of Catholicism may have changed over the course of the RCIA process. In formal catechesis and in formation through liturgy and experience, especially the experience of the rites of initiation themselves, those becoming Catholic are supposed to be socialized into the Catholic tradition. Sociologists examining the contemporary Catholic church, such as Jerome Baggett, Tricia Bruce, Michele Dillon, and Andrew Greeley, highlight the many different ways to study the Catholic tradition—or, more accurately, plural Catholic traditions—empirically.[50] Recognizing that there is no single way to operationalize this outcome, I approach this issue by asking people directly, "What does it mean to be Catholic?" Examining the extent to which individuals' understandings of what it means to be Catholic grow and develop over the course of the RCIA process is suggestive of one dimension of the difference it makes.

Second, recognizing that becoming Catholic is not just about "talking the talk" but is also (and for many, more importantly) about "walking the walk," I also examine how religious *practices* change from the start of the RCIA process to after its conclusion. I look at both spiritual practices, such as prayer and scripture reading, and ecclesial involvement, such as Mass attendance, involvement in spiritual groups, and volunteering for church ministries. Growth in these practices is an indicator of key outcomes of the initiation process: formation as an apprenticeship in the faith and incorporation in the church body. In assessing this growth, and its relationship to the initiation process itself, I use the unique quantitative data described above to connect changes at the individual level to aspects of the RCIA process at the parish level. The brief conclusion to these analyses is that the RCIA process often does make a difference, both in individuals' understandings of and involvement in the Catholic tradition.

Conclusion

I conclude this introduction by reminding readers that *Becoming Catholic* is a case study. It is not a random or even a representative sampling of all parishes in the United States. It is not designed to causally explain nominal changes in religious affiliation in a representative sample of Americans. Existing articles do a fine job of this.[51] Rather, I look into the complexity that lies beneath the surface of religious affiliation and the organizational realities of parish life that structure it. In examining the meaning and process of finding Rome in the American religious landscape, I show that "Catholic" is not just a label to be applied or a box to be checked on a survey, but an identity to be achieved. For new Catholics, this identity is negotiated in a lengthy, formal initiation process that mimics the ancient model of adult initiation in the church and follows the pattern found by van Gennep in rites of initiation in very different times and places. The initiation process itself is implemented differently from parish to parish and therefore provides insight into the lived reality of Catholicism as it is produced at the local level. All of this takes place in the context of the centrifugal and centripetal forces of modern society—forces that have a significant effect on individuals and churches and the relationship between them.

CHAPTER ONE

VATICAN II AND THE REINVENTION OF ADULT INITIATION

The Rite of Christian Initiation of Adults (RCIA), as it is practiced in the United States today, is a direct result of the Second Vatican Council. Like other developments in the Roman Catholic church following Vatican II, the liturgical changes that were implemented were revolutionary and truly transformed Catholicism.[1] They also most directly affected the average Catholic in the pews, whose main connection to the universal church was through the Mass. These changes were inspired by the first of the four major Vatican II constitutions, *Sacrosanctum Concilium* (the Constitution on the Sacred Liturgy). This document, approved by a vote of 2,147 to 4 and promulgated by Pope Paul VI on December 4, 1963, famously declared, "The liturgy is the summit toward which the activity of the church is directed; at the same time it is the font from which all her power flows" (no. 10). It also insisted that "the faithful take part fully aware of what they are doing, actively engaged in the rite, and enriched by its effects" (no. 11). And expressing perhaps its most famous phrase, it held that "Mother Church earnestly desires that all the faithful should be led to that *fully conscious, and active participation* in liturgical celebrations which is demanded by the very nature of the liturgy" (no. 14, emphasis added). Extending from these general principles, a number of reforms were proposed, leaving no part of the sacred liturgy untouched.[2]

Michael McCallion and David Maines summarize some of the major changes forwarded by *Sacrosanctum Concilium*:

This document represents nothing less than a radical redefinition of the methods and meanings of worship, especially with respect to ritual practices. For example, the document stated that Mass could be conducted in languages other than Latin; it emphasized the Liturgy of the Word, or Biblical sources of sacred meanings, as well as the Eucharist; it mandated that the Homily (sermons) always focus on scriptural interpretation in an attempt to bring new spiritual understandings to the laity; it embraced enculturation—that the liturgy should be flexible and can be modified to fit variations on cultural practices and modes of expression.[3]

As Melissa Wilde recounts in her book *Vatican II*, the results were immediate and dramatic:

On November 29, 1964, the first Sunday of Advent, Roman Catholics walked into their parishes around the globe and, for the first time since the fall of the Roman Empire, participated in a mass that was given largely in their native tongue. Not only did parishioners find themselves responding to the priest in words they spoke every day, but they spoke more often than they had at any Catholic service they had ever attended. Many Catholics saw the strange sight of their priest consecrating the Eucharist facing the congregation rather than the crucifix behind the altar, along with other new practices meant to make the mass and liturgy more participatory by incorporating the "people of God."[4]

And these were just the immediate changes. Soon enough the faithful would receive the Eucharist in their hand rather than on the tongue, and standing rather than kneeling. They would be confronted, for better or worse, by guitar-based folk music rather than organ-based hymns. In many churches, communion rails would be removed and altars would be pushed out into the center of the congregation and surrounded by seating "in the round." Often statuary would be minimized if not removed altogether, and tabernacles would be moved to side altars or entirely separate chapels. Taken together, these changes amounted to a "Copernican revolution in Catholic worship."[5]

A less well-known—though significant and enduring—product of *Sacrosanctum Concilium* is the revision of the process by which adults are initiated in the church. Chapter III of *Sacrosanctum Concilium* addresses the sacraments other than the Eucharist, including the two nonrepeatable sacraments of initiation (baptism and confirmation).[6] Three somewhat oblique paragraphs mandate revision in the process of initiation for adults:

> 64. The catechumenate for adults, comprising several distinct steps, is to be restored and to be taken into use at the discretion of the local ordinary. By this, means the time of the catechumenate, which is intended as a period of suitable instruction, may be sanctified by sacred rites to be celebrated at successive intervals of time.
>
> 65. In mission lands it is found that some of the peoples already make use of initiation rites. Elements from these, when capable of being adapted to Christian ritual, may be admitted along with those already found in Christian tradition, according to the norm laid down in Art. 37–40, of this Constitution.
>
> 66. Both the rites for the baptism of adults are to be revised: not only the simpler rite, but also the more solemn one, which must take into account the restored catechumenate. A special Mass "for the conferring of baptism" is to be inserted into the Roman Missal.

This mandate led to a new book of rites for adult initiation, published in 1972 in Latin under the title *Ordo Initiationis Christianae Adultorum*. A provisional English translation of this new "order of initiation" was introduced into the Catholic church in the United States in 1974, and a final official American English translation of the *Rite of Christian Initiation of Adults* (called the vernacular typical edition) was published in 1988. At that time, the National Conference of Catholic Bishops also issued the *National Statutes for the Catechumenate*, guidelines for the use of the new process.[7]

In the balance of this chapter, I give a short historical overview of adult initiation in the Catholic church and note how the contemporary Rite of Christian Initiation of Adults reflects a return to an ancient model of initiation in the church. I then briefly describe the RCIA process as it is laid out in the guiding texts and commonly practiced in the United States. This material will provide the reader with a broader, bird's-eye view of the RCIA process as background for the more focused, ground-level view that I provide in Chapters 3 through 6.

RESSOURCEMENT AND THE RESTORATION OF THE CATECHUMENATE

The restoration of the catechumenate for adults, called for in the Constitution on the Sacred Liturgy, is an example of what theologians call *ressourcement*: looking to the ancient church for models of liturgy and practice to be implemented in the contemporary church. It is, quite literally, a "return to the sources." In this view, the problems that the church faced in the modern world were best addressed by a return to "the very headwaters of the Christian tradition." Although this approach looks to the past for guidance, *ressourcement* in its essence is "not retrograde, but progressive."[8] Indeed, *ressourcement* and *aggiornamento*—the opening up of the church to the world and its internal updating that Pope John XXIII sought in calling the Council—can be complementary insofar as *ressourcement* uses tradition to *renew* tradition.[9] This recalls Jaroslav Pelikan's famous definition of tradition as "the living faith of the dead."[10]

Ordo Initiationis Christianae Adultorum draws mainly on early sources from the Christian church even before the time of Constantine. According to Paul Turner's history of the catechumenate, initiation in the early church in the West centered on the theological works of Cyprian and Tertullian (ca. 150–220) in North Africa and the Apostolic Tradition as it was carried out in Rome.[11] The Apostolic

Tradition was first composed in Greek by Hippolytus (ca. 215). Fragments turned up in other languages in Syria, North Africa, and Italy. According to the Apostolic Tradition, baptism for adults was to be preceded by a structured period of instruction or catechesis, which could last as long as three years. Individuals undergoing instruction were called "catechumens" ("hearers of the word") and the period of instruction was designated the "catechumenate." The process also called for a number of pre-baptismal rites associated with purification and exorcism in preparation for initiation.[12]

At the time of Ambrose (339–397), teacher and mentor of Augustine, a year-long catechumenate was in place that appears very similar to today's RCIA process in its periods and rites. The period of catechesis began with a public signation that designated the individual as a catechumen. Later, the catechumens submitted their names as candidates for baptism to a minister who smeared mud in their eyes. Thereafter, they were called "the elect." During the final preparations for baptism, in what we now call the season of Lent, the focus was on prayer, exorcisms, scrutinies, and ascetic practices. On the Sunday before Easter, the community presented the Creed orally to the elect. Just before the baptismal rite, the bishop performed the *ephphetha*, or "opening" rite, touching those to be baptized on the eyes and nose. After Easter, the bishop explained to the newly baptized what they had celebrated in a period of post-baptismal catechesis.

Unable to retain its integrity under the weight of the massive number of conversions to the faith after Constantine (280–337), and heavily influenced by Augustine's (354–430) doctrine of original sin, the structured catechumenal model of initiating adults would soon disappear. According to historical theologian Maxwell Johnson, Augustine argued that because of the fall of Adam, "the human will is not free but sick, 'curved in upon itself' (*incurvatus in se ipsum*) and seeks only the gratification of its own self-oriented desires (a condition of concupiscence or lust). Hence, from the moment of birth (if not before), human beings cannot choose, will, or do what is good but are in need of the medicine of divine grace in order to choose, will, and do the good."[13] Baptism of infants was seen as the salve to remove the sickness of original sin; consequently, infant baptism became a regular practice, and concern with the initiation of adults waned.

By the mid-twentieth century in the United States, the process of adult initiation was brief, private, and focused on catechetical instruction, often conducted one-on-one by a priest, though sometimes in "convert classes." *Fr. Smith Instructs Jackson*—an instruction manual by Archbishop John Francis Noll that presents doctrinal instruction in dialogue style, following the order of *The Baltimore Catechism*— was typical of the instructional material and approach of the time. Upon successful completion of the catechesis, the sacraments of initiation were usually administered to individuals outside the context of the worshipping community.

During this same time period, however, other movements were developing that would provide an impetus for a restoration of the catechumenal model of initiation. Missionary evangelization in Africa had led to the development of catechumenal models of initiation in which individuals moved from being "postulants" to "catechumens" and finally to "faithful" over a period of time. This catechesis required a series of rites to move individuals from status to status in the process; in 1959, Joseph Blomjous, bishop of Mwanga in Tanganyika, Africa, submitted to the Vatican a proposal to restore the catechumenal rites to the initiation process. The Sacred Congregation of Rites published the "Order of Baptism of Adults Arranged as a Catechumenate in Steps" in 1962, just prior to the opening of the Second Vatican Council.[14] This laid the groundwork for the Vatican II call for the catechumenate for adults to be universally restored.

As Michael McCallion and his colleagues have observed, Vatican II mandates often "lacked definitive markers or criteria for implementation."[15] In the case of the restoration of the catechumenate, this created a space for some entrepreneurial Catholics to play a leading role in shaping its development. Immediately following the publication of a provisional English translation of the *Ordo* in 1974, people outside the hierarchy took the initiative in charting a path for the implementation of the RCIA in the United States. Central figures included the Belgian theologian Christiane Brusselmans and Father James Dunning. In 1978, Brusselmans invited a small group of individuals (including Dunning) to meet in Senanque, France, to discuss the newly published rite. Later, she and Dunning welcomed some 200 initiation leaders to Estes Park, Colorado, to reflect on the rite and its implementation in North America. This and another meeting in Calgary, Canada, gave birth to the North American Forum on the Catechumenate. Jim Dunning served as its founding coordinator.[16] Thus, by the time the United States bishops mandated the use of the RCIA in 1988, the Forum was already well-established as the leading organization fostering what it called the "full and faithful" implementation of the *Ordo*.

Taken together, the *Rite of Christian Initiation of Adults* (the ritual text) and the United States bishops' *National Statutes for the Catechumenate* paint a general picture of the reinvented adult initiation process in the Catholic church. The broad outlines of the process as it applies to unbaptized adults are summarized in Table 1.1 and described in the next section.[17] (Note: See also the caveat at the end of the section concerning the distinction between unbaptized and baptized individuals in the RCIA process.)

A Brief Overview of the RCIA Process

Like many church documents, the formal texts of the RCIA do not constitute a road map for implementation at the parish level. Much of my work in this book and elsewhere seeks to understand the variations in implementation from parish to parish.[18] But we do well to begin with a description of the normative vision of the RCIA process as described in the guiding documents. As seen in Table 1.1, the RCIA process in the ideal is composed of four distinct periods and three ritual transitions that move individuals from one period to the next.

Period 1, the Period of Evangelization and Precatechumenate, is the opening stage in the RCIA process. It is colloquially known as the inquiry period, and individuals who enter the process here are called "inquirers." The purpose of this period is to ensure that "the beginnings of the spiritual life and the fundamentals of Christian teaching have taken root in the candidates." Those in charge of the process are to look for "the first stirrings of repentance, a start to the practice of calling upon God in prayer, a sense of the Church, and some experience of the company and spirit of Christians through contact with a priest or with members of the community" (*RCIA*, no. 42).

In practice, inquiry usually entails a weekly meeting in which information about the Catholic faith and church is provided to inquirers by a parish staff member (usually the RCIA director, pastoral associate, or parish priest) or occasionally by members of the parish who volunteer as catechists. Inquirers also have an opportunity to ask questions in these initial sessions, which technically are open ended but typically last five or six weeks. Also during this period, inquirers are paired with "sponsors"—Catholics in good standing with the church who are to accompany the individuals on their journey toward initiation. Once the inquirers decide to continue in the RCIA process, they go through their first ritual transition.

Ritual Transition 1, the Rite of Acceptance into the Order of Catechumens, is the ritual transition into the Period of the Catechumenate. During a liturgy, inquirers are asked to declare their intention to continue their faith journey by standing before the gathered parish community and answering two questions: "What do you ask of God's Church?" and "What does faith offer you?" (*RCIA*, no. 50). Standard answers are "Faith" and "Eternal life," respectively, but many parishes allow individuals to give their own personal responses. Inquirers are then asked to affirm their acceptance of the Gospel of Christ, and sponsors and the church assembly are asked to affirm their support of the candidates.

The passage from the status of inquirer to that of "catechumen" is ritually enacted by the tracing of the sign of the cross on the forehead of the candidate by the priest, catechist, or sponsor. In many cases, sponsors will also sign the candidate's other senses—ears, eyes, lips, chest, shoulders, hands, feet—with the cross as the priest or catechist says, "Receive the sign of the cross on your ears, that you may hear the voice of the Lord," "Receive the sign of the cross on your eyes, that you may see the glory of God," and so on (*RCIA*, no. 56). Often, the new catechumens are presented with a cross and/or Bible to commemorate the transition into the Order of Catechumens.

Period 2, the Period of the Catechumenate, or simply "the catechumenate," is the main time of formation for those seeking initiation. The purpose of this period is to give catechumens "suitable pastoral formation and guidance, aimed at training them in the Christian life." The four means of achieving this are: catechesis, community, liturgy, and service (*RCIA*, no. 75). In practice, most parishes achieve this by requiring catechumens to attend a weekly catechetical session, often indistinguishable from the inquiry sessions, as well as Sunday Mass. In many parishes, catechumens are "dismissed" from the Mass prior to the Liturgy of the Eucharist in order to "reflect more deeply upon the word of God which you have shared with us today" (*RCIA*, no. 67). In these dismissal sessions, a catechist leads the catechumens in a discussion of the readings for that particular Sunday.

The ritual text specifies that the catechumenate may last "several years" (*RCIA*, no. 7), though the United States bishops' *National Statutes* more realistically hold that the period "should extend for at least one year of formation, instruction, and probation" (*NS*, no. 6) so that a catechumen is exposed to an entire cycle of the liturgical year. Once catechumens are ready to receive the sacraments of initiation, they must publicly declare this and go through a ritual transition to become one of the "elect."

Ritual Transition 2, the Rite of Election, takes place at the conclusion of the catechumenate and carries the individuals into the final period of preparation prior to initiation. Often, parishes celebrate a Rite of Sending of Catechumens for Election at their Sunday Mass prior to the Rite of Election. The candidates for election are presented

Table 1.1. Overview of the Contemporary Rite of Christian Initiation of Adults

Item	Title	Length/Timing	Focus
Period 1	Evangelization and Precatechumenate (also called "Inquiry")	Unspecified, varies by individual need	Ensure that "the beginnings of the spiritual life and the fundamentals of Christian teaching have taken root in the candidates." Look for "the first stirrings of repentance, a start to the practice of calling upon God in prayer, a sense of the Church, and some experience of the company and spirit of Christians through contact with a priest or with members of the community" (*RCIA*, no. 42).
Ritual Transition	*Rite of Acceptance into the Order of Catechumens*	*Whenever inquirer is ready*	*During a liturgy, inquirers declare their intention to continue their faith journey; the church welcomes them as persons who intend to become its members.*
Period 2	Catechumenate	May be "several years" (*RCIA*, no. 7); "should extend for at least one year of formation, instruction, and probation" (*NS*, no. 6)	To give the candidates "suitable pastoral formation and guidance, aimed at training them in the Christian life." The four means of achieving this are: catechesis, community, liturgy, and service (*RCIA*, no. 75).
Ritual Transition	*Rite of Election*	*Sunday prior to Ash Wednesday*	*Held at a cathedral, presided over by ordinary (bishop or archbishop)*

Period 3	Purification and Enlightenment	Lent (40 days)	This is "a period of more intense spiritual preparation, consisting more in interior reflection than in catechetical instruction, and is intended to purify the minds and hearts of the elect as they search their own consciences and do penance" (RCIA, no. 139).
Ritual Transition	Reception of the Sacraments of Initiation	Easter Vigil	*Baptism, confirmation, and Eucharist, in the same liturgy and in this order*
Period 4	Mystagogy	Eastertime (50 days)	Sometimes called the period of "post-baptismal catechesis" because it seeks to lead the newly initiated more deeply into reflection on the experience of the sacraments and membership in the community.

Note: This is the normative vision of the process specified in the *Rite of Christian Initiation of Adults* (RCIA) and the United States bishops' *National Statutes for the Catechumenate*. This table was inspired by Ron Lewinski, *Welcoming the New Catholic* (Chicago: Liturgy Training Publications, 1983), pp. 12–13.

to the assembly, and their sponsors affirm their readiness by answering questions such as, "Have these catechumens taken their formation in the Gospel and in the Catholic way of life seriously?" and "Do you judge them to be ready to be presented to the bishop for the rite of election?" (*RCIA*, no. 112).

The Rite of Election itself is typically celebrated on the first Sunday of the season of Lent at the diocesan cathedral and is presided over by the ordinary (bishop or archbishop) of the (arch)diocese. This rite brings together individuals in the RCIA process from the entire diocese so that, for the first time, candidates are able to see the scores of individuals from other parishes who are going through the initiation process at the same time. In the rite, God "elects" those catechumens who are deemed by the church to be ready to take part in the sacraments of initiation (*RCIA*, no. 119). During the rite, godparents (often the catechumens' sponsors) are asked by the presider to affirm the candidates' readiness, after which the candidates affirm their desire "to enter fully into the life of the Church through the sacraments of baptism, confirmation, and eucharist" (*RCIA*, no. 132). The candidates are then invited to the enrollment of names: the ritual inscription of their names in the diocesan "Book of the Elect," which will be countersigned by the presiding bishop, who then declares them to be members of the "elect" and ready to begin the final period of preparation prior to initiation.

Period 3, the Period of Purification and Enlightenment, is defined by the 40 days preceding Easter, known as the season of Lent. This is "a period of more intense spiritual preparation, consisting more in interior reflection than in catechetical instruction, and is intended to purify the minds and hearts of the elect as they search their own consciences and do penance" (*RCIA*, no. 139). As part of the spiritual cleansing prior to initiation, the elect undergo three public "scrutinies" during the Masses on the third, fourth, and fifth Sundays of Lent. The scrutinies typically involve prayer over the elect and an "exorcism" enacted by a laying on of hands by the presider and sometimes others (godparents, catechists, and at times members of the assembly).

These scrutinies are meant to encourage "self-searching and repentance" so as to "complete the conversion of the elect and deepen their resolve to hold fast to Christ" (*RCIA*, no. 141). During the week after the first and third scrutinies, the elect are ritually presented the text of the Nicene Creed and Lord's Prayer. Often, as a final step in the process of preparation for initiation, the elect are taken on a day-long (or overnight) Lenten retreat, either at the parish or a retreat center. At the conclusion of this period, the elect undergo the most significant ritual transition: the reception of the sacraments of initiation.

Ritual Transition 3, the Reception of the Sacraments of Initiation, usually takes place during the Easter Vigil Mass on the Saturday night prior to Easter Sunday. The elect are first asked to renounce sin and profess faith, after which they receive the sacrament of baptism. The presider declares, "I baptize you in the name of the Father, and of the Son, and of the Holy Spirit," while pouring water over the head of the candidate, or where the facilities permit, immersing the candidate in the baptismal font. Immediately following their baptism, the "neophytes" (newly baptized) change into white garments and are presented with a candle lighted from the Paschal Candle. They then receive the sacrament of confirmation by a laying on of hands and anointing with oil by the presiding priest or bishop. The celebration culminates with the neophytes' first sharing in the sacrament of the Eucharist. From this point forward, the newly initiated are "raised to the ranks of the royal priesthood" (*RCIA*, no. 217). They have officially become Catholic.

Although the initiation of new members culminates with the celebration of the sacraments at the Easter Vigil, the RCIA process continues through *Period 4*, the *Period of Mystagogy*, which lasts for the 50 days of the Easter season in the liturgical calendar. This is sometimes called the period of "post-baptismal catechesis," because it seeks to lead the newly initiated more deeply into reflection on the experience of the sacraments and membership in the community. According to the ritual text, "This is a time for the community and the neophytes together to grow in deepening their grasp of the paschal mystery and in making it part of their lives through meditation on the Gospel, sharing in the eucharist, and doing the works of charity" (*RCIA*, no. 244). In this final period, neophytes are propelled out of the cocoon of their RCIA experience and into the life of the parish.

Caveat: For the sake of brevity and simplicity, Table 1.1 and this brief overview describe the RCIA process for an unbaptized adult. Although the *Ordo* takes as its norm the unbaptized, uncatechized adult, the reality is that these individuals are a slight minority of all those who join the Catholic church in any given year. In recognition of this, the United States bishops issued (as Appendix I to the *Rite of Christian Initiation of Adults*) additional "combined rites" for situations in which both unbaptized and baptized individuals are present. For example, although only an unbaptized individual can become a "catechumen" and enter the catechumenate by going through the Rite of Acceptance, baptized individuals become "candidates" through a parallel Rite of Welcoming Baptized but Previously Uncatechized Adults Who Are Preparing for Confirmation and/or Eucharist or Reception into the Full Communion of the Catholic Church. This Rite of Welcoming typically takes place in the same service as the Rite of Acceptance, and the baptized Christian seeking to become Catholic enters a period of continuing formation that in almost all cases is no different from that of the catechumen. In practice, the catechesis of baptized candidates and unbaptized catechumens most often takes place in the same catechetical sessions.

Despite issuing these combined rites, the American bishops urge caution in combining the final initiation rites of the unbaptized and baptized. The bishops note, "it is preferable that reception into full communion not take place at the Easter Vigil lest there be any confusion of such baptized Christians with the candidates for baptism, possible misunderstanding of or even reflection upon the sacrament of baptism celebrated in another Church or ecclesial community, or any perceived triumphalism in the liturgical welcome into the Catholic eucharistic community" (*NS*, no. 33). Although combining these individuals into a single process raises both practical pastoral and theological problems, a national study of the implementation of the RCIA in 2000 found that only 19% of parishes nationally receive baptized Christians into the full communion of the Catholic church *outside* the Easter Vigil.[19] Therefore, the Rite of Christian Initiation of Adults in most American parishes is adapted to include both baptized and unbaptized individuals seeking initiation in the Catholic church in the same process. In recognition of this practice, in this book I do not focus on distinctions between the experiences of unbaptized and baptized individuals seeking to become Catholic.

CONCLUSION

The aftermath of a revolution can often involve more struggles—struggles to define the meaning of the revolution itself and the changes it embodies. Not surprisingly, then, the Second Vatican Council has been the source of considerable conflict over the past 40-plus years. "Liberals" and "conservatives" in the church continue to fight over the consequences and, indeed, the very meaning of "the Council." These days, aging liberals—whom Dominican priest Paul Philibert calls "Vatican II Fundamentalists"—frequently lament the failure of the church to live up to "the vision of the Council." Meanwhile, church conservatives decry "what went wrong with Vatican II."[20]

Given these serious divisions in the church, we do well to recognize how widespread the support is for this one product of the Council: the Rite of Christian Initiation of Adults. Although its implementation is not above criticism, the ideal of adult faith formation embodied in the RCIA finds praise in all corners of the church. As Robert Duggan and Maureen Kelley have observed, "At once extremely conservative and traditional, yet forward-looking and progressive, the *Order* has proven to be one of the most dramatic 'surprises' of the Second Vatican Council."[21] The RCIA process has also become an influential model for other Christian traditions. According to the ecumenical North American Association for the Catechumenate, "During the past two decades non-Catholic Christian churches have slowly begun to understand the catechumenate as a process of faith formation and spiritual development for twenty-first century people who have little or no previous association with the Christian faith." Among the denominations that have already implemented a catechumenal process of initiation are the Anglican Church of Canada, Episcopal Church USA, Evangelical Lutheran Church in America, Evangelical Lutheran Church in Canada, Mennonite Church USA, Presbyterian Church (USA), Reformed Church in America, United Church of Christ, and United Methodist Church.[22]

The RCIA process as a model of adult faith formation has also been influential in the Roman Catholic church itself. *Adult Catechesis in the Christian Community*—a 1992 document prepared by the International Council for Catechesis—declares, "According to ancient tradition, every form of catechesis should be inspired by the catechumenal model. Precisely because the catechesis of adults aims at living the Christian life in all its fullness and integrity, the process outlined in the catechumenate seems the most appropriate model and should be encouraged everywhere" (no. 66). This sentiment is elaborated in the *General Directory for Catechesis* published in 1997 by the Vatican Congregation for the Clergy: "The concept of the baptismal catechumenate as *a process of formation and a true school of faith* offers post-baptismal catechesis dynamic and particular characteristics: comprehensiveness and integrity of formation; its gradual character expressed in definite stages; its connection with meaningful rites, symbols, biblical and liturgical signs; its constant reference to the Christian community. Post-baptismal catechesis . . . does well . . . to draw inspiration from 'this preparatory school for the Christian life'" (no. 91).

Its influence as an ideal surely makes the RCIA process more interesting as an object of sociological study. But as a work of sociology, this book is not principally concerned with the ideal of the process of adult religious formation and initiation, but with the real. In the chapters that follow, I trace the actual paths taken by scores of individuals as they make their ways through the diverse RCIA processes in dozens of parishes in the Roman Catholic Diocese of Fort Wayne–South Bend, Indiana. It is precisely these differences in individual motivations and diversity in organizational processes that make the Rite of Christian Initiation of Adults sociologically significant as a window onto American religion and American Catholicism today.

DIANE GALL: FINDING
A HOME IN CATHOLICISM

Sitting in her office with an interviewer, Diane Gall is as genial and composed as if she were speaking to one of her clients at Cooper Financial Services. She speaks of abortion, alcohol abuse, divorce, and betrayal as if they happened to another person, in another life. She displays no scars from experiences that would emotionally disable many. She laughs about the various challenges that she faced in trying to join the Catholic church. She draws strength from the sacrifices she has made. With the crucial support of her husband, his family, and the Catholic Church, and a great deal of individual determination, she has created a new life.

Now 34 years old, Diane maintains that most of her childhood friends would not recognize her. A photograph of her as a teenager reveals only slight external changes. Her hair is no longer feathered—à la Farrah Fawcett—as was fashionable in the late 1970s and early 1980s. Her makeup is more discretely applied. Her clothing is more current and the collar of her shirt no longer appears as if it could support her in flight. But the real changes, she insists, are inside.

Her mother was just 17 years old when Diane was born, and she was not prepared to be married or raise a child. Her parents divorced when she was two years old. Although her father lived only 20 miles away, she saw him mostly on weekends. *Me and my father are a lot closer now. A lot. He hates to see what I went through and he hates the fact that I had to go through all of that, but back then, a father trying to get custody of a daughter was almost unheard of. The mother always got custody. All Dad could do was try to keep in contact with me as close as he could and pay child support.* The fact that her father and his family were from a Pentecostal background and had different moral expectations did not help their relationship when she was younger. *When I turned 14, I decided that I wanted to go live with my father for a while. And I lived with him for about three months, and didn't like Dad's rules. Wanted nothing to do with it. Why can't I talk to guys on the phone? Why can't I go out on dates? I was only 14 years old. I couldn't get what I wanted from Dad. I didn't get my way. So, Mom said I could come back home. So I did.*

Although she bristled at her father's restrictions, Diane returned to a situation with its own, possibly worse, pathologies. *[My mother] was a very young mother. She went out. She was always at the bars. I was left alone quite a bit in my younger childhood years. Once I got into my teenage years, since mom was never around and she was always out with her friends and out at the bars, there was nothing for me. So, I went out looking for people to hang on to.* The year after the failed experiment of living with her father, she met someone who seemed to offer her both the security and the freedom she longed for. As often happens, the freedom was primarily sexual and the security an illusion. *At 15 years old, I got involved with a boy that was four years older. Now I feel the reason I did it was because I was so alone that I wanted to latch onto somebody, and there he was. We had been together for two years, and I ended up pregnant. Our relationship had started growing apart, so I had an abortion, and the relationship ended, pretty much all at the same time. Those are things that I would not want a child to go through. It's rough. It's a very rough life.*

Much of this realization has only come to Diane with age. At the time, the "rough" experiences didn't alter her lifestyle greatly. When her mother decided to move to Arizona after Diane's graduation from high school, she went along for the ride. *I was 18 years old, and my mother moved down there. At the time, I was just the typical teenager, just out for the fun. I was always out with my friends, partying, having a good time. Mom moved to Arizona and I didn't really have any place to go, except to my Dad's. Back then, we weren't that close.*

Mom let me get away with and do whatever I wanted. She didn't care. And Dad was more along the lines of, "You're going to have a curfew." I was 18 years old, I didn't need a curfew. He said, "If you're going to live in my house, here's the rules." I thought, hey, I can move to Arizona! It's nice and warm and never snows. So I went and I ended up living down there for ten years.

During that time, she met and married a man in a ceremony she remembers well to this day. *We were married in a living room by a notary public on a Tuesday night,* she says plainly, then adds more emphatically, *It was horrible!* This memory is certainly colored by the spectacular demise of her marriage. *You know, I went through a tremendous ordeal. Not only when my husband and I divorced, but my husband moved in with my mother and they bought a house together.* That she pauses to add, *these are not ordinary situations,* seems entirely unnecessary at this point.

After this unsuccessful time in Arizona, Diane returned to her childhood home of South Bend. *I came back in December of '97, and I still socialized with the same friends I did as a teenager. But we had all grown over the past ten years. We were all very irresponsible before, but this time we all had jobs, we all had responsibilities. So we got involved in bowling groups and dart-shooting groups. And, so I went to play darts with my friends, and that's how I met Jack. He was a friend of a friend.* It was not exactly love at first sight. To the contrary, Diane recalls vividly, *At first I didn't like him. He was very arrogant. And I didn't need that type of person in my life. I didn't like him because of his arrogance, but I told him so and we became friends. But I still thought he was arrogant, and I would never, ever think of being in a relationship with this man.* So what changed? *About a year after we had been friends, he asked me to go to a formal dinner with him. My reply was, "What? You couldn't find anyone to go with ya?" It wasn't a nice yes or no. He said that he had asked someone and his date had canceled, and he wanted to know if I'd like to go. So, we decided to go just as friends, and that was it. Yeah, once he got out of the bar and away from shooting darts and it was just us in a totally different environment, he was like night and day. Our relationship started growing from there.*

As she grew closer to Jack, she also developed a relationship with his family, the Sullivans, especially his Catholic parents, Patty and Bill. This relationship would prove decisive in her conversion. *Three or four months after I met his parents, his mother called and asked if we would like to meet them for dinner and to go to Mass. So, Jack said, "I'm sure you're not going to want to go, but here's the deal." I said, "Yeah, sure, no problem." And he says, "You want to go?" I said, "Yeah. I'm not Catholic, I don't know what to do, but, yeah, I'll go." And we went to a church downtown and I enjoyed it. I didn't feel comfortable by any means. I'd stand up and sit down and everyone is talking and praying. I'm like, where's this at? I'm looking through a book trying to find all this stuff. But I understood the whole Mass, and so I thought, maybe there is something to this. In Arizona, like 10 years ago, I went to a church. And I only went twice, and each time I felt like an outsider. It just didn't feel right. But when I started coming to Catholic church with Jack—it was like the third or fourth Mass that I'd been to, it was the Mother's Day Mass I think—all of a sudden something hit me. During Mass, with the singing and the prayer, I just started crying. It wasn't a bad cry, it was just kind of like a release type of thing. And that's when I knew, I knew I didn't need to look any further, this is where I belong. Whether or not Jack and I ended up married or not, this is still where I belong.*

That August, Diane decided she would dedicate an entire year to attending Mass and reading the Bible. She thought, *If I can go to Mass for a year and read this Bible, then I'll get some idea of what this religion is about. And that's what I did.* During this year, Patty and Bill journeyed with her, answering her questions and explaining things she didn't understand. But perhaps more important, they guided her in and toward the faith by example. Diane recalls discussing her difficult past with them. *I told Jack's parents everything about me. They know everything about me. And they just turned it around saying, "Well, you've had some things and problems that you've gone through in your life, and now you're where you need to be. And, it's OK." And it made me feel good because I was accepted, even though I wasn't Catholic and even though I went through all of these horrible things in my lifetime. I was still accepted by this family. I wasn't shunned or turned away. They never said, "She's not good enough for you," or that sort of thing. It was never like that.*

Diane attributes that acceptance to the family's Catholic faith. *To me, religious people were always very preachy and judgmental, but Jack's family was always totally the opposite. Very humble and accepting. Very into family.* When asked where she thought that attitude came from, Diane closes her eyes slightly longer than normal, trying to recall something. She suddenly opens her eyes widely and smiles, as if surprised to grasp the memory and excited to be able to share it. *OK, I'm trying to remember something from one of our first RCIA sessions at St. Paul's. [RCIA director] David was welcoming everyone and saying we all come to the meeting from different backgrounds, and that's ok. I can't remember who he was quoting—David was always quoting these great figures in the church and history, God love him—but the words they stuck with me: "Catholic means here comes everyone." It's like the saying from "Lilo and Stich": "Family means nobody gets left behind." To me that is what Catholicism is. And [Jack's family] really shows that.*

Despite her difficult past, Diane is optimistic about the future. Not the false optimism of those who think nothing bad will happen, or the saccharine, bumper sticker optimism of those who suggest, "When life hands you lemons, make lemonade." Diane evidences the realistic optimism of a person who has taken her fair share of blows from life and remains standing. Only now, she has a family and a worshipping community to stand with her. *When something bad comes you make something good out of it. Because if you carry around that bad, then things don't ever get better.*

Do you think you can do that outside the Catholic church? *No, because I tend to carry the things with me. I don't let things go very easily at all. So, if I get stressed or upset, I take everything very personally.*

If somebody upsets me, you hear a lot of people say, "Oh, just let it go. Blow it off and go on." I'm not that type of person—I take it with me. It affects me personally. And it gets to be a pretty heavy load to carry, let me tell ya. And I don't think I'd be able to do it without being Catholic. Going to Masses on Sundays, it's almost like I let everything out. Everything just flows right out of me. Everything that I've carried around with me all week long, that has had me so stressed or upset or worried or whatever, it's almost like when I go to Mass it just kind of flows right on out and you can start all over again. And I like that feeling because for an hour and a half on Sunday morning, and most of the day on Sunday, it's almost like you have that perfect idealistic life. You're spiritually happy, you're emotionally happy, and it's a great day. And then things come along throughout the week and it kind of beats all that down. But then there's always the next Sunday to look forward to.

In comparison with other stories of individuals becoming Catholic, Diane Gall's is both exceptional and common. After having listened to scores of people talk about how and why they have joined the church, I can say that no two stories are identical. I have heard from people, like Diane, whose lives were profoundly changed by becoming Catholic, from people whose life trajectories were altered only slightly or not at all, and everything in between. But in Diane's extraordinary life story, some patterns crystalize. We see the centrifugal forces of contemporary society—especially family dissolution and geographic mobility. We see the centripetal desire for home and stability. We see how she finds a home in Catholicism, and how she finds that home through networks of friends and families. We see how she connects her journey to Catholicism to broader cultural ideals and how those ideals inform her identity. In Chapter 2, I take the lessons learned from Diane and examine them on a broader scale.

CHAPTER TWO

THE CIRCUMSTANTIAL CONVERT AS MORAL ACTOR

In his *Invitation to the Sociology of Religion*, Phil Zuckerman describes two fictitious characters: Tom, a Christian believer living in the contemporary United States, and Mustafa, a devout Muslim living in Saudi Arabia. Zuckerman observes that "had Tom been born and raised in Yemen three hundred years ago he would most likely be a devout Muslim. . . . Conversely, if 'Mustafa' . . . had been born and raised in northern Mississippi two hundred years ago, he would most likely be a Baptist or Methodist Christian." From this, Zuckerman concludes, "Ultimately, religious identity and conviction aren't generally so much a matter of choice or faith or soul-searching as a matter of who and what one's parents, friends, neighbors, and community practice and profess." Put simply, religion is an accident of birth.[1]

Although cheeky, Zuckerman is substantially correct. For most of human history and in most parts of the world, people have become religious by inheriting their beliefs and practices from their ancestors. Even today, individuals are socialized into their religious identities, orientations, beliefs, and practices by those close to them. But the transmission of religion from a community to its residents, from a religious group to its members, and even from parents to children is not perfectly mechanical or entirely predictable.

Religiosity also changes over the course of an individual's life. At times, this entails an individual leaving her religion of origin for a new religion (or, increasingly, no religion at all). Sometimes this change entails a dramatic conversion in which a person's entire identity is transformed and direction in life is turned around. Examples abound, from Saul of Tarsus becoming Paul the apostle of Christianity, to Cassius Clay becoming Muhammad Ali upon his conversion to Islam. One might even go so far as to add Diane Gall becoming Catholic—described in the prelude to this chapter—to this list.

While compelling examples like Diane deserve and receive considerable attention, a comprehensive accounting of individual religious change needs to understand these examples alongside the many others whose distance traveled is not as far and whose change is not as comprehensive. Sometimes called "everyday conversion," this less dramatic religious reaffiliation or denominational switching is increasingly common in American society and has been the subject of numerous studies. Among the largest of these studies is the 35,000-respondent *U.S. Religious Landscape Survey* conducted by the Pew Research Center's Forum on Religion & Public Life and published in 2008. According to this study,

> more than one-quarter of American adults (28%) have left the faith in which they were raised in favor of another religion—or no religion at all. If change in affiliation from one type of Protestantism to another is included, 44% of adults have either switched religious affiliation, moved from being unaffiliated with any religion to being affiliated with a particular faith, or dropped any connection to a specific religious tradition altogether.[2]

As noted in the introduction, 11% of American adults who identify as Catholic today were raised outside the Catholic church (8% were raised Protestant, 2% were unaffiliated, and 1% were raised in other religious traditions). With 23.9% of the total adult population in the United States identifying themselves as Catholic, this means that about 2.6% of the adult population has converted to Catholicism—nearly six million individuals.[3]

What accounts for switching among the millions of Americans who have changed their religious affiliation? There is no single explanation of everyday conversion, but the strongest and most consistent predictor is clearly intermarriage. Individuals who marry outside their religious tradition are more likely to switch (bringing their affiliation in line with their spouse's) than others. This seems to be particularly true of those marrying Catholics. In the 1940s and 1950s, Joseph Fichter found that 75% of converts came to the Catholic church through interfaith marriages. Two decades later, Ruth Wallace found a similar pattern among Catholic converts in Toronto, Canada. They were overwhelmingly likely to have Catholic spouses or to be engaged to Catholics. In a national study of American converts to Catholicism in the late 1970s, Dean Hoge found that family was overwhelmingly the most important factor in explaining conversion, estimating that more than 80% of Catholic converts came into the church due to intermarriage.[4] Similarly, my survey of 167 individuals participating in the RCIA process in 32 different parishes in the Roman Catholic Diocese of Fort Wayne–South Bend, Indiana, suggests that religious intermarriage remains a major factor in conversion. An overwhelming majority (87%) were either married or engaged, almost all of them to Catholic spouses (81% of those married) or fiancé(e)s (84% of those engaged).

Thus, the majority of people are drawn into a new religious tradition, denomination, or organization for circumstantial reasons. As Rodney Stark has observed, "Converts very seldom are religious seekers, and conversion is seldom the culmination of a conscious search— most converts do not so much find a new faith as the new faith finds them." Most often, the new faith finds them through existing social networks. According to Stark's network theory of conversion, "conversion is seldom about seeking or embracing an ideology; it is about bringing one's religious behavior into alignment with that of one's friends and family members." Thus, "conversion tends to proceed along social networks formed by interpersonal attachments."[5] To describe this phenomenon, I have coined the phrase "the circumstantial convert."

In this sense, Diane Gall exemplifies the circumstantial nature of most religious conversions in America: she converted to the religion of her future spouse. She was not a spiritual seeker or religious shopper, yet at the same time she is more than a product of her circumstances. She saw something of value in her fiancé Jack's family, something missing in her own family, and she connected that to the family's involvement in the Catholic church. Her decision to become Catholic reflected her desire to bring her actions in line with the ideal of family they represented and the church supported. Although social networks without question explain the *mechanism* by which she was brought to the Catholic church, they do not explain the *meaning* or *motivation* for her action in becoming Catholic. Indeed, after observing that more than 80% of Catholic converts came into the church due to intermarriage, Dean Hoge was also quick to highlight that "marrying a Catholic is not in itself a motivation for conversion to the Catholic church; many non-Catholics marry Catholics and never change. So the actual decisions are made by other factors than just intermarriage as such."[6] From my perspective, an adequate explanation of an individual's decision to convert must account not only for the mechanisms but also the meaning of and motivation for conversion. Sociologically, this means that we need to begin with a theory of action.[7]

In the sociology of religion today, there are two major theoretical perspectives that speak to the circumstantial convert as an actor. One perspective, advocated by Rodney Stark and his colleagues William Sims Bainbridge, Roger Finke, and Laurence Iannaccone, is that the circumstantial convert is a *rational actor*. As I explain in the following section, this perspective on action does appear to explain some aspects of the decision to convert; however, in the end it is limited in its ability to illuminate my data on the process of becoming Catholic. Therefore, I look to a second perspective, elaborated by Christian Smith, which views the circumstantial convert as a *moral actor*. After discussing Smith's perspective, I apply it to data on the decision to become Catholic, gathered through open-ended interviews with individuals who were in the inquiry period of the Rite of Christian Initiation of Adults (RCIA).

THE CIRCUMSTANTIAL CONVERT AS RATIONAL ACTOR

The discovery of rational choice theory by students of religion and the discovery of religion by rational choice theorists are two of the most important theoretical developments in the sociology of religion of the past 30 years. "Rational" here is not a philosophical or psychological concept referring to the human cognitive capacity for reason. It is an economic concept referring to the human propensity to "seek what they perceive to be rewards and avoid what they perceive to be costs."[8] Or, more specifically, "[i]ndividuals act rationally, weighing the costs and benefits of potential actions, and choosing those actions that maximize their net benefits."[9] Thus, at the individual level, rational choice is a theory of action based on principles of "utility maximization" as understood by economists.

If Stark is the most identifiable spokesman for the rational choice movement, Iannaccone is its chief technician, bringing his University of Chicago econometrics training (under Nobel Laureate Gary Becker) to bear on questions of religion. Contributing to the Beckerian "new home economics," Iannaccone views religion from a "household production" perspective.[10] In this view, religious practice is just one of the many commodities that a household can choose to produce. Households contribute "inputs"—such as money donated to a church and time it takes traveling to and from services—to produce certain religious commodities as "outputs." Although Iannaccone recognizes that religious commodities are "complex and largely unobservable," they include this-worldly religious satisfaction and assurances of otherworldly rewards. Thus, household investments in religion are made in such a way as to minimize inputs (costs) and maximize outputs (benefits).

As part of the household production model, Iannaccone deploys the concepts of "religious human capital"—a person's "accumulated stock of religious knowledge, skills, and sensitivities"—to account for the pattern of religious participation and affiliation that actors exhibit.[11] For example, religious switching is more likely at an early age, before an actor has accumulated so much religious capital that switching is more costly than staying. Once a person has invested 40 years accumulating the knowledge, skills, and sensitivities associated with the United Methodist Church, the cost of associating with (for example) the United Church of Christ is quite high.[12] This is to say nothing of a longer-range conversion to a non-Christian tradition such as Judaism or Islam. Similarly, people will tend to marry those who have similar religious human capital, which allows the couple to produce religion more efficiently within their household. It is more "cost effective" to marry someone who attends a Baptist church, if you do, than to marry someone who attends a Catholic church.

This rational choice model of religious action, therefore, suggests that in cases of religious intermarriage there will be pressure to produce religion more efficiently within the household by having one spouse convert. Without such a conversion, the couple faces several inefficient options. Consider a hypothetical couple, Pat and Kim. Prior to their marriage, Pat attended First Baptist Church and Kim attended St. Leo's Catholic Church. One option for them would be to continue to attend their respective churches. Although they would continue to derive religious rewards from their participation in their respective churches, this would come at the cost of time they do not spend together and possible disagreements over how to allocate their resources (time, money, and talents) in their different churches. These costs become even greater when children enter the equation. A second option would be for Pat and Kim to attend *both* First Baptist Church *and* St. Leo's. This option, too, has significant costs, especially in terms of time and money. A third option is for both to join a third church; however, in doing so they would *both* forfeit their accumulated religious capital. A fourth possibility is to discontinue religious participation altogether. This option reduces the costs of household religious production significantly, but also eliminates the benefits entirely.[13] Thus, a fifth and common response to religious intermarriage would be for Pat to become Catholic and join St. Leo's or for Kim to become Baptist and join First Baptist. As Stark and Finke have observed, "When mixed marriages occur, the couple maximizes their religious capital when the partner with the lower level of commitment reaffiliates or converts to the religion of the more committed partner."[14] This pattern is so commonly seen that it has been dubbed by some "Greeley's Law," after the sociologist Andrew Greeley, who first observed it.

Although the rational choice perspective does provide a surface-level explanation for some empirical regularities observed in patterns of religious switching, it cannot account for many of the complexities that I find in my data on Catholic converts. For example, although people clearly do convert for spousal reasons, it is equally clear that there is no simple relationship between getting married and switching. In the prelude to Chapter 6, I introduce Les Burns, a baptized Protestant who had been attending the Catholic church with his wife Mary for 48 years prior to entering the RCIA process at Queen of Peace parish. In my survey of individuals entering the RCIA process, the length of marriage ranged from 2 months to 42 years, with an average length of 10.8 years. The presence of children in a family is also connected with the decision to switch, as I discuss at length later. Again, however, there is no "one size fits all" explanation for when and how children factor into the decision to become Catholic. Some decide when they are pregnant, some decide when their children are baptized, some decide when their children start Sunday school, some decide when their children enroll in Catholic schools, some decide when their children receive their first communion, some decide when their children ask them to, some decide when their children get married, and some even decide when they are babysitting their children's children (their grandchildren!). How can we understand the varying timing of these decisions to convert from the rational choice perspective? Rational choice theory would suggest that the decision to convert comes when the benefits of changing outweigh the costs of remaining, but that is a thin sort of explanation.

The rational choice perspective also neglects the changing cultural contexts within which religious decisions are made. Cultural contexts are crucial, however, because they shape motivations for action and render action meaningful for the individual. For example, historically there have been strong cultural norms for marriage within one's religious tradition, and for switching in the event of religious intermarriage. Speaking to Catholics of a certain age, one frequently hears stories about how "When I was growing up in the 1950s, we weren't even allowed to have dinner with our Lutheran friends, much less marry them." Such were the pressures to marry within the faith. But Catholics were not alone in wanting to marry their own kind. Religious homogamy in marriage—cultural norms prescribing marriage within one's religious group—has been a fact of American life for some time. A 1951 Gallup Poll found 54% of Americans agreeing that "two young people in love who are of different religious faiths— Protestant, Catholic, or Jewish—should *not* get married."[15] Not surprisingly, in 1955, only 12% of Protestant women and 16% of Jewish women married someone of a different faith. Since then, religious intermarriage has dramatically increased as social and cultural differences between people from different religious backgrounds have diminished and as social stigmas against religious intermarriage have faded. By 2005, the rate of religious intermarriage increased to 25% for Protestant women and 38% for Jewish women. During this same time period, the percentage of Catholic women who married non-Catholic men rose from 33% to 46%.[16]

As the rate of intermarriage has increased, so too has the rate of religious switching. Given what we know of the connection between the two, it makes sense to draw a causal connection (more intermarriage is causing more religious switching), and the rational choice theorist would explain the causal mechanism in terms of maximization of household religious capital. However, Robert Putnam and David Campbell find that over the past several decades marital switching as a proportion of all switching is going down and nonmarital switching is going up. Putnam and Campbell estimate that today about 60% of Americans marry someone from another religious tradition (including from two different Protestant traditions). Of these, roughly two-thirds are still mixed. Thus, over the course of the twentieth century, "both the 'is' and the 'ought' of religious intermarriage" changed considerably. Working in tandem, rates of religious intermarriage and the acceptability of religious intermarriage both increased significantly.[17]

This is not to say that intermarriage is no longer a significant predictor of religious switching. It is, especially among those becoming Catholic. The point here is that the process by which religious intermarriage leads to switching is not at all mechanical. Social norms today are such that one doesn't *have to* switch simply because of intermarriage. The cultural context in which the decision to switch is made needs to be understood and factored into the analysis, including in cases of martial switching.[18]

Moreover, these efforts to craft a sociological rational choice perspective are still based on the essential core assumption: "Within the limits of their information and understanding, restricted by available options, guided by their preferences and tastes, humans attempt to make rational choices."[19] To be sure, the best rational choice theorists recognize that utility maximization is an assumption rather than an empirical fact. Following Becker, Iannaccone notes that maximizing behavior is the "fundamental" assumption, but also observes:

> One must, however, emphasize its status as a simplifying *assumption* to be employed and assessed within the context of predictive models that are themselves simplified representations of reality. One may assert its usefulness without for a moment believing that people always act logically, efficiently, or in accordance with their own self-interest. I do not claim to *know* that people truly are rational.[20]

James Coleman, one of the pioneering sociologists in employing a rational choice perspective, clearly recognizes that his theory "is constructed for a set of abstract rational actors. It then becomes an empirical question whether a theory so constructed can mirror the functioning of actual social systems which involve real persons."[21] In fact, at some times and places, people act rationally. Rational action is a contingent property of human action, but it is only universal in the abstract.

That rational choice theory is explicitly a theory of action—a general theory of how and why people do what they do—is to its credit. But for the sociology of religion, it is a very partial theory of action. From my perspective, it is not what rational choice theory tells us but what it does not tell us that is its key limitation. It holds constant as a pragmatic assumption that which most sociologists seek to explain, and in doing so it turns into a universal principle of action what is clearly a contingent property of action. We certainly make rational choices at times, even in the religious sphere. Do I sleep in on Sunday and go to the 11:00 a.m. service, even though I don't particularly like the contemporary music at that service? Or do I get up early for the 9:00 a.m. service with the traditional music I like better, even though the sermons at that service are boring? Balancing the "costs" and "benefits" of different solutions to these calculations does mimic the rational choices that people make when deciding what mustard to buy or whether to invest in the stock market. Some people at some times may also seek to maximize their household religious capital by making rational choices about which religious tradition to affiliate with or which congregation to attend. But in my experience and my analysis, most do not.

A more nuanced sociological analysis of religious choice must be built on a more accurate "descriptive anthropology of human personhood," in Christian Smith's language.[22] Following Smith, I postulate that human beings are *moral, believing animals,* a point I elaborate further in the next section. As I will demonstrate, adopting the perspective that converts are *moral* actors rather than *rational* actors allows us to see how and why interfaith marriages actually lead to religious conversions, and the real but limited place of utility maximization in the process.

THE CIRCUMSTANTIAL CONVERT AS MORAL ACTOR

In *Moral, Believing Animals: Human Personhood and Culture*, Christian Smith suggests that "every theory and analysis inevitably . . . assume[s] some account of human motivations, and that we will do well to acknowledge and evaluate these assumptions."[23] In contrast to the assumption that human beings are utility maximizers—or the more general social psychological perspective of human beings as cognitive information processors—Smith argues that we are moral actors. Our actions are "moral" in the sense that they are oriented toward "understandings about what is right and wrong, good and bad, worthy and unworthy, just and unjust."[24] These moral understandings "are . . . powerfully shaped by, if not derived from, larger systems of moral order." Thus, "to enact and maintain moral order is one of the central, fundamental motivations for human action."[25]

From this perspective, we need to examine the moral orders—the culturally provided schemas—that shape the meaning of and motivation for individuals' changing religious traditions, and to understand how these changes reflect action oriented to those moral orders. The complexity of this non-mechanical perspective on religious choice is a strength and challenge. In any complex society like the United States, there are multiple culturally provided schemas for moral action, and hence multiple motivations. In the following analysis, I highlight the three dominant schemas I find operative in my interviews with individuals considering becoming Catholic: familism, expressive individualism, and utilitarian individualism (see Table 2.1).

In analyzing these interviews, I pay particular attention to expressions of identity and self. One of the major ways that moral orders provide meaning and motivation for action is by setting up ideals of identity and self that propel action toward the realization of those ideals. Answering the question "what must I do?" very often requires an actor also to answer the question "who am I?"[26] For example, a tree branch has fallen in my neighbor's driveway during a storm. Even though it is still raining heavily, must I go outside and

Table 2.1. Distribution of Respondents by Dominant Cultural Schema Expressed

Schema	% of Respondents
Familism (n = 40)	72
Expressive Individualism (n = 12)	21
Utilitarian Individualism (n = 4)	7
TOTAL (n = 56)	100

help him move it? My answer depends in part on my understanding of neighborliness and how being a good neighbor fits into my self-concept. A homeless couple stands on the side of the road at an intersection. Do I slow down and hand them some money? Do I give them a bottle of water? Do I drive by? My answer depends in part on my understanding of my obligation to other human beings and whether a sense of obligation to others is part of my identity. A rational choice theorist would examine these choices in terms of costs and benefits, but it is descriptively more accurate to view these decisions as fundamentally moral rather than utility maximizing. It is not a matter of whether helping my neighbor is a greater benefit than the cost of my time, energy, warmth, and dryness. It is not a matter of whether the benefit I receive from handing a homeless couple a dollar outweighs the marginal utility of that dollar to me. It is a matter of how those actions articulate my identity and sense of self, which itself is embedded in moral orders that define and direct my actions.

A second focus in my analysis is on human emotions. A perspective that sees action as fundamentally moral rather than essentially rational draws attention to emotions as "indicators of the moral assumptions, convictions, and expectations that pervade and order our personal and collective lives." When as analysts we see individuals express feelings of guilt, annoyance, gratitude, anger, embarrassment, elation, outrage, contentment, betrayal, indifference, offense, shock, and awe, we are seeing "signs of moral orders fulfilled and moral orders violated."[27] When individuals talk about their decisions to enter the process of becoming Catholic, their language is often loaded with emotion, as we will see in the following sections.

Familism

The dominant cultural schema upon which individuals draw in explaining their decision to become Catholic is familism.[28] Seventy-two percent of respondents drew primarily on this schema (Table 2.1). According to Penny Edgell, familism sees religious involvement as "an appropriate expression of a family- and community-oriented lifestyle." Religious commitments are seen as expressing the "desire to put family first, as a way to be anchored in the local community, and as a way to achieve the moral instruction of children."[29] Emphasis is on what "good families" are or do, or the proper way to enact the roles associated with family ("good father," "good mother," "good husband," "good wife").

Although the specifics of his story are unique, the way in which Stephen Smith draws on familism in explaining his decision to become Catholic is typical. Although Stephen is only 40 years old, his work as a salesman has taken him to five different employers and eight different residences since he graduated from Ball State University as a 22-year-old. Changing jobs and moving every two to four years was exciting at first for Stephen, especially when he was single. But even after he married his college sweetheart, Lynn, in 1990, when he was 28 and she was 26, they both experienced the moving and changing positively. In fact, they were so caught up in work that they delayed having children until Stephen was 35 and Lynn 33. In 1997, their son Drew was born. To that point, church had not been a part of Stephen and Lynn Smith's family life. Stephen was baptized in the Disciples of Christ and Lynn had been raised Catholic, but both had stopped practicing when they were students at Ball State. When Drew was born, Lynn had him baptized, and for a time the family attended a Catholic church. But Stephen was never really into it, and when the family moved again for his work, it was a good excuse to stop attending.

After their most recent move, to Fort Wayne, Indiana, the constant change in their lives centered on Stephen's work began to conflict with the new family reality of Lynn being a stay-at-home mom with their young son. *When our son Drew was about four years old, I was home from work during the week for some reason, and I saw someone I didn't recognize passing by our house several times that day. With all of the stories you hear on the news about people hurting kids, I got all nervous. I called to my wife and said, "Hey, who is that guy? Do you think he's safe?" My wife said, "Stephen, that guy lives two doors down from us." We had lived in Fort Wayne for about 18 months by then, and I didn't even know one of our closest neighbors. I thought to myself, "What kind of family man am I?" I was so disconnected from what was going on with my family because of work that I didn't even know this guy.*

But this moment of insight about not knowing his neighbors—and especially his desire to be a good "family man"—stimulated Stephen to explore joining the Catholic church. *Of course I felt like I was missing out on something, when I didn't even know who was who in our neighborhood. But I also thought that Drew and Lynn must be missing out on something, too. I was depriving my loved ones of something important. I was providing for them financially, but that was it. That's like being half a father or half a husband. So, I asked Lynn if she wanted to start going to church again, and if she knew how I could join the church. I didn't expect it at all, because she had never pushed me to join, but she started crying when I asked. She said she had prayed for this, because she often felt lonely and out of place with our moving around so much, and she thought being a part of a church would help.*

So Stephen went through the RCIA process at St. Mary's Catholic Church in Fort Wayne, with Lynn as his sponsor. He was received into the full communion of the Catholic church and has been active at St. Mary's since then. *It's been great. Even though I still work a lot, making St. Mary's a priority has really helped our family. At this point, St. Mary's has really become my main community. Outside of work, that's where most of my friends are, where most of Lynn's friends are, and where most of Drew's friends are. I felt like joining the church would* . . . At this point in the interview, Stephen's voice cracks and he asks for a moment to compose himself. He leans his face into the crook of his arm to absorb the tears. He looks back up and forces out, *I feel like I am truly providing for my family now.*

Not everyone interviewed had as elaborate a characterization of his or her experience or relived the emotions so vividly, but the same themes are evident even in briefer discussions. Craig Stevens is a 27-year-old who enjoys sleeping in on Sundays. His wife, Katherine, was raised Catholic, always maintained a strong Catholic identity, and went to church as much as she could. When she became pregnant with their first child, Katherine increased her Mass attendance to two to three times per month in anticipation of having the child baptized. Katherine's increasing attendance made the late-sleeping Craig feel "like more of a bum." He recalled waking up one Sunday morning and *for some reason I thought of my dad. He wasn't a Super-Dad or anything like that. But I remember him going to church almost every week with us. I guess something about that thought stuck with me because as Katherine went to church more, I started to go more. As I sat in the pew with [Katherine], her being really pregnant, I thought of my dad. I thought of being like my dad. Him being there for my mom and for me and my sister and brother. By the time Sophie was baptized, I already decided that I would join the church, too. I think my dad would be proud of me for doing that for my family.*

Zack Williams is a matter-of-fact 49-year-old machinist who had worked for one of the many small companies that supply the recreational vehicle manufacturing industry in nearby Elkhart. Zack gave one of the most succinct summaries of the connection between a familialist moral vision and motivation for becoming Catholic: *It became more and more awkward for me to stay in the pew while my wife and kids go up for communion. One day I realized that a good husband and good father would not do that. I really feel like a bad dad to my kids. I should be up there with them, as a family.* So, Zack entered the RCIA process and became Catholic.

Although I do not include this data in Table 2.1, I find that men are somewhat more likely than women to draw on familism as a cultural schema to situate their motivation for becoming Catholic, though a majority of women also do (72% of men and 55% of women). Among them is Michele Patrick, a 34-year-old mother of two boys, Brendan and Sean, both of whom attend St. Mark's School. She was raised Presbyterian but has attended St. Mark's with her husband Dan for many years. *It's funny. All those years I attended Mass with Dan, and then with Dan and the kids, and I never once thought of joining the Catholic church. Even though I only attended the Presbyterian church when I was visiting my family, or when my family was visiting me, I still thought of myself as a Presbyterian who was attending this Catholic church with my husband and then my family. But when Brendan started school at St. Mark's, I started to spend more time at the school, and then I started to get to know more of the other families at the parish, and then I started to talk to Sister [Mary Frances, the school's principal] and Father [Craig O'Malley, the church's pastor] more, and then at some point I started feeling more a part of the parish community. By the time Sean started school two years after Brendan, I really felt like the school and the church were part of my extended family. But I wasn't a member of the church. So what did that say about me? I felt a bit like a fraud, to be honest. Volunteering in the school, helping the teachers, being with the children, but being in between being a Presbyterian and a Catholic. For a long time, Father Craig was asking me, "Why don't you join the church? What are you waiting for?" And one day when he said something about the RCIA, I said, "You know what, Father? I am going to do it. This is the year for me. This church is my family, my extended family, and I have been selfish in not giving all of me to this family. My kids really showed me the way, and I wanted to live up to the example they showed me. So, here I am, and even though I haven't gone through the whole process,*

I feel like I can walk through that school with my head up high and when I see my kids in their class or the lunch room I know they are proud of me." Although the familial role is different for Michele as a woman as compared to Stephen or Craig as men, the underlying logic of the familist cultural schema is evident here. Where Stephen and Craig felt shame for their shortcomings as husbands and fathers, Michele felt pride for better upholding the expectations she felt based on her ideals of what it meant to be a part of a church family.

These illustrative stories are meant to show that family does matter in the process of becoming Catholic, though not in the way that the rational choice theorists suggest. The particular circumstances in which individuals find themselves—married to a Catholic spouse or raising children in the Catholic church or putting children through Catholic schools, to name just a few—are not sufficient to motivate religious change. Rather, these circumstances have to be mediated by a familistic cultural schema that motivates action by placing family at the center of religious decisions. Change comes when individuals start to see themselves as "half a father" or a "bum" or a "jerk." Change comes because people want to avoid feeling "ashamed" in the eyes of their spouses or children; they want to be able to walk with their "head up high" and to be "proud" of themselves as mothers or fathers, wives or husbands.

Although familism is the dominant cultural schema in framing the meaning and motivation for the decision to convert, it is not the only cultural schema that guides people's understandings and actions. Two other languages were seen in these interviews with some frequency. Following Robert Bellah and his colleagues in the classic analysis of American culture *Habits of the Heart,* I call these cultural schemas "expressive individualism" and "utilitarian individualism."

Expressive Individualism

In the introduction to this book, I mentioned Sheila Larson, a young nurse interviewed by the authors of *Habits of the Heart,* who described her faith as "Sheilaism," her "own little voice." For Robert Bellah and his colleagues, Sheilaism reflects the strong hold of "expressive individualism" in American culture. Expressive individualism as a cultural schema "holds that each person has a unique core of feeling and intuition that should unfold or be expressed."[30] In the religious domain, expressive individualism emphasizes spiritual practice as an expression of and path to realization of one's "inner self" or "true self." It is easy, therefore, to see strong affinities between Sheilaism and the increasing popularity of being "spiritual but not religious." In both there is a conscious rejection of organized religion in favor of more personalized forms of spiritual belief and practice. Spirituality in this sense is seen as a quality of an individual whose inner life is oriented toward God, the supernatural, or the sacred. Spirituality is considered primary, more pure, more directly related to the soul in its relation to the divine, while religion is secondary, dogmatic, and stifling, often distorted by oppressive sociopolitical and socioeconomic forces. Some scholars have argued that in the new millennium there is a "divorce" between spirituality and religion, with more personal forms of spirituality destined to replace traditional, organized forms of religion.[31]

However, the relationship between spirituality and religion is not quite as simple as that. To the contrary, spirituality has long been historically connected to religion. Individual forms of piety such as prayer, meditation, or other devotions (often with a mystical component) have long been part and parcel of many major religious traditions. Sufism in Islam, Kabbalah in Judaism, and Benedictine, Franciscan, and Dominican spirituality in Roman Catholic Christianity are well-known examples. Therefore, "spiritual but not religious" may be the epitome of expressive individualism today, but just as spirituality has always existed within religious traditions, so too is expressive individualism as a cultural schema employed by individuals in traditional religious organizations.[32]

In the context of meanings and motivations for the decision to become Catholic, expressive individualism puts the individual and his or her feelings at the center of the decision-making process. One-fifth (21%) of the individuals interviewed employed expressive individualism as the dominant cultural schema through which they understood their decision to become Catholic. Gail Hirsch, a 31-year-old divorced woman and a lifelong faithful Lutheran, provides a clear example. She encountered Catholicism through a retreat that a co-worker invited her to attend. The retreat was a profoundly transformative experience for her, one that she understood very much in terms of the development of her personal spirituality. *In almost 30 years of being a Lutheran, I'd never experienced anything so moving spiritually. And that really made an impression on me. People talking about their spiritual journeys and how God has worked in their lives kind of opened me to how God has worked in my life, and gave me an awareness that I never had before. I started to take a pretty critical look at my life and I realized that God has always been in my life. I just hadn't realized it. It just sparked me to want to pray more. It made a huge impression on me and I found myself going to Mass. I got more out of it and I wanted that to continue so I found myself going to Mass more and more and looking critically at the path I had been taking for so long. So I felt like I was closer with God.* She concludes by reflecting: *I feel so much better about myself today than I did a year ago. Catholicism gives me that.*

In contrast to the familist cultural schema, which often motivates through negative emotions like shame and guilt, expressive individualism is primarily associated with positive feelings. When something feels good to the self, then that is sufficient evidence that the action is right.[33] Like Gail Hirsch, positive self-feelings also figured prominently in Rachael Stroud's decision to become Catholic. A 42-year-old mother, she and her religiously apathetic "cradle" Catholic husband planned to enroll their daughter Emily in the local Catholic school for the *values and morals she would be exposed to and taught about that she wouldn't get in the public school.* When they took Emily to register for school, Rachael was in for a surprise. *The day we went over to the church, everything just felt so right. It wasn't even like there was any thought process to it, it just felt right. I was lost, kind of floundering out there, and didn't know what I was missing.* Attending Mass at the parish *was like a whole new world opened up for me. I found myself again. I thought Rachael was long dead. You know, I'm a mom, I'm a wife, and at the time I was a nurse. There wasn't any time left for Rachael. And I found Rachael by getting closer to God and examining that relationship and perfecting that relationship in the Catholic church.* In contrast to the familist cultural schema, here familial roles like "mom" and "wife" were not ideals to be pursued but impediments to be overcome.

Of course, not everyone highlighted positive emotions in their descriptions of their motivations for becoming Catholic. At times, the self was suffering and the desire to get beyond negative feelings drove the decision. This was the case for Philip Cat, a 51-year-old engineer from Fort Wayne, who said he had been thinking about becoming Catholic for a while. *Something wasn't right. Like I spent an awful lot of time angry at the world and, you know, that was a change. I used to be a pretty happy-go-lucky guy. And I thought, you know, there's something that you're missing, and maybe its church. I was just not in tune with the inner me, I guess. I spent a lot of time upset and I didn't like that. I was looking for some inner peace in my life.* Like others, becoming Catholic helped Philip get in touch with his "inner me."

Utilitarian Individualism

The third cultural schema I identified among interviewees I call "utilitarian individualism," following Bellah and his coauthors. This schema "takes as a given certain basic human appetites and fears . . . and sees human life as an effort by individuals to maximize their self-interest relative to these given ends." If this sounds like the rational choice theory described above, it should. "Utilitarian individualism has an affinity to a basically economic understanding of human existence."[34] Seeing utilitarian individualism as a cultural schema puts us in a position to revisit the place of rational choice in human action.

Christian Smith argues that "to the extent that people today actually do act clearly in pursuit of rational self-interest, they do so much less as a reflection of some innate, natural impulse and much more in conformity with a socially and historically particular moral order that tells them that the way they *should* act is precisely in a rationally self-interested manner." Smith's perspective, therefore, "reinterprets rational choice theory as describing one particular mode of human motivation and action that reflects and embodies a specific moral order situated in a particular place in history and culture."[35] In short, rational choice is a cultural schema (utilitarian individualism), not a universal principle of action. In this context, utilitarian individualism puts the maximization of the individual's resources—especially time and energy—at the heart of the decision to become Catholic. Individuals who use this cultural schema see "saving" time and energy not as a simple description of what they do, but as the *right* thing for someone in their circumstances to do.

Historically, religion has been the one social arena that has most resisted colonization by the logic of utilitarian individualism, so it is not surprising that very few respondents (only 7%) draw on this cultural schema to describe their motivation for becoming Catholic (Table 2.1). Bill Buxley is one of them. Bill is married with three children under seven years of age, and has been attending St. Mark's Catholic Church with his wife, Anna, off and on for a number of years. As his children got older, he felt more motivated to join the church. He does not connect this decision to familial ideals or to his "inner Bill," though. Instead, he treats it as a matter-of-fact calculation that anyone in his circumstances would make. *You know, I'm not really doing this because I want to turn Catholic. I'm just doing it because my wife is Catholic and my kids are coming up Catholic. So, I mean, I don't really have a problem with being Lutheran. I just decided that having two churches didn't make sense now that the kids are getting older. What are we supposed to do? Go to one one week and another another week? Or go to both in the same day? No way! I got better things to do with my time. Don't you? So just to have one church—it's a no brainer.*

Twenty-two-year-old college student Sophie Smith approaches her decision to become Catholic from a similar perspective. Baptized in the Methodist church, she was introduced to Catholicism by her fiancé. *Just all my experiences, you know, I've just basically come to think that I don't really care what I call myself as long as it's Christian, you know, whatever. And [my fiancé] was a little more leery of leaving the Catholic church so I said, "Fine, whatever, I'll switch." It's just easier that way, less of a hassle than if we were two different religions. As long as one of us switches and we don't have to deal with that hassle, I'm good. I guess some people would say my view is wrong, that you shouldn't change just to avoid a hassle, but to me it just makes sense. I'm, like, the exact opposite. I don't see how you could do it different.*

Unlike Buxley and Smith, Paul North appears to take more seriously the substantive uniqueness of the church he is joining, but he nonetheless frames this in utilitarian terms. A 32-year-old married civil engineer and father of two, North observes, *There's some churches that we've gone to that we've gone through the ritual and you walk out of the church and realize that you wasted an hour of your day. At this point we're in a church community that doesn't feel that way. We feel that we're getting a fellowship of worship out of the Mass. So, we're in a win-win situation. Who wouldn't want that?* When the interviewer observed that he could get the fellowship benefit without becoming Catholic, North elaborated on a related benefit of formally joining the church. *Well, it doesn't make sense for me to go to Mass and not receive [communion]. It's, like, a waste of my time to put in an hour or two every Sunday and not get the payoff, you know? It isn't an efficient use of my resources, you know? I do like the fellowship, but communion is a big payoff, a big highlight of the Catholic ritual.*

CONCLUSION

By the time individuals begin the Rite of Christian Initiation of Adults, most are strongly motivated to become Catholic. To be sure, some are still deciding, and not everyone who begins the RCIA process will complete it. But in my analysis there are very few true religious seekers involved; most are products of their circumstances. My interviews with individuals becoming Catholic through the RCIA clearly show that most, like Diane Gall, encountered the Catholic church through personal connections, especially family. This is in line with Rodney Stark's network theory of recruitment. The fact that individuals' circumstances were the mechanism connecting these individuals with the Catholic church, however, does not address the motivation to become Catholic that affects so significantly the decision to act. We see people becoming Catholic at all stages of the life course. Even looking just at family formation processes, which are clearly important, we see considerable variation. Some become Catholic upon engagement, some upon marriage, and some upon childbirth. For those whose conversion is associated with their children's life course development, we see people becoming Catholic after enrolling their kids in elementary school, after their kids receive their first communion, after their kids are confirmed, after their kids leave for college, after their kids get married, and even after their kids have kids and make them grandparents. To understand this great variation in the timing of circumstantial conversion, I look not to the mechanisms of religious recruitment but to the meanings of and motivations for religious change. Following Christian Smith, I see the decision to become Catholic as a form of moral action.

Having decided to become Catholic—or at least to consider becoming Catholic—individuals in most Catholic parishes in the United States enter the Rite of Christian Initiation of Adults. As explained in the Introduction and Chapter 1, the RCIA process consists of four periods and three rituals which transition individuals from period to period. The following chapters follow these circumstantial converts through this process of initiation in the Catholic church, examining how the individual biographical trajectories that I began to look at in this chapter intersect with highly elaborate and variably implemented RCIA processes at the parish level. Because my previous work found significant similarities in how the first two periods of the RCIA process are implemented,[36] Chapter 3 considers the Period of Evangelization and Precatechumenate and the Period of the Catechumenate—the two main catechetical periods—together.

ST. MARY'S AND ST. MARK'S:
A TALE OF TWO PARISHES

Located in Pleasanton, Indiana, St. Mary's Catholic Church is one of the newest parishes in the Diocese of Fort Wayne–South Bend. The approach to Pleasanton from three sides takes one through fields of corn and soybeans. Driving on a narrow country road from the east, the farm fields give way abruptly to outcroppings of new houses in developments with names like Forestmound Run, Forestmound Lakes, and Forestmound Estates. In many of these developments, the most prominent aspects of the landscape are the large water runoff ponds. Few of the perfectly and unnaturally spaced trees are larger than six feet tall. Closer to St. Mary's, the modest homes give way to fields of McMansions—brand-new, 5,000-square-foot brick behemoths on courts and cul-de-sacs that follow the layout of the Forestmound Country Club.

The church at St. Mary's was built after Vatican II and exemplifies some of the changes advocated by liturgists and architects in the spirit of the Council. The pews are arranged in a fan shape, with four aisles dividing the five sections. The choir area takes up a large space in the left front of the church. Beyond that, the sanctuary is plain. There are no statues or icons, no tabernacle or ambry. There is not even a fixed crucifix in the sanctuary. At the same time, the church is not completely modern. In the back of the church there is a statue of Mary with devotional candles. There is an organ. There are stained-glass windows depicting the life of Jesus. Although the tabernacle is not on the main altar, neither has it been completely removed to a separate chapel. It is still visible from nearly every pew. To be sure, no one would mistake this church for a Gothic cathedral; but it is not exactly a nondenominational chapel either.

* * *

St. Mark's Catholic Church was established in the 1950s in recognition of the growing Catholic population in Montara, Indiana, and the surrounding area—a part of the diocese that was and is not particularly Catholic. Although it is only 100 miles away, St. Mark's is a world apart from St. Mary's. Whereas St. Mary's physically and spiritually embodies a post–Vatican II Catholic ethic, St. Mark's is a product of an earlier age of American Catholicism, and in many ways it still resembles the church of the 1950s.

In the beginning, St. Mark's consisted of a four-classroom school with an enrollment of fewer than 100 students and a modest rectangular hall-church serving some 200 families. The hall was outfitted with items donated from other area churches, parishioners, and groups such as the Knights of Columbus and Daughters of Isabella. Not able to build a new church, the parish instead expanded the number of Masses offered on Sunday, from two to five, before its tenth anniversary. All the while, parishioners at St. Mark's were active in the Rosary Society, the National Council of Catholic Women, study clubs, and the Holy Name Society. The parish eventually did build its new church, dedicated in the 1960s for the 700-plus families of the parish. Now nearing its sixtieth anniversary, as St. Mark's moves into the future, it does so with an eye toward the past—to its own history and to the church's tradition. Appropriately enough, one piece of literature produced by St. Mark's offers as a parish motto, "Being Faithful to the Past . . . While Connecting to the Future."

St. Mark's church itself reflects the traditional attitude of the parish. Although not excessively ornate—there is almost no gold—the sanctuary at St. Mark's is busy. Scanning from right to left, one sees all of the following: the papal flag, the priest's chair, a small baptismal font, a statue of Mary, a large stone altar on a riser two levels up from the main altar floor, a statue of the Good Shepherd, the tabernacle, the ambry containing sacramental oils, the ambo, and a US flag. In addition, the sanctuary has as bookends two side altars, one for devotion to Mary and one honoring Joseph. When the altar rail was removed after the Second Vatican Council, two sections of it were placed in front of these side altars, which seemed to appease those parishioners who objected to its removal in the first place. Paintings of Mary surround her altar, and a print of the Divine Mercy Jesus—with red and blue rays of light beaming from his heart—watches over Joseph's altar. Not far from these, on either side of the church, are shrines with statues of St. Mark and St. Paul. Devotional candles are ubiquitous.

* * *

Like the community in which it is located, St. Mary's as a geographic parish and church is resource rich, and this is reflected clearly in the RCIA process. The RCIA week at St. Mary's begins at the 6:30 p.m. Mass on Wednesday nights, which many of the eight to ten regular RCIA team members attend. This is followed at 7:00 p.m. by a team meeting, led by Elizabeth Ann Starr, the parish's full-time director of adult faith formation. The team members trickle in as the evening Mass concludes, greeting each other jovially and warmly. They check their folders in a portable file box for the meeting agenda and other handouts—announcements of diocesan programs, relevant essays from *Catechumenate* magazine, information about new inquirers. On this Wednesday immediately following the Labor Day weekend, the team is preparing for a session with individuals who are nearing the one-year anniversary of their entrance into the catechumenate. Once everyone is settled, the meeting begins with a series of group prayers and petitions. In fact, almost half of the entire team meeting is dedicated to prayer. After the prayers, the team discusses who is responsible for what and when, raises scheduling changes and problems, and chats about the recent events in everyone's lives. The tone throughout the meeting is informal—more a group of friends chatting than colleagues working. It evidences the familiarity and love born out of years of service together as a team.

Near 7:30 p.m., the group starts heading to the meeting room next door. The catechetical sessions are held in a large, new multipurpose room across from the church. Though a large space, the room fills up quickly. The RCIA director and eight team members are joined by five sponsors and eight people seeking initiation. The topic for the night is "The Mass and the Eucharist," as dictated by the "New Catholic Vision" series of pamphlets that St. Mary's has adopted. As at every catechetical session, a different team member has volunteered to lead the opening prayer, the catechesis, and the closing prayer. Tonight, Roseanne Jones offers the opening prayer, and Kate Winters leads the session. To facilitate her presentation, Kate has set up a mini-altar before her. On the table in front of her is a white cloth, and to her left is a side table with a green cloth over it. On top of the table is the group's candle, a chalice and paten, and on a shelf underneath the side table are a vase of water, a dish, and a towel. She has all of the necessary accoutrements to mimic the Liturgy of the Eucharist.

Kate's presentation is taken from a book by Father Alfred McBride called *Celebrating the Mass*. She has gone through the small book and highlighted various sections, and in her presentation she reads those sections and intersperses ad hoc comments along the way. Although it is clear that at times she is reading from the book, her presentation is not at all stiff. She seems comfortable presenting to the group as she elaborates the written material in the text with personal reflections. After speaking about the Eucharist, Kate turns to the Order of the Mass. Everyone has leaflet missals for this exercise. Kate works her way through the Mass, cribbing explanations from McBride and reflections from her personal experience, as everyone else follows along in the missals.

As she works her way through the Liturgy of the Eucharist, Kate actually begins to "perform" the service, saying the words and doing the ritual actions that a priest would do in an actual Mass. She brings the empty chalice and paten forward and sets them on the white cloth in front of her. She raises the chalice in front of her, standing at her makeshift altar, saying: "Blessed are you Lord, God of all creation, through your goodness we have this wine to drink, fruit of the vine and work of human hands, it will become for us our spiritual drink." To which all of the Catholics in the room instinctively respond, "Blessed be God forever." In this way, she enacts every last detail. She reads the Eucharistic prayer and then at the proper moment and quite naturally (it seems), makes the sign of the cross over the imaginary bread and wine. After the "consecration," she raises the host and chalice as high above and in front of her as she can reach and says, "Through Him, with Him, in Him, in the unity of the Holy Spirit, all glory and honor is yours, almighty Father, forever and ever." Most respond, "Amen." She continues to explain what she is doing, trying to point out where she is in the temporal sequence of the Mass. She says, "Now the bread and wine are the body and blood of Christ." Then, realizing what she has implied she quickly adds, "Not here," motioning to the altar in front of her. "It doesn't do any good if a priest isn't saying it. It doesn't change."

The active and participatory nature of Kate's presentation encourages people to start discussing changes that have taken place in the liturgy over the years. Other team members get involved, offering their perspectives on the Mass. Someone mentions that people used to fast for long periods before receiving the Eucharist. This generates a number of additional questions and comments from sponsors and students, and soon there are three or four different conversations going at the table on various topics related to the Mass. Elizabeth Ann calls for a break and encourages people to continue their conversations over refreshments, which most do. Including this break, the session will last an hour and 45 minutes, though many of the team members have logged closer to three hours this (and almost every) Wednesday night in service to the RCIA process at St. Mary's.

* * *

The RCIA process at St. Mark's reflects the more modest resources of the parish. Rather than operating year round, it runs on a "school year" model—beginning in August and concluding in the third week of Easter. There is no RCIA team. Although the RCIA process at

St. Mark's is technically overseen by a part-time lay volunteer RCIA director, Meaghan Donovan, the structure and process are heavily influenced by Father Craig O'Malley, who also attends most catechetical sessions and leads many. Rather than sitting at the front of the room co-presiding with Father Craig, Meaghan often sits at the back of the classroom with others in the process. The fact that most of those going through the RCIA process see Father Craig as responsible for the RCIA process confirms the hierarchical relationship here between clergy and laity, part of St. Mark's faithfulness to the past. Father Craig's teaching style reinforces this as well. The vast majority of catechetical sessions are given over to lecturing. Although Father Craig recognizes that people have questions when they are going through the RCIA process, even the way that questions enter the sessions at St. Mark's is typically from the top down.

A session in the early fall finds a group of 15 inquirers, along with about 10 companions (spouses, fiancées, boyfriends, girlfriends), gathered for catechesis in a nondescript multipurpose meeting room in the church's parish hall. Father Craig begins the meeting by reading part of Chapter 15 of the Gospel of Luke—which includes the Parable of the Lost Sheep ("there will be more rejoicing in heaven over one sinner who repents than over ninety-nine righteous persons who do not need to repent"), the Parable of the Lost Coin ("suppose a woman has ten silver coins and loses one. Doesn't she light a lamp, sweep the house and search carefully until she finds it?"), and the Parable of the Prodigal Son ("we had to celebrate and be glad, because this brother of yours was dead and is alive again; he was lost and is found"). After reminding everyone that this will be the pattern for the meetings, Father Craig asks everyone if they want "the long or the short version" of the Gospel. There is no answer. He asks for a show of hands. "How many for the long version?" No hands. "How many for the short version?" No hands. "The long version it is," he concludes.

Father Craig reads Luke 15:1–32 from the Lectionary and begins a series of questions meant to lead people through an engagement with the text:

"In the story of the lost son, who ran to whom?"

"The father ran to the son."

"What does the church do that's like this?"

"Reconciliation?"

"Yes. I'm sure some of you are wondering, 'What about confession?' The bottom line is that this is being welcomed back into God's arms. What else was in the story?"

"Sheep."

"Are sheep smart animals?"

"No."

"What are sheep like?"

"Dumb."

"What do they do?"

"They walk into walls."

"What do sheep need?"

"Someone to herd them."

"Which is called a . . . "

"Shepherd."

Although initially it seems that Father Craig is trying to encourage reflection on the Gospel, in the end he is really lecturing through questions. There is no personal reflection, dialogue, or questioning. Father Craig is a shepherd leading his sheep to the "right" answer.

The opening Gospel reading and reflection take about 25 minutes, after which Father Craig takes 15 minutes to review the schedule and other administrative items. At 7:40 p.m., he transitions into the main substantive topic for the night. Father Craig writes "Sacramental Plan of Salvation" on the board and asks the group, "What does this mean?" At first it seems the question is rhetorical, because who early in the process of becoming Catholic can answer this? His question is met with silence, so he elaborates: "Whose plan? Who is being saved? From what?" Again, silence. "Don't all speak at once." When he says this, it becomes clear that he is actually expecting a response. After a couple of attempts by participants to offer ideas about the sacraments and the steps to being saved, Father Craig directs the group to the Book of Genesis. The questioning is pretty fast paced, as Father Craig seeks to elicit the correct answers from the group. "In the Garden of Eden, we were what from God?" "Separated." Father Craig draws on the white board "God" on the far left and "Us" on the far right. Father Craig: "Did God turn his back on us?" The group, sheepishly: "No." At this point, people are responding so quietly it is as if they are speaking only to themselves, or perhaps to the person next to them. The people assembled here literally have no voice. "Who did he send?" On this question the group manages, with much urging from Father Craig, to get out "Jesus" (which he wrote on the board half way between "God" and "Us"). Father Craig then fills in the gap on the white board between "Jesus" and "Us." Father Craig: "A baby is baptized into what?" Someone: "Christianity." Father Craig: "O-Kaaaaaay." Pause. He writes down "CH," pauses, then fills in "URCH." Then he erases the UR leaving CH__CH. Father Craig: "What's missing?" Bobby, a cradle Catholic attending with his converting wife, responds excitedly: "U R!" Father Craig: "That's right: you are." In the end, Father Craig has written on the white board:

God – O.T. Prophets – Jesus – Church – Sacraments – Us

He concludes by summarizing the Sacramental Plan of Salvation: "God welcomes us home."

It is 8:00 p.m. now and Father Craig suggests a snack break. After 15 minutes, in which people sit silently or chat with someone they came with, Father Craig calls the group's attention back to the front of the class, to himself, and covers more administrative details relating to choosing sponsors ("dos and don'ts"). He then hands out a letter he drafted that speaks to "marriage situations" among those seeking initiation. ("For someone to JOIN our tradition, if they are now married, this marriage needs to be VALID in the eyes of the Catholic church.") He asks everyone to read the letter and let him know if they have any questions. At 8:25 p.m., Father Craig leads the group in praying the "Our Father" and people quickly head for the parking lot. Meaghan Donovan stays behind to touch base with Father Craig, who tells her he will be leading the session again the following week and so she does not need to do anything other than be present. By 8:30 p.m., Father Craig is back in his office and Meaghan is driving home to her family.

In this tale of two parishes we see the same Rite of Christian Initiation of Adults being implemented in quite different ways. This is perhaps not surprising, given how different the parishes are even at first glance. To be sure, in both cases we see catechists teaching those who are becoming Catholic the elements of the faith. But the means used to do that teaching—what education scholars call the "pedagogy"—differ considerably. And these differences are not trivial. Using concepts drawn from the sociology of education, in Chapter 3 we will see that they represent not just different ways of teaching but different visions of Catholicism itself.

CHAPTER THREE

VISIONS OF CATHOLICISM
IN RCIA CATECHESIS

As we have seen, individuals come to the Rite of Christian Initiation of Adults (RCIA) at all ages and stages of the life course, and
for various reasons. Although I begin this book with individuals, in
the contemporary Catholic church they are immediately drawn up
into the collective process that is the RCIA. Initiation is always about
both the individual being initiated and the initiating community. The
religious changes sought by both individuals and parishes necessarily happen at the intersection of the individual and the collectivity.
Therefore, it is vital to understand how the process of initiation encountered by individuals seeking to become Catholic is shaped by different parishes' unique social and organizational contexts. Because,
as Jerome Baggett has observed, Catholicism is a living tradition subject to local interpretation, we want to understand how different visions of the Catholic tradition are transmitted in different parishes'
RCIA processes.[1]

The first two periods of the RCIA process—the Period of Evangelization and Precatechumenate (colloquially known as "inquiry") and
the Period of the Catechumenate—center on teaching and learning
about the core beliefs and practices of the Catholic tradition.[2] According to the ritual text, the purpose of the first period is to ensure that
"the beginnings of the spiritual life and the fundamentals of Christian
teaching have taken root in the candidates" (RCIA, no. 42). There is
no specified length of time for this period, but in practice it usually
lasts five or six weeks. At that point, inquirers are asked to declare
their intentions to continue their faith journeys by standing before the

gathered parish community and going through the Rite of Acceptance into the Order of Catechumens.

The Period of the Catechumenate, or simply "the catechumenate," is the main time of formation for those seeking initiation. The purpose of this period is to give catechumens "suitable pastoral formation and guidance, aimed at training them in the Christian life" (*RCIA*, no. 75). In practice, most parishes achieve this by requiring catechumens to attend a weekly catechetical session, as well as Sunday Mass. Some parishes practice a Rite of Dismissal during the catechumenate in which, between the Liturgy of the Word and Liturgy of the Eucharist, the catechumens in attendance leave the Mass with a catechist to reflect on the Mass readings. The ritual text specifies that the Period of the Catechumenate may last "several years" (*RCIA*, no. 7), though the United States bishops' *National Statutes* state that the period "should extend for at least one year of formation, instruction, and probation" (*NS*, no. 6).

Although there is a single, universal normative text for the entire church—the *Ordo Initiationis Christianae Adultorum*—the implementation of that text in different parishes varies considerably.[3] For example, only 15% of parishes nationally and 34% of parishes in this study, including St. Mary's, require individuals becoming Catholic to spend at least a year in the catechumenate, as specified in the *National Statutes*. In most cases, a "school year" model of the RCIA—beginning the process in the fall and holding a "graduation" at Easter, as at St. Mark's—is typical in the United States.[4] Other differences in implementation will be explored throughout this book, but this chapter focuses on catechesis, particularly differences in substance and style, like those seen between St. Mark's and St. Mary's in the prelude to this chapter.

There are many ways in which an analyst could approach these catechetical differences. In this chapter, I approach them from the perspective of the sociology of education. Efforts to transmit religious traditions often look like other secular forms of schooling, with students attending classes and teachers instructing them in the ideas and information essential to the subject.[5] This is certainly the case with the RCIA, in which those seeking to become Catholic meet on a regular basis as a group with teachers ("catechists") for classroom instruction in the faith ("catechesis"). Like education generally, RCIA catechesis can be "read" for the beliefs, values, and understandings that it explicitly espouses or implicitly conveys. It is during inquiry and the catechumenate that we see most clearly the differences from parish to parish in visions of what Catholicism is as a tradition, what the Catholic church is as an organization, and what it means to be Catholic as an individual. Without claiming to reduce all the many differences between parishes to a single explanation, in this chapter I highlight *social class* as a key factor affecting the differences.

CLASS MATTERS IN RCIA CATECHESIS

Much of the sociological attention to class differences in religion is focused on differences *between* traditions. The field's debt to Max Weber here is clear. Weber's observation that Protestants tended to occupy higher-status positions than Catholics in virtually all industrial societies led him to conclude famously that there is an "elective affinity" between the ethic of Protestantism and the spirit of modern capitalism. More recently, James Davidson and Ralph Pyle have highlighted religious stratification emerging from the colonial period in America, when Episcopalians, Congregationalists, and Presbyterians came to so dominate business and politics that they were known as "the Protestant Establishment." Although the American religious stratification system has changed some over time—for example, Jews and Hindus have the highest average education and income levels today—the historically elite groups remain so, while Baptists and Pentecostals continue to occupy the lower rungs of the ladder. A number of good empirical studies have been published explaining this latter reality, emphasizing especially the role of such factors as hostility toward secular education, anti-intellectual orientations, and lower verbal abilities among fundamentalist Protestants in mediating their lower economic status.[6]

The place of Catholics in the class hierarchy of the American denominational system has undergone considerable change over time. A small, often persecuted religious minority in most colonies during the seventeenth and eighteenth centuries, Catholics became a larger but still marginalized minority with the waves of immigration from Ireland, Germany, and elsewhere in the nineteenth century. As the Catholic church grew through this immigration, it became predominantly urban and working class. Social isolation and cultural hostility led to the ghettoization of many Catholics and the development of parallel Catholic institutions like schools, hospitals, and fraternal and community organizations. Over the course of the twentieth century, the social, cultural, and economic gap between Catholics and Protestants closed, a phenomenon that preoccupied the attention and publications of scholars like Andrew Greeley from the 1960s onward. Today, American Catholics are "at or just above national averages with respect to educational attainment, occupational status, and family income." They "live in the same neighborhoods . . . [and] read the same books and see the same movies . . . [and] belong to the same associations" as other Americans. In a word, they are "thoroughly assimilated."[7]

This social history tells a familiar story about the Catholic church in America. It is, however, just one story of many. There are stories of American Catholicism that begin in Florida or Louisiana or California or Texas, rather than in New England or New York or Maryland. There are stories of Catholic immigrants from Vietnam, the Philippines, South Korea, and Haiti, rather than Europe. As historian Timothy Matovina has argued recently, there is a major story to be told about Latino Catholics, "America's largest church."[8] Paying attention to this regional and racial diversity in the American Catholic experience also highlights the importance of considering class diversity. Beneath Catholics' middling national averages on educational attainment and income, there is a story to be told about class differences *within* Catholicism. In this particular case, I focus on class differences and their implications for RCIA catechesis and understandings of Catholicism.

Table 3.1 shows some of the organizational and demographic characteristics of the six parishes in which Sarah MacMillen, Kelly Culver, and I conducted fieldwork. Although not exhaustive, education, income, and occupation are the crucial determinants of social class position in the United States. Lacking data on the class composition of the parishes themselves, I use as a proxy data from the US Census Bureau on the zip codes in which the parishes are located. In the bottom half of the table, I list the median household income, percentage of individuals holding college degrees, and the percentage of individuals with professional jobs for each of the six parishes. These data reveal considerable differences between the parishes, which were evident to us during the year we spent observing them. I have arranged the parishes in the table so that the highest social class parishes (St. Innocent and St. Mary's) appear on the left and the lowest social class parishes (St. Mark's and St. John Bosco) appear on the right. The fact that social class is an important, but not the only, factor affecting the implementation of the RCIA can be seen in the class similarity of, but RCIA differences between, Queen of Peace and St. Peters, the two parishes in the middle.

Of what consequence are these class differences between parishes? In terms of the organizational characteristics of their RCIA process, seen in the top half of Table 3.1, even though these parishes initiate roughly the same number of people per year, the higher social class parishes have more resources available to them than lower social class parishes. In the four highest social class parishes, full-time lay ecclesial ministers are responsible for the RCIA process; in the two lowest, ordained clergy and volunteers (Deacon Zeke Williams at St. John Bosco is himself a volunteer). In the higher social class parishes, the number of hours that leaders devote to the RCIA process are much higher than in the lower social class parishes. The higher social class parishes also multiply their catechetical resources by building RCIA

Table 3.1. Organizational Characteristics of RCIA Processes and Class Characteristics of Study Parishes

	St. Innocent	St. Mary's	Queen of Peace	St. Peter's	St. Mark's	St. John Bosco
Organizational Characteristics of RCIA Process						
RCIA Leadership	Pastoral associate	Director of adult faith formation	Pastoral associate	Pastoral associate	Pastor (with volunteer RCIA dir.)	Permanent Deacon
Hours Spent on RCIA Weekly	10	15	20	5	6 (combined)	3
Size of RCIA Team	7	8–10	8	1	0	0
Others Regularly Involved	Both priests, liturgist	No	Both priests, deacon, seminarians	No	No	No
Adults Initiated Annually	5 unbaptized, 10 baptized	3 unbaptized, 5 baptized	4 unbaptized, 5 baptized	4 unbaptized, 5 baptized	5 unbaptized, 10 baptized	4 unbaptized, 5 baptized

Class Characteristics of Parishes

Median Income in Zip Code (National Percentile)	80,351 (96)	60,069 (87)	43,225 (62)	43,160 (62)	45,619 (67)	38,589 (49)
% College Degree in Zip Code (National Percentile)	48.8 (93)	39.0 (88)	28.2 (78)	26.7 (76)	17.6 (56)	16.0 (50)
% Jobs Professional (National Percentile)	50.0 (93)	44.6 (88)	36.0 (76)	36.5 (77)	26.5 (43)	25.5 (38)
Average National Percentile	94	87	72	72	55	46

Note: Demographic data are from the 1990 US Census and were generated using the website zipwho.com.

teams. St. Innocent, St. Mary's, and Queen of Peace all have RCIA teams with seven or more members to support those charged with leading the process, while St. Mark's and St. John Bosco have no team at all. Being able to hire a leader who can spend more time on the RCIA process is a simple material difference between parish budgets. But having a team of volunteer catechists is not. Financially, it would not cost St. John Bosco any more money to have a *volunteer* RCIA team than it costs St. Innocent: nothing. Instead, the presence of large RCIA teams at three parishes and not at three parishes in this study is more reflective of different class-based cultures in three parishes. When I first called St. Innocent and asked for the name of the person who headed their RCIA process, I was told that it was not a person but the RCIA team as a group. Only after some additional questions was I referred to the pastoral associate who coordinated the team. St. Innocent does not simply have more financial resources than St. John Bosco; it has a different vision of the role of lay people in the catechetical process and in the church.

This points to the second and more significant difference that class makes between parishes. Catechetical processes reflect broader understandings of the church itself. Here we return again to theologian Aidan Kavanagh's assertion that the process of initiating new members "defines simultaneously both the Christian and the Church"[9]—it embodies a vision of the church itself. In this chapter, I tie class differences between parishes not to different understandings reflected in RCIA catechesis of *what to believe* about Catholicism, about which there is some unity across parishes, but to differences in *how to believe* as Catholics.

Like the sociologist of education studying schools, to access these visions or understandings of "what it means to be Catholic" we need to examine religious education in the RCIA process in terms of its *curriculum*. True to its Latin root ("running course"), at a very basic level, the curriculum can be defined as the syllabus that specifies the beliefs or knowledge to be transmitted in a course of study. It specifies *what* is being taught in an educational setting. This is vital because "curriculum is a microcosm of the culture: its inclusions and exclusions are an index of what the culture deems important."[10] It also explains why the curriculum is often a battleground on which culture wars are fought, as in the 1980s and 1990s when the question of whether to include diversity courses in the core curriculum was debated strenuously in American higher education.[11]

Sociologists of education, however, have long realized that the overt, explicit curriculum expressed in a syllabus is just one part of what is taught in schools. There is also a "hidden curriculum" that teaches more general orientations and approaches to beliefs, knowledge, and authority. Education scholar A. V. Kelly defines the hidden curriculum as the lessons students learn "because of the way in which the work of the school is planned and organized, and through the materials provided, but which are not in themselves overtly included in the planning or sometimes even in the consciousness of those responsible for the school arrangements."[12] Common examples of the hidden curriculum in schools include lessons about passivity and obedience to authority that students learn by being required to sit at desks attentively, stand in line quietly, and raise hands and wait to be recognized before speaking in class.

Understanding religious education, therefore, requires attention to both the explicit and hidden dimensions of the curriculum. Put simply, we need to understand *what* is taught and *how*. Empirically, this requires an examination of not only *what* those becoming Catholic are taught to believe explicitly, but also what implicit lessons they are taught about *how* they should believe. This distinction between *what* and *how* is essential to grasping the similarities and differences between parishes in their visions of Catholicism.

The Explicit Curriculum of the RCIA Process

English professor E. D. Hirsch famously defined "cultural literacy" as "what every American needs to know."[13] Although he caused a firestorm because of what he included and excluded in his list of necessary knowledge, the idea that there are some things people should know is usefully applied to this case. What does everyone who is becoming Catholic need to know? Is there broad agreement, or is there substantial diversity on what constitutes the core of Catholic cultural literacy? I answer these questions by examining the explicit curriculum of the RCIA process, beginning with RCIA leaders' visions of the Catholic faith they are trying to convey, followed by an examination of the topics covered in the RCIA process in six parishes.

One way to get at RCIA leaders' visions of what it means to be Catholic is to identify what aspects of the church's teachings and practices they hold to be most central to the faith. Obviously, a closed-ended survey is a blunt instrument with which to measure nuanced theological positions, but it does provide a good starting point from which to examine visions of the church. Table 3.2 gives the percentage of RCIA leaders who deem each of the listed characteristics as *essential* "to the vision of the Catholic faith you seek to convey to those participating in RCIA in your parish." Despite considerable attention in the Catholic and secular media to divisions within the church, these data suggest widespread agreement on the essential elements of the Catholic faith to be passed on.

Clearly, sacramental life and devotional practices are the heart of the church, according to those responsible for adult initiation. The highest level of agreement among respondents centered on the presence of God in the sacraments, especially in the Eucharist (100% agreement on both), weekly Mass attendance (94%), the importance of the sacrament of confession (87%), and daily prayer (85%). Beyond the sacramental life of the church, the levels of agreement on the structure of the church hierarchy, sexual ethics, and social teachings vary more widely.

The church hierarchy is frequently identified by RCIA leaders as essential to the vision of the church to be conveyed to those becoming Catholic. Eighty-nine percent deemed the need for a Pope essential and 82% called the authority of the bishops essential. There is

Table 3.2. RCIA Leaders' Identification of Essential Elements of Catholic Faith to be Conveyed to Those Becoming Catholic (N = 45)

Item	% Essential
Unanimous Agreement	
God's presence in sacraments	100
Christ's presence in Eucharist	100
More than 75% Agreement	
Obligation to attend Mass weekly	94
Need for a Pope	89
Confession to a priest	87
Daily prayer	85
Catholic Church is universal	85
Teachings that oppose abortion	82
Authority of bishops	82
More than 50% Agreement	
Opposition to contraception	65
Belief that homosexual acts are sinful	61
Charitable efforts toward the poor	56
Devotion to Mary	55
God's presence in the poor	53
Less than 50% Agreement	
Eliminating causes of poverty	45
Opposition to death penalty	43
Devotion to saints	41
Celibate priesthood	40
Male-only priesthood	38
Having religious orders	24

considerably less agreement on the present eligibility requirements to serve as clergy. Less than half (40%) of respondents see the *celibate* priesthood as essential, and only 38% view the *male* priesthood as essential. Church teachings on issues of sexual ethics were deemed essential a majority of the time. For example, 65% hold opposition to contraception to be essential and 61% see the belief that homosexual acts are sinful as essential.

There is uneven support for conveying what the late Cardinal Joseph Bernardin called the "consistent life ethic" to RCIA partici-pants;[14] to wit: while 82% of respondents identify opposition to abor-tion as essential, only about half as many (43%) see opposition to the death penalty as essential. Other social teachings such as the belief in God's presence in the poor, charitable efforts toward the poor, and the need to eliminate the causes of poverty are considered essential by only about half of respondents (53%, 56%, and 45%, respectively). Although certain aspects of devotional life—such as Mass attendance and daily prayer—are widely held to be central to the Catholic faith, other types of devotions are seen as less essential. Notably, devotion to Mary is held to be essential by 55% of respondents, while devotion to the saints is only deemed essential by 41% of the respondents.

In the end, RCIA leaders' vision of the Catholic faith to be con-veyed to RCIA participants shines through clearly. It centers in the first place on the sacraments, especially the Eucharist, which is cel-ebrated in the context of the Mass. The church is also catholic ("uni-versal") and apostolic, with the Pope, bishops, and priests playing a very special role. Of course, whether this clear vision translates into a specific curriculum for the RCIA catechesis is an empirical question. What are the key topics actually taught to aspiring Catholics? Is there as broad an agreement on topics as we saw in the RCIA directors' survey responses?

To answer these questions, I analyze the syllabi for the six parishes observed in this study. In Table 3.3, I rearrange the topics listed in the syllabi by grouping them into major categories, then listing the categories from most to least common. Not surprisingly, every parish begins their catechesis by introducing the faith journey in various ways, often focusing on God's "call" or "plan" and the individual's response. From there, every parish moves to a consideration of the nature of God (theology) and of Jesus (Christology), and how God is known through Divine Revelation in the sacred scriptures. As is clear from the table, not every parish treats these issues under the same topical heading or in the same order, but they do all cover these topics at the outset. This suggests, once again, a broad common ground of agreement on Catholic literacy, on "what every Catholic needs to know."

The two elements of the Catholic faith that RCIA leaders unanimously agreed on in the survey are God's presence in the sacraments and Christ's presence in the Eucharist. Not surprisingly, then, issues of the liturgical and sacramental life of the church are commonly covered in the RCIA catechesis, albeit under somewhat different headings at different parishes. Less universally treated under this broad heading are issues such as the liturgical year, sacraments other than the Eucharist, and prayer. The omission of prayer as a core topic is surprising since 86% of RCIA leaders consider this essential to the Catholic faith. Of course, prayer is something that can be modeled in many sessions regardless of the topic, and also taught within the context of other topics (e.g., teaching the rosary in a session on Mary).

More than 75% of RCIA leaders agreed that the universality of the church, the authority of the bishops, and the need for a Pope are essential elements of the Catholic faith, and this too is reflected in the RCIA syllabi. The organization of the church—its structure, hierarchy, four marks (one, holy, catholic, apostolic)—is a topic universally covered in the six parishes observed. Interestingly, although devotion to Mary and to the saints is not as widely considered essential to the Catholic faith in the survey of RCIA leaders, Mary and the saints are two of the topics that are also covered by all six parishes. Church structure, Mary, and the saints are among the topics that individuals considering becoming Catholic have the most questions about, so it makes sense for RCIA directors to preemptively address these issues— especially Mary and the saints, which in the grand scheme of things are not considered as essential to the faith as other elements.

Overall, the analyses presented in Tables 3.2 and 3.3 suggest a great deal of commonality and standardization in the way the leadership

Table 3.3. Catechetical Topics Covered by Six Parishes (Session # in Parentheses)

Queen of Peace	St. Innocent	St. John Bosco	St. Mark's	St. Mary's	St. Peter's
The Faith Journey					
"The Call" (1)	Our Desire and Capacity for God (1)	Desire for God (1)	Sacramental Plan of Salvation (1)	God Calls/We Respond (1)	Faith Journey (1); Faith: Our Response (3)
Theology/Christology/Scripture					
God with Us (2)	Trinity (2)	Mystery of God (2)	Who is God? (2)	Holy Spirit and Trinity (7)	Trinity (4)
Scripture (3); Old Testament Images of God (4)	Old Testament (3); New Testament (4)	Divine Revelation (1)	The Bible (6–7)	Divine Revelation (2); Bible, Scripture (10)	Divine Revelation and God's Love (2)
Images of Jesus in the Gospels (5)	Jesus (5)	Christ as Fulfillment of God's Promise; Incarnation (4); Christ's Ministry; Redemption (5); Paschal mystery (6)	Jesus (3)	Jesus (3); Death and Resurrection (9)	God's Revelation in Christ (4); Incarnation (7); Ministry (8); Redemption (9); Resurrection, Ascension (10)

Living in the Spirit: The Christian Communities (Acts/Paul) (6)		Holy Spirit (6)	The Holy Spirit (5)		Holy Spirit and the Church (11)
Church Structure					
One, Holy, Catholic, Apostolic Church (10)	Church Hierarchy (6)	Church—One, Holy, Catholic, Apostolic (7)	The Church (9)	Church Structure (9); Church: One, Holy, Catholic, Apostolic (12)	Church: One, Holy, Catholic, Apostolic (12)
Liturgical and Sacramental Life					
	Eucharist (10–11)	Eucharist: Theology and Structure of Mass (11)	Mass (10)	The Mass (4)	Structure of Mass (6)
The Living Church/A Sacramental Overview (11)		Liturgical/Sacramental Life of the Church; (9)	Grace and the Sacraments (14)	Sacraments (8)	Liturgical/Sacramental Life of the Church (15)

(continued)

Table 3.3. (Continued)

Queen of Peace	St. Innocent	St. John Bosco	St. Mark's	St. Mary's	St. Peter's
Church Tour (2)		Church Tour (9)	Church Tour (4)		Church Tour (6)
Liturgical Calendar (12)	Liturgical Year (9)		Liturgical Year (11)		
Prayer (7); Evening of Prayer (9)		Prayer in the Christian Life (15)	Prayer (13)		
	Marriage (12)	Healing, Matrimony, Holy Orders (12) Baptism, Confirmation (10)		Holy Orders and Matrimony (12)	
Catholic Distinctives					
Mary, the Mother of God (13)	Mary (7)	Mary (7)	Mary (12)	Mary (11)	Devotion to Mary (14)
Call to Holiness/ Communion of Saints (8)	The Saints (7)	Saints (7)	Communion of Saints (8)	Christian Models, Saints (15)	Communion of Saints (14)
Sin and Grace (14)	Sin and Forgiveness (8)	Creation and Sin (3)			Creation and Sin (5)
Four Last Things (15)		Four Last Things (8)			Four Last Things (13)

Morality

Catholic Morality
and Dignity of the
Human Person (13)
10 Commandments
(14)

Christian Moral-
ity (13)

Christian Deci-
sion Making
(14)

in different parishes conceptualize the essential elements of Catholicism to pass on to new members during the period of inquiry and the catechumenate. This is true despite different demographic and organizational characteristics of parishes, different leaders, and different approaches to the RCIA process. Of course, the explicit curriculum is only one aspect of what is taught in the RCIA process. In addition to *what* is being taught about Catholicism, we also need to pay attention to *how* it is being taught.

The Hidden Curriculum of the RCIA Process

Whereas the explicit curriculum is most clearly found in the syllabus of topics to be covered, the hidden curriculum is best examined through the *pedagogy* employed to teach the syllabus. Pedagogy has to do with how instruction is organized and how content is delivered to students.[15] Most discussions of pedagogical differences focus on the relative effectiveness of different teaching methods for student learning (i.e., which instructional methods best promote student learning). I adapt this focus by looking not at substantive student learning outcomes (e.g., can the person explain the concept of the Trinity?), but at the way that different pedagogies suggest different orientations to authority. This perspective comes from the critical pedagogy movement most associated with Brazilian educator and philosopher Paulo Freire. In his famous work *Pedagogy of the Oppressed*, Freire distinguishes between traditional pedagogy based on a "banking model" of education, in which students are open accounts to be filled with official knowledge by teachers, and critical pedagogy, in which students and teachers are co-learners in a more open-ended process of discovery. The hidden curriculum of authority relations in traditional pedagogy is more hierarchical and in critical pedagogy, more democratic.[16]

Not surprisingly, these concepts developed to understand secular schooling can be applied more or less directly to the religious education that takes place in the RCIA. I do this by re-conceptualizing

Freire's traditional-critical pedagogy dichotomy as a continuum. The underlying dimension of this continuum is *extent of student engagement with the material*. More traditional pedagogies like *lecturing* and *seat work* create a separation and hierarchical relationship between teacher and learner, and put the learner in a passive role with respect to learning the material. In lecturing, the teacher stands in front of the class and tells students what they are supposed to know. In seat work, students answer lists of questions or do assignments without any interaction with or guidance from a teacher. Slightly more interactive and engaging for students is a *question and answer* pedagogy. This type of instruction has a tripartite structure, consisting of a question posed by the teacher, a student response, and the teacher's evaluation of the response. As we will see below, this pedagogy is not the most participatory for students, but it can be done in ways that are more hierarchical and ways that are less hierarchical.

A still more engaging pedagogy is *discussion*. This occurs when classroom discourse transcends the typical question-response-evaluation sequence of question-answer sessions to exhibit free-flowing comments among students and teachers. Some, like education professors Stephen Brookfield and Stephen Preskill, have connected discussion-based pedagogies with the cultivation of democratic sensibilities. "Taking discussion seriously," they write, "moves the center of power away from the teacher and displaces it in continuously shifting ways among group members. . . . In this sense, classroom discussions always have a democratic dimension" because both discussion and democracy "imply a process of giving and taking, speaking and listening, describing and witnessing—all of which help expand horizons and foster mutual understanding."[17]

The most engaging and collaborative pedagogy is experiential learning—put simply, learning by doing. This is not a new idea. Indeed, Aristotle wrote in *The Nicomachean Ethics*, "For the things we have to learn before we can do them, we learn by doing them, e.g. men become builders by building and lyreplayers by playing the lyre." Correspondingly, people become Catholic by engaging in Catholic practices such as *liturgy* and *prayer*. This idea does not only follow from educational theories of experiential learning, but is something recognized and promoted by the Catholic church itself, as when Pope Paul VI declared at the Second Vatican Council that "liturgy is . . . the first school of the spiritual life" (an idea to be discussed further in Chapter 4).[18]

These five pedagogies—liturgy and prayer, discussion, question and answer, lecture, and seat work—represent a continuum of the hidden curriculum of authority from most participatory and democratic to most passive and hierarchical. In this continuum we can see different conceptions of what it means to be a Catholic in relation to the locus of authority in the church. On the one pole, authority in the church is more democratic; to be Catholic, one actively engages the beliefs and practices of the tradition. On the other pole, authority in the church is more hierarchical; to be Catholic, one simply shows up, pays attention, and follows the rules.

Having this continuum as a tool with which to analyze pedagogical practices in RCIA catechesis allows me to examine whether there are systematic differences across parishes, and if so, to consider what explains those differences. To this end, Sarah MacMillen, Kelly Culver, and I systematically coded the amount of time devoted to different pedagogies in three catechetical sessions at each of our six fieldwork parishes. The results are presented in Table 3.4. In this analysis we can see some telling differences between parishes. Most notably, St. Mark's and St. John Bosco—the lower social class parishes—rely more on hierarchical and passive pedagogies like question and answer and lecturing (90.6% of the time at St. Mark's and 95.9% of the time at St. John Bosco). The three higher social class parishes—St. Innocent, St. Mary's, and Queen of Peace—reveal more diversity in their pedagogies, and significantly more focus on participatory and engaging pedagogies like liturgy and prayer and discussion. This accords with sociological studies that consistently show greater emphasis on autonomy among the middle and upper classes and on obedience and respect for authority among the lower and working classes.[19]

Table 3.4. Time Allocated to Various Instructional Activities during Catechetical Sessions (in %)

	St. Innocent	St. Mary's	Queen of Peace	St. Peter's	St. Mark's	St. John Bosco
Liturgy and Prayer	5.8	13.8	16.5	1.8	3.4	3.0
Discussion	31.3	29.7	34.9	18.9	6.0	1.1
Question and Answer	9.2	0.4	6.6	14.4	20.2	5.3
Lecture	53.7	56.1	33.6	54.2	70.4	90.6
Seat Work	0.0	0.0	8.3	10.7	0.0	0.0

Note: Small group discussion is coded as "discussion," not "seat work," which is passive and individualized.

To put some flesh on the skeleton of data in Table 3.4, we can consider typical sessions in two different parishes. Consider first St. John Bosco Catholic Church in the downtown area of Owego, Indiana, a small city with a population of around 45,000. The city's closed storefronts and "property for sale" signs testify to the disheartened character of small downtowns in an age of suburban sprawl and declining domestic manufacturing. St. John Bosco is Owego's first Catholic parish (founded in the late 1840s), and its silhouette has long been a prominent figure in the city's skyline. Today, the church sits as a reminder of Owego's once-thriving industrial past, resplendent with architectural accoutrements donated by its immigrant parishioners. It is difficult to imagine a church as massive and ornate as St. John Bosco in a city of such small size and with the economic hardships of Owego, but the building literally stands out as a testimony to the hard labor and determination of its working-class parishioners.

The Old World character of the parish and its diminishing resources are embodied in the RCIA process. At St. John Bosco, Zeke Williams *is* the RCIA process—no RCIA director, no catechetical team, just a tall, cheerful, pastorally paunched, white-haired, grandfatherly figure, with a deep voice and warm laugh. Indeed, as a permanent deacon, Zeke is in many ways at the center of parish life at St. John Bosco generally. It is hard to imagine the church functioning without him. He performs many of the essential duties during the Mass, including offering prayers and giving homilies. He also directs a number of the parish's programs in addition to being fully responsible for adult initiation. No wonder, then, that he spends only three hours per week on the RCIA process (Table 3.1).

In many ways, Deacon Zeke is a perfect representation of St. John Bosco. He is a hard-working parent, grandparent, and a devoted husband for over forty years. Zeke worked for years at a plant in Fort Wayne and then for 18 years as a manager in material flow at the local Owego car plant. He has some college education, but no formal degree in theology. His approach to the faith is dismissive of "high-falutin' theology" in favor of a plain-and-simple, "just do it," task-oriented pragmatism aimed at presenting the material and completing the steps dictated by the Diocese of Fort Wayne–South Bend for the initiation of adults. In this way, he models obedience to authority at the same time that he conveys the sense of the Catholic tradition as individuals accepting correct belief as established by the church hierarchy.

As already noted, catechetical sessions at St. John Bosco are almost wholly given over to Deacon Zeke lecturing (90.6% of the time). Most of the time, when he does ask a question—like "How does God reveal Himself to you?"—he does not get or even seem to expect the students to respond. He fills in the dead spaces himself with more lecturing. His lectures come from what he calls his "notebook" for the class. The notebook actually consists of an RCIA catechetical course book, commissioned by the bishop for use in the RCIA in the diocese, *Making Disciples: A Comprehensive Catechesis for the RCIA Catechumenate. Making Disciples* was edited by Sister Mary Jane Carew, director of the diocesan Office of Catechesis, and published by Our Sunday Visitor Publishing of Huntington, Indiana, located in the Diocese of Fort Wayne–South Bend. It covers topics taken from and organized in the order of Pope John Paul II's universal *Catechism of the Catholic Church*.[20] Each of the 35 chapters provides the outline for a typical RCIA session, including an opening hymn, silent prayer, oration, and scripture reading. A three- to four-page intensive outline of topics to be discussed follows, complete with scriptural citations. Each chapter concludes with focus or discussion questions and a list of resources on the topic.

When *Making Disciples* was issued in 1997, the bishop "request[ed] that every parish use it." Many RCIA directors, either actively or passively, have ignored this mandate. My survey data show that 25% of RCIA processes in the diocese "use" *Making Disciples* in some way, including 17% who use it as their primary text. Many of the other RCIA directors seem unaware of its existence, perhaps because there is considerable turnover among them and the bishop does not remind parishes every year to use the text. Deacon Zeke, then, is one of the few RCIA directors in the diocese who truly use *Making Disciples* as the central text for the structure and content of catechesis.

The Thursday-night catechetical sessions at St. John Bosco last for no more than 60 minutes. In a typical session, Deacon Zeke presents one to two chapters from *Making Disciples*. His presentation on the Holy Spirit, the four marks of the church, Mary, and the communion of saints (all in one session) is typical of this. At 7:00 p.m., as always, Deacon Zeke takes his place at the front of the classroom, with his students dispersed around the room sitting at tables facing him. Because he did not finish his presentation on the Holy Spirit the previous week, he does not begin this session by gathering the group together with a prayer. Instead, he simply picks up where he left off, naming the seven gifts of the spirit, as written in Isaiah—"this is what they'll teach you in the Catholic Church"—and then listing a few more from I Corinthians—"wisdom, faith, healing, prophecy." He continues, "The Holy Spirit is also celebrated in confirmation, in the gift of tongues, and it has many titles: paraclete, grace, adoption, glory." Finally, he pauses to ask, "Do any of you recall how you might have seen the Holy Spirit, or heard it referred to?" This question is not his own, but comes from the lesson plan in *Making Disciples*. There is no answer, so he continues on. "OK, one is water, the sacramental sign of new birth. Another is fire, which happens on Pentecost. Another is a seal, a sign of anointing. Another is a laying on of hands." After a few more examples, Zeke concludes the material on the Holy Spirit, and without asking if anyone has any questions or encouraging any discussion or other engagement, he goes straight to the next topic, the next chapter, the next lesson plan in *Making Disciples*.

"OK," Zeke says by way of transition, "now let's start with a prayer." Without encouraging anyone else to pray along with him, he reads a prayer that asks for an increase of spiritual gifts and invokes the gift of the church as the eternal Temple. He begins his presentation, introducing it as "the Mystery of the church and why it is One, Holy, Catholic and Apostolic." As instructed in *Making Disciples*, he reads from St. Peter, "writing to those in Galatia, etc. etc., wherever they are." And then he reads from his notebook: "The body of Christ is a spiritual community and a visible earthly society. . . . Communion is from the Latin for *communio*, unity in togetherness. . . . It has four characteristics: it is one, holy, catholic—that's with a lower case c—and apostolic." He proceeds to go through each of the four characteristics, after which he pauses for questions: "Anybody got any questions? Anybody got any *problems* with any of this?" Hearing none, he moves on to the next topic.

In less than half an hour, Zeke has already finished up the Holy Spirit and cruised through the discussion on the four characteristics of the church. Now he has moved on to Mary. After 10 or so minutes on Mary, he moves to the call to holiness. "Which means we are a communion of saints," Zeke clarifies. At this point, the students are models of disengagement. Rick is nervously shaking his leg, fidgeting. Amanda is sitting with her chin firmly pressed up against the lower palm of her hand. Sara's arms are folded firmly across her middle. Anna is playing with her nails. Zeke asks, "Can any of you think of someone here on earth that is a saint?" There is no answer for a bit, then Rick responds, "You. You're teaching us!" Zeke laughs heartily and responds, "I'm no saint!" He asks if anybody else has anything to share, and hearing nothing, concludes: "Well, I think that's good for tonight."

In a typical catechetical session at St. John Bosco, as Zeke lectures from "the notebook," his students are not visibly responsive: no acknowledgment of what he is saying with facial expressions, nods of the head, or audible confirmations. Even when he asks questions, he usually gets no or only a minimal response. Although Zeke seems to be encouraging participation by asking questions, the authority he conveys through his lecture-based pedagogy—the hidden curriculum—effectively teaches these future Catholics that he is the authority in charge of catechesis, the possessor and deliverer of certain information (required by the bishop through the book he mandated in his diocese, though they do not know this). Their role, then, is to sit quietly, hear and accept as part of their faith what Deacon Zeke is saying. Or if they do not accept it, at least they should not challenge it. Questioning, participation, and engagement are not part of this vision of the church.

In stark contrast to St. John Bosco, the RCIA process at Queen of Peace parish is notable for how little time is spent lecturing (33.6%) and how much time is spent in discussion (34.9%) and liturgy and prayer (16.5%). This pedagogy is reflective of the parish's embrace of the idea of the church as the "People of God." The Second Vatican Council (1962–1965) made the image of the "People of God" the dominant image for the church, drawing on the guiding theme found in St. Paul's Letter to the Hebrews. A major shift in the church's self-understanding can be seen in the Council document *Lumen Gentium*, the Dogmatic Constitution on the Church. Significantly, the chapter on the "People of God" precedes the chapter on the hierarchy, stressing the church as a community of people living out their Christian vocations. Every individual member is "called to the fullness of the Christian life."[21] Sharing in the one and same baptismal call, the faithful in their various states of life—lay, religious, and priestly—nurture their faith as members of the sacramental and liturgical community and dedicate themselves to the renewal of the church as they strive to build God's kingdom.[22]

At Queen of Peace, this ethic is embodied as the pastor shares responsibility with lay ministers, both professional and volunteer. All of the parish activity is overseen by a full pastoral staff: the pastor, two associate pastors, a deacon, director of religious education, youth minister, liturgist, and a pastoral associate who serves as RCIA director. In addition, many individuals volunteer to serve the church, making the proclamation that the church is the "People of God" a reality. Unlike at St. John Bosco, where Deacon Zeke was the entire RCIA process in himself, the entire parish staff at Queen of Peace is invested in the RCIA process. Most members of the staff, from the pastor to the liturgist, lead sessions in their particular areas of expertise. The pastor, a scripture scholar, presents the three classes specifically focused on the Bible. The liturgist walks the group through an overview of the liturgical year and seasons of the church. The deacon, fresh out of seminary, shares his story of faith development, specifically his experiences of prayer. All of this is coordinated by Jill Turnock, whose 20 hours per week devoted to adult initiation are almost seven times what Deacon Zeke spends on it.

Aside from these professionals, regular parishioners also contribute to the process as the RCIA team. The backgrounds of team members range from stay-at-home moms to engineers to salesmen. Despite these differences, they are all quick to say that they "get so much out of it" and love to serve their parish in this way. Currently, the team consists of eight parishioners who have been serving in this capacity for an average of four years each. Thus, although Jill serves as the RCIA director, the RCIA is not just "Jill's thing." It belongs to the whole pastoral staff, the RCIA team, and ultimately to the entire parish. Together, they bring individuals into the People of God as manifested in the Catholic church and this particular parish.

The vision of the church as the People of God is reinforced in the hidden curriculum of the RCIA process at Queen of Peace, reflected in the pedagogical approach taken by the catechists. A session on the subject of Mary exemplifies this. The session begins at 7:00 p.m. with Jill presiding, but she immediately gives the floor to one of the RCIA sponsors, Greg, who reads the Biblical account in Luke of Mary's visit to her cousin Elizabeth. Greg then leads the group in praying the "Memorare" together from a typed page passed out before class began.[23] This establishes from the start the authority of lay Catholics to lead prayer and also the importance of praying itself as central to Catholic life. It stresses participation and engagement.

George Lopez, a seminarian who serves on the RCIA team, then takes over. He was asked to present on the adoration of Mary, the use of the rosary, and intercessory prayer. As a graduate student presenting for the first time, George is nervous, rocking back and forth and speaking quickly. He begins with a personal story of deciding to enter the seminary and how he would ask for Mary's help in making that decision, but then falls back into a dry, academic presentation on the distinction between adoration and veneration of Mary and Mary's role as an intercessor and protector. After several minutes of this, the group begins to fidget, looking around and down. Seeing that he does not have their full attention, he invites questions. Unlike at St. John Bosco, this opens things up significantly. "I am not sure what you meant when you said that if you were persistent in your prayers to Mary, you would be granted what you wanted," Suzi, a team member asks. "Is this true?" George responds by using scripture to break open what he was saying. "Scripture says that whatever we ask of Jesus will be given," he explains, though this is not about literal, material answers to our prayers. Another sponsor, Carmen, jumps in saying, "I just wanted to correct you. God does give material things. Look at the homeless shelter [that was recently built]." She says that if the requests help build up the work of God, they could be granted. "If you wanted to build a house of ill-repute, I do not think you would be answered, no matter how many time you prayed." The group laughs at her example. Suzi and Carmen then begin talking back and forth about prayer, clarifying and sharing. This is an actual dialogue. It is not simply people talking to the presenter, but sharing with one another their insights. Although those going through the process are not yet actively involved in this conversation, as lay Catholics Suzi and Carmen are modeling for them the engaged People of God envisioned by the Second Vatican Council.

The session continues with George passing out handouts for small group discussion. Each table is given a biblical passage that involves Mary, for example the annunciation, the visitation, and the wedding at Cana. They have to answer questions about images of Mary given in the passage, images of God gleaned from them, and what connections can be drawn to their own lives. It also asks them to write a prayer to Mary based on the passage, which is remarkable for what it conveys both about the importance of prayer and also the power of individuals to create prayers and not simply recite prayers like the Memorare that have been handed down from the tradition. In this small group setting, it is easier for those going through the RCIA process to have a voice and active role, and several of them raise questions and offer contributions in ways that they did not in the larger group setting. This approach to teaching also allows the students to discover something about Mary in a different way from an academic lecture on church dogma concerning Mary. The group is able to see who Mary is and why Catholics use her as intercessor. For example, Jesus listened to her at the wedding at Cana, so he will listen to her as she intercedes for us. This message comes across in a fleshy way.

After the discussion of images of Mary, George moves the group to a consideration of ways of relating to Mary. He talks about pictures, hanging one up on your wall and praying with it. "You can take a Christmas card you get and frame it," he advises. "I have done this. This can look very nice." "The Martha Stewart of the seminary," Suzi shouts out. The group laughs. George laughs, too, and continues on, talking briefly about pilgrimages, before turning to his final major topic for the night, the rosary. George asks Father Samuel, the associate pastor, to help him with the actual rosary beads. Father Samuel blesses the rosaries and passes them out. This is significant in highlighting the special role that the ordained priesthood has in Catholicism, as servants of the People of God rather than members of a superior class by virtue of their ordination.

As the rosaries are being distributed, George talks about the history of the rosary and its use. He teaches the group how to pray the rosary, walking them through the beads and what to say. Although it is approaching 9:00 p.m.—two hours on Mary at Queen of Peace, compared to 10 minutes at St. John Bosco—the group is still actively engaged in the session. The evening ends with the group praying "Hail Holy Queen" (the *Salve Regina*), the prayer commonly said at the end of the rosary.[24] As the group prays, the volume is high. The group is fully present and alive. There is no mumbling as everyone speaks up and out. The RCIA director Jill, seminarian George, Father Samuel, team members, sponsors, and those seeking initiation into the Catholic church pray alongside each other, together. There seems to be power in their prayer—the power of the People of God.

The differences in the hidden curriculum between Queen of Peace and St. John Bosco cannot be entirely explained by the social class differences between the parishes. As Sean McCloud keenly observes, "Class should not be seen as the sole, deterministic basis of everything. Class always matters, but sometimes it matters less than other things."[25] Because this study focuses on parishes in a single diocese and does not include any parishes that are dominated by a linguistic minority (e.g., Mexicans, Vietnamese), class may matter more than other things in this case. That class matters is reinforced by the fact that the same dichotomy we see between these two parishes we also have seen in the brief descriptions of the more affluent St. Mary's and the less affluent St. Mark's in the prelude to this chapter.

CONCLUSION

In approaching the issue of how American Catholics live their faith, Jerome Baggett gained considerable insight from reflecting on the work of Belgian surrealist artist René Magritte. Baggett was drawn in particular toward Magritte's famous work *The Treachery of Images*, which is a painting of an ordinary pipe against a plain background. What makes this work so lasting, however, are the words Magritte painted below the pipe: *Ceci n'est pas une pipe* ("This is not a pipe"). Gazing at a reproduction of this work in his office, Baggett agreed. "It is not a pipe; it is a representation of one. This distinction is evocative of culture in the representational sense because the painted pipe is a symbolic means of presenting a reality that is often mistakenly taken to be completely encapsulated by the representation itself."[26] The lesson from Baggett's reflection for the material just presented is that what is being transmitted in RCIA catechesis is not Catholicism, per se, but particular visions of a vast and diverse Catholic tradition that cannot be completely encapsulated in any singular representation. What is interesting is how the different visions of Catholicism that we see in RCIA catechesis, particularly those in the hidden curriculum, are tied to social class differences between Catholic parishes.

The way in which the RCIA process is implemented in different parishes—especially the religious education that takes place in the initiation process—has the potential to tell us a great deal about unity and diversity in understandings of Catholicism today. The class differences on which I focus in this chapter do not shape understandings of *what to believe* about Catholicism, about which there is considerable agreement, but *how to believe* as Catholics. Concepts drawn from the sociology of education, especially those based on Freire's distinction between traditional and critical pedagogies, help illuminate the class-shaped approaches to authority that are reflected in RCIA catechesis.

One final commonality among parishes that cuts across class lines bears mentioning. Sarah MacMillen, Kelly Culver, and I spent nearly a year in each of six different parishes. Considering the period of inquiry and the catechumenate, on only a handful of occasions did we observe any teaching that took place outside a classroom setting. The most common non-classroom session during these periods was a tour of the church. Activities entirely outside the church itself were nonexistent. Thus, whether the parish process was more participatory and democratic or more passive and hierarchical, RCIA catechesis remained firmly situated within the walls of the classroom. What Queen of Peace was able to do within the walls of their classroom—blending catechesis, community, and prayer—was exceptional, in both senses of the term. There are limits to what can be done in a classroom.

Dorothy Bass, director of the Valparaiso Project on the Education and Formation of People in Faith, explains why extending catechesis beyond classroom walls is important. All congregations engage in religious education "to teach tradition in a sustained and deliberate way." However, the fact that "living traditions are socially embodied suggests that the classroom transmission of ideas and texts can play only a limited part in congregations' bearing of traditions." Instead, "it is the group of practices intrinsic to that tradition . . . that need to be learned."[27] Those becoming Catholic not only need to learn *about* Catholicism, but also how to *be* Catholic. In colloquial terms, they need to learn to "walk the walk" and not simply "talk the talk."

Although not common, it is possible to break down the walls of the RCIA and liberate it from the classroom, in the same way that service-learning pedagogies seek to educate students in secular schools by getting them off campus and into the community to learn by doing.[28] The experience of RCIA director Jay Landry suggests as much. During the catechumenate at his parish, he would lead his catechumens and candidates on five or so "field trips":

For example, we go to the Center for the Homeless. We clean toilets, we scrub floors, we do all kinds of things there. We do a tour and we hear testimony from some of the guests about their life stories. The testimony is always a very riveting time, when the catechumens and candidates realize how human these people are, how they're not bums, and how this could be them. They truly reflect the image and likeness of God, and with a little help anybody can get back on their feet. It's really a great experience. As a matter of fact, we went about three Thursdays ago, and one of our catechumens bumped into a good friend of hers there. And she was just overwhelmed; she just couldn't believe this friend of hers was homeless. And that's had a huge impact on this catechumen and somewhat on the larger group as well. We also go to the St. Vincent de Paul store to see what they do, and we have somebody from our St. Vincent de Paul Society come and talk to us about this outreach ministry. We do different things like going to the Women's Care Center, a crisis pregnancy facility. We take diapers to them, we take baby clothes to them, we take any number of things to them. We get a tour from them, we hear what they do, what their mission is in trying to support and serve pregnant women and families in crisis.

As valuable as hearing a lecture about the dignity of the human person or having a classroom discussion of Catholic Social Teaching might be, they cannot replicate the types of learning *experiences* that are facilitated by these field trips. The significance of experience, particularly as it is fostered in liturgy, and its relationship to formation in the Catholic tradition is taken up in detail in Chapter 4, which examines the next stage in the RCIA process, the Period of Purification and Enlightenment.

THE RITE OF ELECTION: THROUGH THE CATHEDRAL TO PURIFICATION AND ENLIGHTENMENT

On consecutive Sundays in February, the Diocese of Fort Wayne–South Bend celebrates the Rite of Election and Calling of Candidates to Continuing Conversion at its two cathedrals. On the first Sunday of the church's season of Lent, over 250 catechumens and candidates for full communion with the Catholic church from some 30 parishes gather at the Cathedral of the Immaculate Conception in Fort Wayne. The following week, a similar number gathers at St. Matthew's Cathedral in South Bend. Along with at least three times as many sponsors, catechists, clergy, family, and friends, they pack the cathedrals to near standing-room-only capacity both Sundays.

Many, like Queen of Peace team member Dan Lackman, have to park blocks away in order to find a space. As Dan enters the cathedral, he is a bit overwhelmed by the sea of people as he tries to find where those from Queen of Peace are sitting. An usher informs him that catechumens are with their sponsors on the left side of the center aisle, candidates and sponsors on the right, and a person from every parish to introduce these individuals is seated behind the altar in the sanctuary. Steve Gallagher, a catechumen, and his fiancée Amy are all smiles as they stand up and wave Dan over. When he sits down with them, the pew is full. Dan sees that many RCIA directors are still looking around, searching out their last few candidates and catechumens, to check them off the list and help them find their seats.

St. Innocent's large team allows them to control the situation more easily, to the point that one team member manages to corral every catechumen and candidate in the hallway to snap a photo for the parish prior to the liturgy. Sister Marie Smith, RCIA director at St. Peter's, is on her own. She is looking up until the last few moments before the service for one of her catechumens, Betsy Gonzalez. Betsy enters right at 2:30 p.m., with her sponsor, Stacy Barrett. Sister Marie guides her quickly into a pew, and then moves herself as stealthily as possible into a seat behind the altar.

During this commotion, prelude music fills the sanctuary. The music fades and Bishop John D'Arcy waits in the narthex for the liturgy to begin. After some opening instructions by the master of ceremonies, Office of Worship director Beverly Rieger, Bishop D'Arcy, Auxiliary Bishop Daniel Jenky, and two other priests process in. Many heads turn excitedly to watch the shepherds of the local diocese enter, symbolizing the significance of this moment for the individuals and the church. After arriving on the altar, Bishop D'Arcy welcomes the assembly and notes that the ceremony is intended to "confirm what Christ has chosen." The Liturgy of the Word includes readings from Ezekiel, Peter, and John, upon completion of which "Thanks be to God" and "Praise to you Lord, Jesus Christ" booms and echoes through the sanctuary. The response highlights how large and engaged the assembly is.

At the conclusion of the homily, Beverly Rieger resumes her role as MC, asking the presenters from each parish to stand and come to a microphone at the far right of the sanctuary to present their catechumens. She then addresses the bishop, presenting to him those who are asking to be baptized and confirmed at Easter. The bishop calls up those who are "chosen by Christ," along with their sponsors. Sister Marie represents St. Peter's at the microphone. "Bishop D'Arcy, I present to you the catechumens from St. Peter's parish. Deb Ceffalio. Doris Ford. Betsy Gonzalez." Her voice is strong and clear, and as she says the name of each individual they step forward and shake the bishop's hand. While this is happening, St. Peter's adult education coordinator, Bill Symanski, presents the parish's Book of the Elect to the bishop's helper. Jill Turnock from Queen of Peace, true to the parish's emphasis on being the People of God, deviates from the words used by most and says instead, "The people of Queen of Peace have blessed and sent Steve Gallagher and Rick Commons." Sister Marie and Jill do a good job of linking the names they are saying to the individuals stepping forward to shake the bishop's hand. Others, like Deanna Koehler from St. Innocent, nervously race ahead, finishing all of the names on their list while people are still waiting for their moment with Bishop D'Arcy.

After shaking the bishop's hand, the catechumens and their sponsors fill the area behind and in front of the altar. As more parishes are presented, more names are read and more people are stuffed into the limited space. By the end, they are standing seven or eight rows deep, numbering 20 or more across. Although they appear uncomfortable in front of the assembly, the large size of the group presents an impressive image to those still in the pews. Bishop D'Arcy then faces the group, and addresses the sponsors specifically: "God's holy church wishes to know whether these candidates are sufficiently prepared to be enrolled among the elect for the coming celebration of Easter."

> *Have they faithfully listened to God's word proclaimed by the Church?*
> They have.
> *Have they responded to that word and begun to walk in God's presence?*
> They have.
> *Have they shared the company of their Christian brothers and sisters and joined with them in prayer?*
> They have.

He then turns and addresses the assembly, asking them if they will support the catechumens in "prayer and affection" as they move toward Easter. "We will." After addressing the sponsors and assembly, Bishop D'Arcy turns back to the catechumens and asks, "Do you wish to enter fully into the life of the church through the sacraments of baptism, confirmation, and the eucharist?" They respond quietly, "We do." To which Bishop D'Arcy replies, "A little louder." They try again: "We do!" Slightly louder, but not enough to satisfy the bishop. "One more time with all your heart." "WE DO!"

After these questions, Bishop D'Arcy signs each Book of the Elect that was presented to him. As there are some 30 parishes, this takes time, as several piles of books are given to him, open and ready for his signature. After signing each book, the bishop declares the catechumens to be members of the elect, ready to be initiated at the Easter Vigil. The elect are admonished to be faithful to God's call. Their godparents are instructed to place a hand on the shoulder of their elect and are admonished to sustain them. The people then flood back to their seats and the entire process is repeated, with some changes in the language, for the already baptized Christian candidates who are celebrating the "Call to Continuing Conversion" in anticipation of their reception into the full communion of the Catholic church.

Even to someone who has attended many liturgies, the Rite of Election is impressive. For those becoming Catholic, being in the presence of the bishop and having the opportunity to shake his hand could inspire awe. Rachel Stroud used this exact phrase to describe her experience, while the younger Max Anderson characterized it as "awesome." Several people identified being addressed by name as a highlight. Others noticed the impressive stacks of the Book of the Elect. Jean Raddatz astutely observed that signing the Book of the Elect "puts your name right in there with everyone else who's signed it from this church. That's big. And then you put our book in with all of the others. That's a lot of people. And then the bishop signs them all. That puts a ribbon on it." The other aspect of the celebration that most stood out to people was the sense of commonality in being brought together in a single location and single liturgy with people going through the RCIA process in different parishes from across the diocese. Reflecting on what stood out most in the ceremony, Melissa

Lodge commented that she felt "such a sense of community. From a small group, add sponsors, add team, then go beyond the parish to see the diocese. It promoted a sense of community and belonging." Someone else built on this idea, adding, "It was a symbol of the church growing."

These reflections suggest that the Rite of Election accomplishes something more than just ritually moving individuals from one stage in the RCIA process to the next. In reflecting on their experience of the liturgical celebration, these elect and candidates are also learning some important lessons about the nature of the church they are seeking to join. These are lessons—like what it means to say the church is "one, holy, catholic, and apostolic"—that are taught in regular catechetical sessions. But divorced from personal experience, these classroom lessons are often lost on the students. Taking what is directly learned from liturgy and experience and connecting it to broader understandings of the tradition are central to the task of forming individuals as Catholics. The Period of Purification and Enlightenment is the most liturgically and experientially intensive stage in the RCIA process. As such, it provides an opportunity to explore not how people learn about Catholicism, but how they learn to be Catholic. The key is not information, it is formation.

CHAPTER FOUR

LITURGY, EXPERIENCE, AND FORMATION

If our understanding of initiation were limited to what is taught in the Periods of Inquiry and Catechumenate, we might conclude that becoming Catholic is principally a cognitive process, a matter of learning doctrine and accepting beliefs (albeit using different class-based pedagogies). But we know from many other studies of American Catholicism that doctrine and belief do not constitute a common ground in the church generally. The broad agreement on the central-ity of certain beliefs and the core of topics to be taught evidenced by RCIA directors (see Chapter 3) is not reflective of the views of lay Catholics. Five waves of American Catholics Today (ACT) surveys, beginning in 1987 and most recently in 2011, have documented that lay Catholics maintain their own ideas about what it means to be "a good Catholic," ideas that are often quite distinct from official church doctrine. To take just one example, while 94% of RCIA leaders be-lieved the obligation to attend Mass weekly is an essential element of the Catholic faith, in the most recent ACT survey, 78% of Catholics answered that one can be a good Catholic without attending Mass each week. This is not to say that Mass attendance is unimportant to lay Catholics, but it shows a great variance between what the church teaches—Mass attendance is obligatory—and what Catholics believe. Similar gaps can also be found with respect to church teachings on birth control, abortion, and charitable efforts toward the poor.[1]

To be sure, some will still point to the teaching authority of the church hierarchy (known as the "Magisterium") as clearly specifying what Catholics should believe. Someone looking for a single, universal source for church teachings can turn to the *Catechism of the Catholic Church*, promulgated by Pope John Paul II in 1992. An alternative view, however, suggests that one does not become Catholic by reading a catechism, any more than one becomes a dancer by reading *The Fred Astaire Dance Book*.[2] Attention must be paid to Catholicism as a living tradition, as embodied in the lived experience of Catholics. As Jerome Baggett argues, "People learn how to be Catholic by being told the story of how they are connected to the sacred, by putting that story into practice in their daily lives, and crucially, by interacting with and comparing themselves to other Catholics." By doing this, they develop "a feel for the game."[3]

Similarly, in her study of members of groups such as the highly orthodox Catholic League for Religious and Civil Rights and of pro-change groups like Dignity and the Women's Ordination Conference, Michele Dillon found, alongside their clear doctrinal differences, a substantial realm of commonality between the members of the two groups. Dillon argues that what really brings Catholics together is the church's "sacramental-liturgical tradition," especially the core sacramental ritual of the Mass, which "would seem to offer a bridge over some of the doctrinal differences between these divergent groups."[4] Dillon's arguments are further substantiated by some questions added to the ACT survey in 2011 (when she joined the research team). Rather than just asking about the most important church doctrines or what makes a good Catholic, new questions were introduced that asked Catholics what aspects of Catholicism are meaningful to them. Very large majorities indicate that the Mass (84%) and the grace of the other sacraments (80%) are meaningful to them. This helps explain why the personal hold of Catholicism is quite strong for many Catholics, despite their doctrinal disagreements with and general disregard of the church hierarchy. Seventy-five percent of respondents to the 2011 ACT survey said that "being a Catholic is a very important part of who I am," 68% "cannot imagine being anything but Catholic," and 75% say that it is important to them that the younger generations of their family grow up as Catholics.[5]

Baggett's and Dillon's studies suggest that becoming Catholic is not only a matter of cognitive learning and acceptance of the official teachings and beliefs of the Catholic church. It is also about "socialization in the 'remembered trajectory' of the Catholic tradition that anchors Catholics as a group."[6] The RCIA, at least potentially, is about the *formation* of individuals into Catholics and not simply the passing on of information about Catholicism. According to religion scholar and medical educator Margaret Mohrmann, formation into any social identity or practice "is a matter of giving form to that which is . . . not yet ordered." Under the guidance of mentors or teachers, it builds on what is previously given, giving shape to it and adding onto it. Mohrmann continues,

> Formation refers to the method by which a person is prepared for a particular task or is made capable of functioning in a particular role. One forms, as well as educates, priests, soldiers, nurses, and doctors in a process that moves beyond the knowledge content of those crafts to the moral content of the practices—the obligations entailed, the demands imposed—and thus to the moral formation of the practitioners.

To this list of practitioners we could add well-formed Catholics, who understand not just what Catholicism is but what Catholics do. Thus, Mohrmann concludes:

> A better metaphor [for formation] is dance: having and displaying integrity is more a matter of being able to move in ways that are consistent with the originating and developing themes of our lives. Teachers, guides, and practice make us better dancers because they help us listen more carefully and follow the music we hear more confidently. We learn which movements fit the rhythms and which do not.[7]

Taking off from the distinction between learning about something and learning to do something, there is wisdom in the *Rite of Christian Initiation of Adults* with respect to formation. Like many rites of passage, its periods and ritual transitions are designed to lead people gradually into a deeper faith and practice in the church, culminating in the crossing of a final threshold of initiation into skillful membership. Although formational practices and experiences can take place throughout the entire RCIA process, they are especially prominent in the Period of Purification and Enlightenment. The centrality of catechetical instruction in the classroom seen in the Periods of Inquiry and Catechumenate gives way—to some extent, imperfectly, as I have written about elsewhere[8]—to a greater emphasis on liturgical practices, personal experience, and interior reflection in the final period of preparation for the rites of initiation to be celebrated at the Easter Vigil.

At the conclusion of the Period of the Catechumenate, those individuals who wish to receive the Easter sacraments must publicly declare their readiness and go through a ritual transition to become one of the "elect." This Rite of Election, described in the prelude to this chapter, is the gateway into the final period of preparation prior to initiation. Celebrated at the diocesan cathedral and presided over by the bishop of the diocese, it brings together individuals in the RCIA process from the entire diocese so that, for the first time, candidates are able to see the scores of individuals from other parishes who are going through the initiation process at the same time. When, at the climax of the rite, the presiding bishop declares those gathered to be members of the elect, they enter the third and penultimate period of the RCIA process.

Although they are now just weeks away from receiving the sacraments, the joy of election is tempered by the reality of more work to be done, including retreats, exorcisms, presentations, and preparatory rites that are part of the Period of Purification and Enlightenment. This period is defined by the 40 days preceding Easter, known as the season of Lent. Like Lent itself, this period of the RCIA process is designed to be a time of testing, of devotional discipline, of prayer and abstinence with the goal of strengthening faith. According to the normative vision of the process articulated in the ritual text, this is "a period of more intense spiritual preparation, consisting more in interior reflection than in catechetical instruction, and is intended to purify the minds and hearts of the elect as they search their own consciences and do penance" (*RCIA*, no. 139). As part of the spiritual cleansing prior to initiation, the elect should undergo three public "scrutinies" during the Masses on the third, fourth, and fifth Sundays of Lent. The scrutinies ideally involve prayer over the elect and an "exorcism," enacted by a laying on of hands by the presider, though in some parishes godparents, catechists, and even members of the assembly are also encouraged to lay hands on the elect. These scrutinies are meant to encourage "self-searching and repentance" so as to "complete the conversion of the elect and deepen their resolve to hold fast to Christ" (*RCIA*, no. 141). As part of the elect's deepening exposure to the Catholic tradition, there are separate rites that can be celebrated in which the elect are presented the Nicene Creed and Lord's Prayer in the context of a liturgical celebration. According to the ritual text, "With the catechumenal formation of the elect completed, the Church lovingly entrusts to them the Creed and the Lord's Prayer, the ancient texts that have always been regarded as expressing the heart of the Church's faith and prayer. These texts are presented in order to enlighten the elect" (*RCIA*, no. 147). As a final step in the process of preparation for initiation, many parishes take their elect on a day-long (or overnight) Lenten retreat, either at the parish or a retreat center. At the conclusion of this period, the elect are considered prepared for the rites of initiation.

In this chapter, I highlight two ways in which formation is emphasized over information in this period of the RCIA process. First, I explore the ways in which people learn what it means to be Catholic beyond the classroom, through participation in various rituals like the Rite of Election. Although four of six parishes we observed dedicated an entire catechetical session to the topic of "Church: One, Holy, Catholic, Apostolic," for many the "four marks" of the church were more alive and more real in the liturgy than even the best-run classroom session. In the liturgy, individuals are not told what the church is. Rather, they experience it directly for themselves, in the feeling of common purpose from seeing other people going through the process (one), and the awe and excitement (holy) of seeing the stacks of the Book of the Elect representing their place in the broader church (catholic), and shaking hands with the bishop (apostolic). That they learn about and feel a part of the church in a way they could not do in the classroom highlights the formational potential of liturgy.

Second, the shift in emphasis from catechetical instruction to interior reflection in the Period of Purification and Enlightenment also opens up to a consideration of personal experience, and how experience is or is not shaped in the initiation process. As we saw in Chapter 2, the motivation for people to begin the process of becoming Catholic was generally not a purely religious one. It was most frequently connected to family concerns. But this does not mean that religious experience plays no role in the process. On the contrary, even though not everyone who goes through the RCIA process has transformational experiences, activities in the Period of Purification and Enlightenment (especially) help cultivate such experiences and connect those experiences to some individuals' trajectories toward becoming Catholic in very profound ways. Taken together, liturgy and experience are central to the formational process. They are, as this chapter will show, two of the most significant schools of spiritual life for those becoming Catholic.

FORMATION AS LEARNING BY DOING

The notion that involvement in ritual has formational potential is not proprietary to sociologists of religion. Folk wisdom often stresses the importance of learning by doing. Notable in this regard is the Chinese proverb, "I hear and I forget; I see and I remember; I do and I understand." Again, in the prelude we see the development of an understanding of the "four marks" of the church that results from the active participation of individuals in the Rite of Election. This is what was meant by Pope Paul VI when he declared at the Second Vatican Council that "liturgy is . . . the first school of the spiritual life."[9] Later, Pope Benedict XVI wrote in his 2007 apostolic exhortation on the Eucharist, "By its nature, the liturgy can be pedagogically effective in helping the faithful to enter more deeply into the mystery being celebrated. That is why, in the church's most ancient tradition, the process of Christian formation always had an experiential character."[10] From this perspective, it is in the ritual life of the church, more than in any lecture, class, or program, that people learn the Catholic faith. It is worth recalling that the contemporary RCIA process itself resulted from ideas raised in the Vatican II document that addressed reform of the sacred *liturgy* (see Chapter 2).

The Period of Purification and Enlightenment is the best period of the RCIA process in which to consider the role of liturgy in the formation process because it is the most ritually intensive. Of course, the enactment of the various rites specified in the *Ordo* varies from parish to parish, both in number and quality. At St. Mary's, for example, the celebration of the many different rites is a strength of the RCIA process. The RCIA team knows the rites and does not cut corners in their celebration. The director of liturgy ensures that the music for the Mass is coordinated with the rites, and the RCIA team does an excellent job of preparing those participating in the rites, both spiritually and practically. At the other end of the spectrum, at St. John Bosco the rites proper to the period are not even celebrated. So the question is: Where they are celebrated, what effect do these rituals have on the formation of those who go through them?

As noted, the core liturgical rites of this period are the "scrutinies." Scrutinies are celebrated within the Mass on the third, fourth, and fifth Sundays of Lent. The first scrutiny centers on the story of Jesus and the woman at the well (John 4:5–42), the second scrutiny on the man born blind (John 9:1–41), and the third scrutiny on the raising of Lazarus (John 11:1–45). Although the substance differs according to these Gospel readings, the structure and enactment of each scrutiny is the same from week to week. The second scrutiny as celebrated at

Queen of Peace is typical of these rites. The two elect who will be scrutinized, Steve Gallagher and Ricky Commons, arrive earlier than many attendees. They check in with RCIA director Jill Turnock, who shows them the pews reserved at the front of the church for them and their sponsors. They are quiet and, although this is the second scrutiny they have experienced, they are clearly anxious. When the service begins with an announcement about how the church all around the world is celebrating the second scrutiny, Steve and Ricky look at each other with knowing and nervous smiles. After the homily, Father Samuel walks from the ambo to the front and center of the sanctuary. He explains the scrutinies to the assembly. "The scrutinies are a period of self-searching. They uncover and heal weaknesses. They are meant to deliver the elect from sinfulness and temptation." At this point, Father Samuel invites the elect and their sponsors to come up.

Ricky and Steve move slowly from the pews and take their place just outside the sanctuary, facing the assembly, while their sponsors stand on the first step behind them. Deacon Matt is Ricky's sponsor and stands over six feet tall without the step's help. On the step, he towers over Ricky. Standing behind Steve are Amy (Steve's fiancée and sponsor) and Mike (Steve's parish-appointed sponsor). When they are settled in, Father Samuel invites everyone to pray for these elect. The entire assembly kneels as Steve, Ricky, Amy, and Mike also turn and kneel on the first step facing the altar and crucifix. At this point Deacon Matt moves to the ambo to read the Mass intentions. Each addresses a particular problem and seeks divine intervention, such as: "In our fast-paced world of busy work lives and busy home lives, it is hard to find time for God. Help the elect to learn to put God first in their lives."

With the elect still kneeling, Father Samuel begins the exorcism by reading a prayer from the ritual text:

> *Father of mercy,*
> *you led the man born blind*
> *to the kingdom of light*

through the gift of faith in your Son.
Free these elect
from the false values that surround and blind them.
Set them firmly in your truth,
children of the light for ever.
We ask this through Christ our Lord.

It is clear at this point that the bare marble steps are beginning to take their toll on Steve and Ricky. While trying to maintain their reverential posture, they shift from side to side periodically, to relieve the pressure one knee at a time, and also rock back on their heels to save both knees at once. When Father Samuel finishes the prayer with an "Amen," both Ricky and Steve pop back up on their knees and become more erect. He then approaches Steve very deliberately. Both men bow their heads and Father Samuel solemnly lays his hands on Steve's head. He holds them there for some 30 seconds, his body motionless except for his lips, which are mouthing an inaudible prayer. At some point Amy places her hand on Steve's shoulder. Father Samuel then repeats this same process with Ricky. After the laying on of hands, he invites "the entire community and the sponsors to extend your hands in blessing over these elect." The community, almost everyone, extends one hand as the final prayer is read.

This general pattern can be seen in other scrutinies, with some minor variations from parish to parish. At St. Mark's, for example, pews are not set aside for the elect and no special intentions are read for them, but sponsors are invited to lay hands on them after the priest—an action that personalizes the experience but also extends the discomfort of kneeling on the top step of the sanctuary. At St. Mary's, the experience is made more personal by Father Paul asking each of the elect individually if there is something in particular they would like him to pray for when he lays hands on them. At St. Peter's, the entire scrutiny, including the hand laying and exorcism, is performed with the elect standing rather than kneeling before the presider.

When considering the formational effect of experiencing these scrutinies, we do well to remember that, just as there are variations in the ritual, so too are there variations in how people experience and interpret the ritual. This fact is highlighted in Susan Ridgely Bales's study of children's interpretations of their First Communion experiences. Official understandings of the meaning and intended effects of various rites can be garnered from the ritual texts, other church documents, and those charged with implementing them. But the reality of those rites and individuals' interpretations of them may vary.[11] In the case of the RCIA scrutinies, we have one rite but three different responses: a lack of any notable experiential engagement; a significant experience but without any immediate formational implications; and a coming together of experience and interpretation in a significant formational moment.

The first response highlights the fact that formation requires both a concerted action on the part of a mentor/teacher and attentiveness and effort on the part of the person being formed. For example, while most of the elect at St. Mary's appreciate the small gesture of personalization in the laying on of hands, when I ask Max Anderson what his response was to Father Paul's prayer request, he tells me he said to Father Paul, "Not right now." Clearly the type of interior reflection being sought is not happening in his case. Similarly, a week after the first scrutiny, St. Mary's RCIA director Elizabeth Ann Starr asked if anyone who went through the ritual had any thoughts about it. People go around the room offering their ideas, and then attention turns to Christina Poole, who responds, "Not really. I haven't really thought about it during the week." She is much more interested in the *People* magazine she brought to the meeting. Christina is entering the period of final preparation for initiation, but the first scrutiny does not move her to greater reflection.

The second response demonstrates the opposite: the individual being formed is attentive and connected to the ritual, but the formational possibilities are not capitalized upon by the mentor/teacher. At St. Mark's, the second scrutiny looks very similar to Queen of Peace's ritual, except that the elect kneel on the top step of the altar, with their sponsors kneeling behind them. Among those being scrutinized are Craig Stevens and Paul North. Because they are facing away from the assembly, it is impossible to see their faces during the exorcism, but when they turn around, Craig's smiling face is flushed and Paul is dabbing his eyes with the sleeve of his shirt. Something is clearly going on here. Following the rite, the elect are "dismissed" from the Mass since they do not participate in the Eucharist—a common practice specified in the ritual text (*RCIA,* no.169). As they are processing out of the church, when they have just cleared the last row of pews, Craig leans over and says quietly to Paul, "I see you got a little teary eyed from having to kneel so long." To which Paul responds, "Yeah, *that's* why." And they both share a quiet laugh. Judging from these emotional responses, they clearly had experienced *something* in the rite.

The excitement quickly fades, however, as the elect process downstairs into a cramped band practice/storage room, where RCIA director Meaghan Donovan has arranged for them to view a Lenten reflection video, "God Sees into the Heart." In the video, Father Michael Himes reflects on and spins out the significance of the story of the man born blind. Of course, this connects clearly to the scripture readings for the day, but the elect have already heard Father Roth's homily about the man born blind prior to the scrutiny. So, although the video is fine, as far as videos go, forcing the elect to sit passively for 20 minutes kills the excitement that was generated by the experience of the ritual. After the video ends, Meaghan gets up and asks the group, "What do you think? Anyone care to share?" No one says anything, so Meaghan makes some organizational points and the session ends.

Because I did not attend the first scrutiny at St. Mark's, I make a point of lingering after the session to chat with the elect, to see what they thought of the first two scrutinies. I want to know what their experience was like since the dismissal session effectively disengaged them. "You looked excited," I say to Craig. This seems to break the spell of the "videopium" and bring him back to life. "Oh my God, yes.

Yes. I was. I . . . I don't know why I was smiling. Was that the right response? My knees hurt so much. Why was I smiling?" I look to Paul and say lightly, "*You* weren't smiling." "No," he replies, "something must have got in my eyes. They were burning. That's why I was rubbing at them." We all laughed knowingly, but rather than continuing to reflect on these experiences and what could be learned from them, the conversation drifted to where I had been the previous week, if I would be attending the following week, and other mundane topics. The formational opportunity in the wake of a significant rite was lost.

The third response successfully brings together both sides of the formational equation: the interaction between what the students bring to the table and what the teacher helps to make it. A specific goal at St. Mary's is to take what otherwise might remain inarticulate and to develop it, both in the immediate dismissal session that follows the scrutiny and in the catechetical session the following week. As at St. Mark's, after the exorcism the elect are dismissed from the Mass. Father Paul hands the Lectionary to RCIA team member Hannah Impink, who leads the procession from the church sanctuary into the daily Mass chapel. Hannah's husband, Mark, falls in line behind the elect. The group arrives at the chapel to find seven chairs arranged in a circle around a small table with a lit candle on it. Hannah sets the Lectionary down on the table and uses the ribbon to open it to the Gospel reading on the man born blind. Everyone else settles into their chairs and look to Hannah and Mark to start the session.

Both Hannah and Mark are very soft spoken, and in this instance that is a strength. Other times when she has been a lead catechist, Hannah was better at lecturing than at facilitating discussion, but in this case she does an excellent job of getting the group to open up. She first has everyone recite together a short, simple prayer. This gets everyone involved from the start. Next, Mark reads the Gospel to refresh everyone's memory.

"As long as I am in the world, I am the light of the world." As he said this, he spat on the ground and made clay of the spittle and anointed the man's eyes with the clay, saying to him, "Go, wash in the pool of Silo'am" (which means Sent). So he went and washed and came back seeing. . . . Jesus said, "For judgment I came into this world, that those who do not see may see, and that those who see may become blind." Some of the Pharisees near him heard this, and they said to him, "Are we also blind?" Jesus said to them, "If you were blind, you would have no guilt; but now that you say, 'We see,' your guilt remains."

Neither Hannah nor Mark jump in immediately following the reading. They let the words linger in the air, and the words combine with the scent of the burning candle to create a calm and reverential atmosphere. Everyone sits quietly, prayerfully, for a moment, and then Hannah invites people to share their experiences of the scrutiny. Notably, she does not suggest people immediately connect their experiences to the Gospel; this allows people time to build up to that connection. Asking people to connect their experiences to broader themes from the start could have been a conversation stopper.

Hannah simply asks the group, "Who would like to begin?" Philip Cat jumps in first, noting that he "got more out of this [scrutiny] than the first one." He spoke of how anxious he was before the first scrutiny, not being entirely certain of where he was supposed to stand, what he needed to say (if anything), what the priest was going to do, how the assembly was going to react, and how long it would take. Knowing the second scrutiny would be structurally the same as the first allowed Philip to relax and experience the ritual more fully. He describes the energy he felt coming through Father Paul's hands when he placed them on his head. At this point, another one of the elect, Rachel Stroud, takes advantage of a pause in Philip's story to interject something about the energy coming from the pain she felt from kneeling so long. With knowing laughter the 51-year-old Philip adds, "Oh, I'm not gonna lie and say my knees weren't on fire. But I tried to tell myself it was the Holy Spirit or something."

During the dismissal session, all six of the elect contribute. Even Christina Poole and Max Anderson are more engaged than they were following the first scrutiny. Not fully letting go of her interest in the mundane—like her *People* magazine—Christina begins by joking about how all she could think of in the first scrutiny was how Father Paul was going to "mess up" her hair by putting his hands on her head. This week she knew it was coming so she did not spend as much time putting "stuff" in her hair. With less to mess up, she could pay more attention to what was happening in the scrutiny. Reflecting on this in a tone that suggests she is surprised at her own insight, Christina observes, "I guess that was me opening my eyes to see what was really most important." Max talks about how before the first scrutiny he did not think it was that big of a deal and so he didn't really think about what he was doing and why. This time, he said, he knew what he was in for—he knew that Father Paul was going to ask him what he wanted him to pray for, and he knew he would have a better answer than the previous week (not disclosing to the group his answer the first time around). So he focused hard on the Gospel reading prior to the scrutiny and came up with an answer: "That I not be like the Pharisees." Seeing a rare opportunity to draw Max out, session leader Mark Impink asks Max what he means by that. Max responds, "They are in the dark but they think they can see. I'm like that too. I always think I know best. I guess I'm not very humble, so maybe I am asking to be more that way."

One of the more profound comments I heard during my research is then offered by Jean Raddatz. Jean tells the group that when she was kneeling down she wanted to take her mind off the pain in her knees and so she called to mind the image of the blind man with mud caked on his eyes. "I imagined that my eyes had mud caked on them too. When Father Paul asked me if there was anything special I wanted him to pray for me, I just said 'open my eyes.' After he took his hands off my head, I opened my eyes and something seemed different. I looked back at [my husband and sponsor] Ron and he looked like when I first met him. [The scrutiny] feels like a renewal of the spiritual part of our relationship, which has been put on the back burner for various reasons. And this time I can play a bigger role." When she finished this reflection, hers were not the only eyes with tears in them. In this dismissal session, we can see the formational process at work. Individuals begin to internalize Catholic Christianity by forming their experiences in dialogue with the tradition and shaped by their teachers. In doing so, they are learning to dance, getting a feel for the game.

WHITHER SACRIFICE?

In the same way that dance forms and styles of game play change, so too does the tradition into which those becoming Catholic are socialized. In this chapter and the previous one, I have explored some of the aspects of the Catholic tradition that are front and center in RCIA catechesis and formation. But what about aspects I *expected* to be front and center but were not? One aspect I expected to see emphasized more during the Period of Purification and Enlightenment was sacrifice. This period of the RCIA process corresponds with the 40 days in the liturgical calendar known as Lent. In fact, as Mark Searle has explained, "From the fourth century, the 'forty days' (*quadragesima*) before Easter became a time of asceticism for the whole Christian community, as bishops encouraged the faithful to associate themselves with the catechumens. . . . Such were the origins of Lent."[12] In the Lenten season and hence the Period of Purification and Enlightenment, I thought a natural topic would be sacrifice, and related ideas of sin, penitence, and reconciliation. I thought wrong.

Catholics' conceptions of God have undergone dramatic change over the past several decades. "Gone, it seems, is the God of judgment, who, in keeping scrupulous tally of the faithful's venial and mortal sins, was ultimately punitive as well." Today's more personal, loving, and understanding God is "there for you." As Jerome Baggett concludes from this observation, there has been "such a remarkable de-emphasis on sin that . . . people may soon fail to 'get' the long-told collection of jokes that end with punch-line allusions to 'Catholic guilt.'"[13] All joking aside, theologian David Wells has described religion in contemporary society as "weightless." Weightlessness, he writes, is "the common form in which modernity rearranges all belief in God."[14] The metaphor suggests that religion does not bear heavily on believers. In my observations, I found this to be true over and over.

This broader change can be seen clearly in the changing place of *sacrifice* in the Catholic tradition. In his doctoral dissertation, "A Place for Sacrifice: American Catholics and the Religious Value of Sacrifice," Thomas Landy argues that "American Catholics are heirs to a church that long regarded sacrifice as *integral* to religious life and practice. . . . In terms of theology, ritual, popular piety and practice, Catholicism was essentially and consciously built around and upon sacrifice." In particular, Landy observes that the "explicitness, extent, and breadth of reference to Hebrew cultic sacrifice is astounding" in the Tridentine Mass—established at the Council of Trent in 1564 and the normative service until the liturgical reforms of the Second Vatican Council were implemented in the mid-1960s. The *Baltimore Catechism*, foundational to the education of American Catholic school children from the 1850s until the 1960s, explained the Mass in terms of sacrifice: "What is the Mass? The Mass is the Sacrifice of the New Law in which Christ, through the ministry of the priest, offers himself to God in an unbloody manner under the appearances of bread and wine." Along with the centrality of sacrifice in understanding the Mass, the notion of personal sacrifice as renunciation, as a way of imitating Christ, was evident up through the 1950s in popular practices such as Lenten renunciations, fasting and meatless Fridays, and devotions to particular saints.[15]

It appears, however, that the tradition of sacrifice—so deeply rooted in Jewish and Christian scripture and traditions—has not easily made the transition into late modernity. The changes "that have contrived to loosen the connection between religion and sacrifice for American Catholics" include ecclesial, theological, and social changes that are not strictly American.[16] It seems, however, that sacrifice is particularly ill-suited to the current American situation, to what Alan Wolfe has called "how we actually live our faith." Wolfe's central thesis concerning the transformation of American religion is that "American faith has met American culture—and American culture has triumphed." Older conceptions of religion, with their strong understandings of sin, have passed, trumped by an increasingly mass-mediated American culture that is dominated by a "tamed" view of God as understanding and empathetic.[17] We see this in Catholic churches, where "the Holy Sacrifice of the Mass" has become a "celebration" of the Mass and the altar of sacrifice has become a communal table. Officially, the Eucharist is still considered a sacrifice, but for ordinary Catholics "that understanding has largely been replaced, or at least tempered, by the image of the Eucharist as a celebratory banquet."[18]

For individuals, as Landy points out, "no act is inherently or definitionally sacrificial" because "sacrifice is fundamentally an interpretation, a form of explanation, imposed upon events to give them meaning." People need to have a language or a framework of understanding, or even just a notion of sacrifice, in order to make sense of their actions as sacrifice. In his interviews, Landy found such notions foreign to most contemporary Catholics, at least as a religious principle. People still use the term "sacrifice," but it does not have the same meaning it once had. Younger Catholics especially "tended to talk about sacrifice solely as a choice guided most of all by the preference, circumstance and the needs of desires of the individual," though the language of preference was seen in all cohorts. As one older interviewee put it, "If my neighbor wants to sacrifice, there's nothing wrong with that. It's up to him." These sorts of responses led Landy to conclude, sounding very much like David Wells and Alan Wolfe, that "emphasis on preference had gone a long way to domesticate sacrifice and take away any sting it might ever have."[19]

The religious value of sacrifice among Catholics has become so marginal that major surveys, such as American Catholics Today, do not even ask questions about it. And perhaps that is just as well. In open-ended interviews conducted as part of this project, I asked individuals—both as they were beginning the RCIA process and after they completed it—about the place of sacrifice in their understanding of being Catholic. I could not use any of the data because the respondents simply did not *get* the question, talking instead about all of the "benefits" they would experience from being Catholic. Searching the field notes from all six parishes in this study for references to sacrifice yielded only slightly more useful data. One exceptional case, that of Meaghan Donovan, I take up momentarily. More often I found occasions when I thought sacrifice *would be* discussed but was not.

A session at St. Mary's was enlightening in this regard. In addition to the Sunday scrutinies and dismissal sessions to reflect on them, St. Mary's continues to have a weekly meeting for the elect on Wednesdays during the Period of Purification and Enlightenment. Unlike the dismissal sessions, the purpose of these meetings is not to reflect on the scrutinies in relation to the Mass readings, but to think about them in the context of some broader Catholic themes. This week, the theme is sacrifice and reconciliation. Elizabeth Ann is leading and asks all of the elect, then sponsors, then team members to reflect on their experience of the second scrutiny. In a departure from the more lecture-oriented sessions in the Period of the Catechumenate, she asks the simple, open-ended question, "What stood out for you?" The sharing goes around the circle three times, and everyone in the group says something. Although the elect have already shared their experiences in the dismissal session, they have not shared with any of the sponsors and team members, other than Hannah and Mark. So, their reflections echo some of the themes that emerged in the dismissal session. Christina jumps in to say that in the first scrutiny, "I kept thinking, you're messing up my hair! What am I going to look like after?" But this time around, she was more relaxed and in the moment. Jean Raddatz gives an abbreviated version of her comments at the dismissal session, as does Max Anderson. The reflections are again very personal and even moving at times, but they do not bear on the theme for the day. Neither Elizabeth Ann nor any of the other team members at the meeting seek to focus the reflections and connect them to ideas of sacrifice and reconciliation. Consequently, the experiences are not brought into dialogue with tradition. Instead, Father Paul comes in toward the latter half of the meeting to make a presentation. As his style is very didactic, no one is encouraged to engage with his ideas, and no one does. The formational opportunity is lost.

Another telling example from St. Mary's comes from an earlier classroom discussion of Lent. During the discussion, Christina asks, "Why should I give up chocolate for Lent when I know I'm not going to be able to?" This view sees Lenten sacrifices as akin to New Year's resolutions that are made and broken every year, rather than as renunciations undertaken in imitation of Christ. Recalling that acts are not inherently sacrificial in a religious sense—I give up chocolate annually on January 1 in order to lose weight—having the language with which to understand certain acts as sacrificial is key. Christina did not have this language. But as telling as her comment was, in light of Landy's work, even more significant was the response of the RCIA team. There was no response. Christina's view was not corrected, developed, or taken up in any way by her teachers. An opportunity to help form Christina's understanding of this aspect of the Catholic tradition was lost—perhaps because this aspect of the Catholic tradition is lost even to the catechists, who are, after all, part of the broader movements that Landy discusses. Catholics in the pews and would-be Catholics in RCIA sessions are simply not taught very often about the religious value of sacrifice. As Landy observes, "Interviewees of all the generations tell me that serious discussion about sacrifice is no more forthcoming from pastors, bishops, and other church ministers than it is from other influences in their lives. . . . Priests and others who minister to Catholics appear to have as difficult a time turning to the language of sacrifice as do lay people."[20]

In this regard, RCIA director Meaghan Donovan's presentation of her faith at St. Mark's is exceptional, and her audience's response is remarkable. Whatever else Catholicism is to her, it is anything but "weightless." This was evident throughout the school year when I observed the RCIA process at St. Mark's, and it was brought home once again at her final presentation prior to Easter. In concluding her discussion of the sacrament of reconciliation, Meaghan is moved to

tears while imploring the assembled to confess their sins and be rec-
onciled with God so as to be able to partake of the Eucharist. It matters that much to her. Her entire vision of the Catholic faith centers
on sin, sacrifice, and penitence. For Meaghan, sins come with costs.
The sacrament of reconciliation forgives our sins, but does not allevi-
ate the related temporal punishments that sinners must endure as a
consequence. Sinners must be purified of these before they can have
eternal life, and this is where penance and purgatory come into play.
Talking about how to get into Heaven, Meaghan claims that "Protestants believe that all people go directly to Heaven, and Catholics do
not believe this. Some people wonder why we have to be good all the
time when we can repent at the end of our lives and get into Heaven
at the last minute." Meaghan's answer to the potential problem is
to raise the issue of purgatory. Last-minute converts and others who
have residual punishments for their sins spend time being purified in
purgatory. What is important is to sacrifice through penitential acts
while we are here on earth in order to lessen the time we spend in
purgatory after our earthly demise. Here she gives two examples: of
St. Francis of Assisi throwing himself into a rose bush (amazingly, all
of the thorns fell off the bush and he was unaffected) and of seeing a
woman at the Marian shrine in Fatima, Portugal, praying the rosary
while circling the shrine—*on her knees!*

Not all penance needs to be so extreme, though. During her presentation on prayer, Meaghan gives out a handout on "Devotion
to Divine Mercy." On the cover is the image of the Divine Mercy
that has frequently been depicted as a white-robed Jesus with two
rays of light emanating from his heart. (As noted in the prelude to
Chapter 3, this image is hung inside St. Mark's Church.) The image
is a representation of what Sister Faustina Kowalska saw when Jesus
appeared to her in the 1930s. Sister Faustina was "an uneducated
Polish nun from the Congregation of Sisters of Our Lady of Mercy in
Poland" whose years in the convent "were filled with extraordinary
gifts, such as revelations, visions, hidden stigmata, participation in the
Passion of the Lord, bilocation, the reading of human souls, prophecy,

and the rare gift of mystical espousal and marriage." She received the Divine Mercy message directly from Jesus in encounters between her soul and Him. In April 2000, when he canonized her Saint Faustina, Pope John Paul II declared the Second Sunday of Easter to be "Divine Mercy Sunday."[21] According to Meaghan, "If you pray the Divine Mercy Novena, your sins will be forgiven and your punishments indulged when you go to Confession that Saturday. This means less time in purgatory after you die. Your soul is almost as clean as when you were baptized." Meaghan follows this up with another related example: on Good Friday, she prayed the Divine Mercy Novena for her mother's shoulder, which had been chronically in pain. Sure enough, a few weeks later, the pain went away.

How do those in the RCIA process at St. Mark's hear this sort of message of sin, sacrifice, and penitence? On the way out of the classroom after the session ends, I get an idea when two candidates, Michele Patrick and Connie Buchanan, eagerly tell me the story of a woman they know who prayed a novena for new carpet. Sure enough, her prayer was answered. Her husband divorced her, she had to move, and the apartment she moved into had new carpet. Be careful what you pray for, they warned me, you just might get it! Although not everyone made a joke out of her presentation, others also had a hard time hearing her message. "She's a real nice lady," reflected Zack Williams. "But some of the things she talks about are real crazy, like out there." Like what? "Like people crawling around on their knees. Just seems weird." When I asked Bill Buxley what he thought, he told me, "I appreciate everything that Meaghan puts into the process, but she's kind of a downer." Of everyone I met during my fieldwork, Meaghan is the only one who was very strong on the idea of the religious value of sacrifice. But to individuals who lack a vocabulary of sacrifice, and who are divorced from any sort of experience that could be the basis for formation, Meaghan's ideas have no salience. They are "kind of a downer" or "just seem weird." Although this is the opposite of what happened earlier at St. Mark's (when Meaghan had the experiential basis of the scrutiny to work from but showed a video instead) and at St. Mary's (where the catechists did not help the elect make the connection between the scrutiny and sacrifice), the end result was the same in each case: there was no formation.

CONCLUSION

The shift in emphasis from "catechetical instruction" to "interior reflection" that is supposed to take place during the Period of Purification and Enlightenment highlights the fact that becoming Catholic is not simply about *knowing* and *believing,* but is also (and perhaps more significantly) about *being* and *doing.* That is, it is about formation. Patricia Benner's observations about formation in professional education are applicable to any desired transformation from an outsider's perspective "to that of a skillful member participant in practice,"[22] including transformation into a member of the Catholic church. Specifically, Benner and her colleagues argue, "Furnishing an experiential learning environment and reflection on that experiential learning . . . supports formation."[23] Both halves of this equation must be present for successful formation. Apprentices' personal experiences must be shaped by mentors, and mentors must ground their teaching in their apprentices' experiences.

Liturgy and experience are both significant schools of faith. For this reason, the emphasis on liturgical practices, personal experience, and interior reflection makes the Period of Purification and Enlightenment the most likely time during the RCIA process in which to see formation taking place. As this chapter has shown, formation takes place unevenly in the RCIA process. There are plenty of false starts and missed opportunities. But sometimes catechists do bring together individual experience and the Catholic tradition in a formational way. In doing so, they help initiate individuals into Catholicism as a set of practices and a way of living. They teach their students how to dance the Catholic dance, to have a feel for the Catholic game.

ST. INNOCENT: "A PEOPLE DESTINED FOR HEAVEN IS BORN HERE FROM HOLY SEED"

St. Innocent parish is in the small but ever-expanding suburban community of Farmington, Indiana, just outside Fort Wayne. Regularly outgrowing their church has been a continuing blessing for St. Innocent as a parish since its founding in the 1950s. Most recently, packed pews forced the parish to construct another new building that was dedicated in 1992, though space constraints in the church and parking lot still require five Masses to be offered every weekend to accommodate the 7,000 members of the parish. What was once a small parish in a farming community is now a burgeoning parish populated by upper-middle-class members who buy housing development homes with large fenced backyards for their vegetable gardens, gas grills, and kids' trampolines.

The architecture of St. Innocent coordinates nicely with the scattered suburban mini-malls and doctors' offices nearby. The building is noticeably modern, inside and out, without any ornate inner wall-work or frontispiece, and minimal stained glass. It is a dull backdrop to the vibrant parish life. Although the action at most Catholic churches takes place around the altar, the narthex at St. Innocent provides a second center of gravity. The narthex is denser with Christian symbols than the sanctuary and buzzes before, during, and after Mass.

The font is the centerpiece of the narthex, though it is not centrally located in terms of spatial arrangement. It is surrounded by an iron fence and has a lower pool deep enough to immerse an adult, and a smaller upper font that is used for infants. Water spills from the upper to the lower pool, and during the quieter parts of services, one can hear the trickle of water. This is a subtle reminder of baptism as a vital sacrament at St. Innocent. It, like the Rite of Christian Initiation of Adults, is a gateway, an entrance through the doorway to the body of Christ. This will be symbolized nicely by the opening of the iron gates to the elect at the Easter Vigil Mass. At the base of the font are bricks with the words of Pope Leo inscribed on them (in Latin): "A people destined for heaven is born here from holy seed. Born of the spirit that hovered over the water. Neither the number nor the gravity of your sins should frighten you; born again in this font you will be holy!"

The immediate buildup to the Easter Vigil begins with a prayer service on the morning of Holy Saturday. The hanging lamp lights at St. Innocent are dim, and the morning sun is the source of most of the light in the sanctuary. The crucifix lies on a pile of red shrouds, in front of the altar, flanked by two lit candles. After singing a series of responsorial psalms and a reading from scripture, the pastor, Father Chuck Fuller, offers a few reflections on the meaning of Holy Saturday. He explains the significance of Holy Saturday as "the day the church has nothing scheduled. Like the theologian Karl Rahner has said, most of our lives as Christians is like Holy Saturday—between the tragedy of Good Friday and the joyous celebration of Easter Sunday. We do nothing except watching and waiting for our Lord." Although they are not the only ones in attendance, Father Chuck addresses the elect directly, saying how important it is for them to stay in the Holy Saturday mode today, to take time to do nothing, to fast and pray, "because after all the hoopla, there'll be no excitement after a while. You'll have to settle into the Holy Saturday of Christian existence."

Father Chuck then calls up the elect for various preparation rites. The Lord's Prayer is "presented" to them through a reading of the prayer in the context of Matthew's Gospel, and then (using "cheat sheets" prepared by a member of the RCIA team) they "recite" the Nicene Creed back to the assembly. In the both of these rites, Father

Chuck declares, "Take this precious gift, and this gift we give to you, give back to us before you go into the baptismal waters." According to the ritual text, this "prepares the elect for the profession of faith they will make immediately before they are baptized" (*RCIA*, no. 193).

Remaining before the assembly, the elect next celebrate the ephphetha rite. This rite is grounded in the story of the healing of a deaf man in the Gospel of Mark (7:31–37), in which Jesus "put his finger into the man's ears and, spitting, touched his tongue; then he looked up to heaven and groaned, and said to him, '*Ephphetha*' (that is, 'Be opened!'). And the man's ears were opened, his speech impediment was removed, and he spoke plainly." One by one, Father Chuck goes to each of the elect, touching their ears and mouth, and saying, "Ephphetha: be opened." He then asks the assembly to extend their hands and pray over the elect. "Let's pray over these good people. . . . Bless these your servants as they prepare for baptism. . . . Amen." Finally, Father Chuck anoints each of the elect with the oil of catechumens—a sacred oil that has been blessed by the bishop at a special chrism Mass during Holy Week. Father Chuck puts oil on the back of each of their necks and explains to the assembly, "what they're doing is putting on oil to ease the yoke of Jesus they are taking on." Following more singing and prayers, the elect are released until the Easter Vigil at 7:00 p.m.

The Vigil Mass begins outside the church, with the assembly gathering around the Easter fire, whose flames soar some 8 to 10 feet above the basin. Night is falling. The end of the sunset leaves a turquoise hue behind the church. Father Chuck asks everyone to stand quietly in a prayerful mode and to pray for "those about to pass through the waters of baptism." A large group of at least 200 people stands around the fire, silent for nearly 10 minutes. Father Chuck then begins to sing a plainchant: "Jesus Christ, yesterday, today, forever." After two or three times through the phrase, it catches on and eventually almost everyone is singing right up until 8:00 p.m., when the Easter candle is lit from the bonfire. The candle is difficult to light (it takes a couple of tries from splinters dipped in the fire) due to the wind whipping across the Indiana plains. But finally it is lit, and the flame is passed to the small white devotional candles being held by the assembly. Father Chuck asks everyone to follow the paschal candle into the sanctuary, and a river of candlelight flows into the church. Once inside, the flame is passed to others who remained in the sanctuary.

The RCIA team, elect, and candidates for full communion sit in the front two pews reserved for them. After the introductory rites and the Liturgy of the Word, RCIA team member Phil Koehler walks up to the ambo and presents the adult elect to Father Chuck and the assembly, calling them by name to the front. Father Chuck asks them to process to the back of the church, inviting sponsors and friends and family to the font. About 25 people can fit comfortably in the back of the narthex for a baptism. With 16 candidates for baptism—including 10 children—each of whom had family and sponsors observing, there are easily over 100 people sardined into the narthex to watch the baptisms.

In his excitement after blessing the water, Father Chuck practically jumps into the tank, not at all concerned about the wireless microphone pinned to his alb. He is beaming, his eyes bright and eager, as he leads the elect through the three-question profession of faith. "Do you believe in God, the Father Almighty, creator of heaven and earth? Do you believe in Jesus Christ, his only Son, our Lord? . . . Do you believe in the Holy Spirit?" He points at each person who dutifully responds, "I do." With these preliminaries completed, Alison Bass steps forward as the first adult to be baptized. Wearing a blue baptismal gown, she passes through the gate tended by an RCIA team member and descends into the font. Standing in three feet of water, she has a look of intensity on her face, even flinching a number of times. Father Chuck holds a jug full of water, which he pours over her head in a circular motion, saying, "I baptize you in the name of the Father." He gets another jug of water, "and of the Son." And another jug, "and of the Holy Spirit."

After Alison, the other five adults to be baptized all kneel, guided by the improvising Father Chuck. For most, this is a family affair.

As Samantha Armstrong takes Father Chuck's hand and steps into the font, her husband Eric is smiling ear to ear, and his eyes are fixed on her the whole time she is in the water. Samantha emerges from the font with a mild, contented smile, which cannot match the wide grin on Eric's face. Next, as Cindy Ford lets her son Jimmy go into the font before her, a smile spreads across her face that will stay there for the rest of the evening—through her own baptism, confirmation, and reception of the Eucharist. The last adult to be baptized is Darin Soriano, a large and typically stoic police officer. Father Chuck has been extremely excited about baptizing Darin, calling out in a number of sessions, "I can't wait to get you in that water!" Contrary to Father Chuck's predictions, the water does not boil when Darin enters the font. And contrary to physically large Darin's warning, the water from the tank does not flood out into the narthex, though even with Darin kneeling in the water, Father Chuck has to stretch to pour the large jar over his head. All the while both Darin and Father Chuck have huge grins on their faces.

After changing into white confirmation robes, the newly baptized process down the main aisle with their godparents to the front of the sanctuary. They are led by RCIA team member Jack Collins, who holds a quilted RCIA banner that is composed of patches from everyone who has been involved in the RCIA process at St. Innocent this year. They are met by those already baptized Christians in the RCIA process who were received into the full communion of the Catholic church while the neophytes were drying off. The newly received also have their sponsors with them, so altogether there are dozens of people crowded on the steps before the altar.

As he did with the font, Father Chuck eagerly wades into the mob of confirmation robes, asking the godparents or sponsors for the name of the individual to be confirmed. Dipping his right thumb in the chrism—an anointing oil blessed by the bishop at the Mass of the Chrism, along with the oil of catechumens and oil of the sick—Father Chuck smears a good amount of the scented olive oil on each of their foreheads, making the sign of the cross and declaring, "Be sealed with the Gift of the Holy Spirit." Afterward, Father Chuck shakes each of their hands and tenderly touches each of the confirmandi temple to temple, saying, "Peace be with you."

Overall, the confirmations seem more moving to the elect than baptism. Perhaps this is because the rite is less physically invasive. It is probably more difficult to be reflective in a three-foot tank of water while you're being doused. The confirmation rite also involves more senses, especially aural and nasal. During the confirmations, the choir sings a very meditative *Veni sancte spiritus* that fills the sanctuary and conveys a "heart in throat" sensation. There is also the power of the balsam scent in the chrism oil, which when used on two dozen people can fill the air in the sanctuary as much as the music. Most of all, Father Chuck's tenderness comes out much more during the confirmations than it could in the baptisms. As a consequence, both the "big tough guys" in the group—Darin and Patrick—are really fighting back tears during the confirmation. Alison takes her glasses off to wipe her eyes at one point. Wendy has a loving smile on her face when Father Chuck comes to her. Jason lets out the biggest smile he can.

After the chrismations, the confirmandi and their sponsors return to their seats and the Liturgy of the Eucharist proceeds as usual. Although they stand out in their white gowns, the newly confirmed do not receive communion before the rest of the assembly. They fall into line with the rest of the assembly, no different from Catholics who have processed through such lines for centuries. As they approach the eucharistic ministers, some of whom are members of the RCIA team, they come to the final step in their initiation. They are shown the consecrated host and told, "This is the body of Christ." In responding "Amen" and receiving the Eucharist, they officially become Catholic.

From a theological perspective, in becoming Catholic through the sacraments of initiation, these individuals are becoming part of the body of Christ on earth, as the church is often called. There is a parallel here in social scientific approaches to initiation, which see the final stage of these rites of passage as *incorporation*—literally, the process by which the individual is made part of the "body" of the group. A difference between the theological and the social scientific approaches, however, is that the social scientist treats the question of incorporation as an empirical one to be investigated, rather than as a matter of faith to be assumed. How and how well individuals are incorporated into the Catholic church through the sacraments of initiation is taken up in Chapter 5.

CHAPTER FIVE

OBJECTIVE AND SUBJECTIVE INCORPORATION THROUGH THE SACRAMENTS OF INITIATION

The third and final phase in Arnold van Gennep's model of initiation is aggregation or incorporation—the process by which the individual is made part of the body of the group. In being incorporated, the individual takes on a new status and is entitled and empowered to act in ways that accord with this new state of being. Some have criticized scholars who study ritual for idealizing the very phenomena they are supposed to be critically examining. Ronald Grimes, for example, takes to task those who "too readily offer glorified accounts or abstracted descriptions rather than candid accounts of actual ritual experience," claiming that their accounts "tend to hide blemishes and ignore flaws." This idealization applied to the study of initiation becomes, for Grimes, "the problem of dissonance: Initiations may not do what either theorists or practitioners claim they do."[1]

In the Rite of Christian Initiation of Adults, incorporation into the church body (normatively and most often) takes place during the Easter Vigil—what Augustine called "the mother of all holy vigils."[2] In and through this ritual, individuals receive the sacraments of initiation and thereby become Catholic. According to the ritual text, "The third step in the Christian initiation of adults is the celebration of the sacraments of baptism, confirmation, and eucharist. Through this final step the elect, receiving pardon for their sins, are admitted to the people of God. They are graced with adoption as children of God and are led by the Holy Spirit into the promised fullness of time begun in Christ and, as they share in the eucharistic sacrifice and meal, even to a foretaste of the kingdom of God" (*RCIA*, no. 206). After spending weeks in the Period of Evangelization and Precatechumenate, months (or in rare cases even years) in the Period of the Catechumenate, and an intensive 40 days in the Period of Purification and Enlightenment, the elect at last become Catholic. Although there is one period that follows—the Period of Mystagogy (discussed in Chapter 6)—the sacraments of initiation are the climax of the RCIA process for the individuals involved and for the church.

The question that Grimes raises with respect to initiations generally can be asked of the RCIA as well. Does the ritual enactment of the sacraments of initiation at the Easter Vigil do what the church claims it does? Are the individuals who are initiated successfully incorporated into the people of God, the church, the body of Christ on earth? The simple answer—which will be drawn out in the course of this chapter—is "yes and no." Or, somewhat more accurately, "yes and sometimes." The emphatic "yes" refers to what I called the *objective* dimension of incorporation. The hedging "sometimes" refers to the *subjective* dimension of incorporation. Both are necessary to a full understanding of incorporation through the sacraments of initiation as the climax of the adult initiation process in the Catholic church.

THE OBJECTIVE DIMENSION OF INCORPORATION

Theologian Edward Yarnold has written of the "awe-inspiring rite of initiation," and certainly there are moments at St. Innocent, described in the prelude to this chapter, that live up to this billing.[3] Equally as certain is that not every parish celebrates the rites of initiation as well. Regardless of the quality of the celebration, through the sacraments of initiation—baptism, confirmation, and Eucharist—individuals become Catholic *in the eyes of the church*. Comparing the Easter Vigil at St. John Bosco to what we saw at St. Innocent highlights this objective dimension of incorporation.

In stark contrast to St. Innocent, the RCIA process at St. John Bosco has no particular liturgical dimension, other than the sacraments of initiation themselves. The Rite of Acceptance into the Order of Catechumens, Rite of Sending, and Rite of Election are not celebrated at all. The three scrutinies are performed, not in the company of the assembly, but condensed into a rushed and weakly conducted separate liturgy just for the elect, their sponsors, and families. Deacon Zeke himself is a bit embarrassed about this lack of ritual in his RCIA process, giggling in discussions whenever he knew he was not doing something the *Ordo* required.[4] Not surprisingly, then, St. John Bosco parish does not celebrate the sacraments of initiation as elaborately as St. Innocent.

Arriving at St. John Bosco 15 minutes before the start of the Easter Vigil, the sanctuary is about one-quarter full with people holding half- and two-thirds consumed candles they received when they entered. All of those to be initiated—Sara, Rick, Kris, Anna, and Cathy—are dispersed enough through the first six rows of the right center set of pews that they do not have to interact with one another. This is reflective of the entire process, in which little collective sentiment is present among the group. Unlike at St. Innocent, there were no preparatory rites performed prior to this moment, no Saturday morning meeting, no real preparation at all. Deacon Zeke comes down the aisle already dressed in his alb and sash, and he tells the candidates and elect to be sure to be sitting at the end of the pew so they can get out easily.

About three or four minutes before eight, Father Post, Deacon Zeke, and the four altar servers walk down the center aisle to the back of the church in preparation for the beginning of the service. At this point, the church is half full. The lights are then turned out, except for those in the entryway. There is no Easter fire. The paschal candle—the large white candle that is blessed and lit each year at Easter for use during the Easter season, as well as at baptisms and funerals throughout the year—is lit by one of the servers with a cigarette lighter. The same server then uses the cigarette lighter, rather than the paschal candle, to light the small devotional candles being held by Father Post and Deacon Zeke. They pass the "light of Christ" to parishioners as they process up the aisle. After the procession reaches the front of the church, one of the servers rather unceremoniously turns all the lights in the church on to almost full brightness, leaving the congregation bathed in incandescent light, candles still lit.

After blessing the paschal candle, readings from scripture, and a brief, four- to five-minute homily by Father Post, Deacon Zeke steps to center stage to lead the initiation rites. He calls the elect and candidates forward by name, and they cautiously approach the altar with their sponsors. Deacon Zeke reads the blessing over the water of the font like an incantation, and then continues with the renunciation of sin and profession of faith. He asks a series of questions of the initiands as a group. "Do you reject sin so as to live in the freedom of God's children? Do you reject the glamor of evil and refuse to be mastered by sin?" They respond as a group, "I do." Although candidates for baptism are supposed to be questioned individually for their profession of faith and then baptized immediately after (RCIA, no. 225), Deacon Zeke asks the baptismal questions to everyone in the group, including those who are already baptized Christians. "Do you believe in God, the Father almighty, creator of heaven and earth? Do you believe in Jesus Christ, his only Son, our Lord . . . ?" They respond as a group, "I do."

Zeke baptizes Rick, Sara, and Kris by having them tilt their heads to the side over the basin he held in his hand while he poured a bit of water from a shell three times, once with each of the three parts of the Trinity: "I baptize you in the name of the Father, and of the Son, and of the Holy Spirit." In comparison with the enthusiastic, full-bodied baptisms at St. Innocent, the mood here is restrained. The only bit of interaction during the entire ceremony comes when Sara turns and smiles in anticipation to her family. After she is baptized, she turns again and smiles. There is no visible reaction from either Rick or Kris following their baptisms. No songs are sung at any point during or after the baptisms.

All of the candidates are then confirmed. As with the baptisms, this is done without any particular ceremony and includes only a liturgically nominal dotting of chrism oil on the forehead. Again, there is no particular physical expression of congratulation between Deacon Zeke and any of the neophytes—no handshakes, no hugs. After all are baptized and confirmed, they return to their seats. The offertory hymn is "Christ the Lord is risen to today, Christians haste. . . . " The celebratory tone of the hymn seems an ironic contrast to the generally subdued tone of the rites that had just taken place. During the hymn, the neophytes chat quietly with their families and sponsors, but only Sara and her sponsor seem particularly animated.

Finally, the neophytes are called forward to receive the Eucharist first, followed by the rest of the congregation. Just before the final blessing, Deacon Zeke asks the congregation to congratulate the neophytes and the congregation claps. The neophytes follow Father Post and Deacon Zeke out, and they stand in the entryway of the church to be welcomed into the church by their fellow Catholics. Brief words are exchanged as individuals file out of the church, but no one stops to speak with the new Catholics. After a time, everyone disperses. There is no reception or gathering, just people getting on with their lives on a Saturday night.

The difference between St. John Bosco and St. Innocent is striking, but is it consequential? From the perspective of objective incorporation, the answer is no. In her systematic analysis of the study of ritual, Catherine Bell notes that scholars have been critical of van Gennep's and Victor Turner's theories of rites of passage for a number of reasons. Among them is what Vincent Crapanzano calls the "ritual illusion" of scholars—the tendency highlighted also by Grimes to accept at face value "that ritual actually does what it says it does." In his study of circumcision in Arab villages in Morocco as a male initiation ritual, Crapanzano concludes that the ritual is fraudulent as it "declares passage where there is in both ritual and everyday life no passage whatsoever—only the mark of passage, the mutilation that is itself an absence, a negation."[5] Along these same lines, Maurice Bloch makes the more general point: "Circumcision ceremonies do not . . . make adults out of little boys, curing ceremonies do not cure, etc., and any attempt to pretend that they do (as is done in the work of so many anthropologists) is wrong from the first."[6] With respect to the rite of passage under consideration here, the question is raised: Do the sacraments of initiation received at the Easter Vigil make Catholics out of non-Catholics, or is this just a ritual illusion?

In answering this question, the variety of different enactments of the sacraments of initiation—from St. Innocent to St. John Bosco, and all points in between—ironically help us to see the universal and efficacious dimension of Catholic initiation. When the officiating minister speaks the words and performs the actions of the sacraments— "I baptize you . . ." and "Be sealed . . ." and "Receive the Body of Christ"—from the perspective of the church, they have the intended effect. The church maintains that it is not the catechists or the priest or the assembly who are acting in the sacraments to realize the intended effect, but God who is the primary actor. Thus, once the sacraments of initiation are received, the individual is, by the grace of God, Catholic. It does not matter if the priest says the words excitedly, sincerely, or in a monotone while yawning under his breath. It does not matter if a team of 20 catechists and thousands of parishioners welcome the new Catholic warmly and profusely, or if a single deacon rushes through a minimalistic ceremony while a few dozen assembled individuals wait impatiently for communion. It does not matter if the symbols of the initiation ceremony are rich or sparse. Although rituals have a performative element, they cannot be reduced to mere performances. The difference between initiation rites and theater, as J. S. La Fontaine observes, is that ritual "is purposeful activity; that is, it aims to affect the world. . . . Whether it is the material world that is to be affected, as in the rituals for rain, at harvest or when bringing new ground under cultivation, or human beings who are to be redistributed among the groups and positions that make up social life, ritual is expected to produce results." She continues, "Insofar as initiation rituals mark the dividing line which distinguishes between social statuses, like adult and child, and between membership of groups and outsiders, crossing it changes one's state." Thus, "a man who has been initiated into a Masonic Lodge is a Mason, though he may not participate much in its activities from then on."[7] In the same way, *the individual who receives the sacraments of initiation in a Catholic church is a Catholic.*

Whether the observer believes that the waters of baptism remove the taint of original sin or the oil of confirmation actually seals the newly baptized with the gift of the Holy Spirit, within the context of the church itself they do have the initiatory power specified. Admission to communion is the final stage in incorporation, in which the individual becomes a part of the church and one with Christ by taking his body and blood. The individual now can check the "Catholic" box, join a parish, receive communion, get married in the church, and so on.

A vignette from St. Innocent highlights this objective dimension of incorporation. On the morning of Holy Saturday, the RCIA team and initiands gathered briefly in the meeting room for a few announcements about the Vigil—what to wear, where to sit, and so on. Father Chuck then came in to give everyone assurance about how the rite would go. "It's not going to look like rehearsal from the other night," he said, recalling the seamless walk-through. "Something will probably go wrong! But you'll be baptized, confirmed, and brought into full communion with the church. So don't worry about it. Everything will go just fine." At the end of the day, people receive the sacraments of initiation and they are Catholic. Regardless of the different aesthetics of the ceremonies, in an objective sense they are incorporated into the church all the same.

The reality of the objective dimension of incorporation does not mean we should turn a blind eye to other dimensions. There is some truth to the criticisms raised in the field of ritual studies: many are content to analyze the objective, structural, and functional aspects of rites of passage, without regard to the subjective, meaningful, sensual, emotional, and experiential dimensions. Susan Ridgely Bales, for example, observes that in *The Ritual Process,* "Victor Turner spends seventeen pages discussing boys' and girls' puberty rites without including one quotation from a child."[8] I myself once criticized another sociologist for studying the "experience" of Navajo rituals without reference to the subjective states of the individuals involved.[9] Resisting the temptation to make an "either/or" choice when "both/and" will do, I do not advocate going so far as to say the objective dimension of incorporation is irrelevant. I do want to say that we should *also* look at the subjective dimension. The normative structure and outcome of adult initiation in the Catholic church is universal, but what individuals actually take from the process of initiation can vary. Do the individuals who have received the sacraments of initiation experience incorporation? Do they feel a part of the church in a way they didn't before?

THE SUBJECTIVE DIMENSION OF INCORPORATION

In her study of children's interpretations of first communion, Bales shows how the participants' understandings of the event can often differ considerably from the institutional church's official definition "found in encyclopedias and the *Catechism of the Catholic Church*."[10] At the same time, she finds considerable evidence that first communion as a rite of initiation does subjectively incorporate many of the children who experience it. They *feel* a part of the church body. She observes that "most children seemed to gain a greater sense of their significance as individuals to both parish and family. . . . The children earned their family's, teacher's, and Jesus' respect, which allowed them to claim their own position within the central congregation in their parish." And, "the children felt that they were being seen by both the adults and by Jesus as fellow parishioners, as members of the adult parish." Overall, "the children seemed to feel that they had passed the test for membership in their parish. . . . The children's feelings of belonging to their parish evolved from their view of their status before and after First Communion."[11]

It is interesting to note, as Bales does, that the children feel connected to their families and the local parish, not the universal church in a more abstract sense. These local connections call to mind the major motivations individuals have for becoming Catholic in the first place. As discussed in Chapter 2, familism dominates the subjective rationales for seeking initiation. Seventy-two percent of individuals interviewed explained their motivation for becoming Catholic in terms of this cultural schema. For these individuals, subjective incorporation is not only about becoming part of the church, it is about bringing themselves, their families, and the church into closer alignment.

Craig Stevens, whom we first met in Chapter 2, is a case in point. Craig entered the RCIA process feeling "like more of a bum" as his wife Katherine increased her church attendance while pregnant with their first child. He thought of his father's role in his family growing up, remembering "him going to church almost every week with us." He equated this with "being there for my mom and for me and my sister and brother." To the extent that he did not do the same, Craig was not there for his wife and daughter, Sophie. After he received the sacraments of initiation at St. Mark's, I asked him how he felt. "Really good," he responded quickly. "It was a long process, but it was good. I'm glad I did it." I followed up by asking, "What's different now?" "Well, I'm part of the church now, for sure." He did not elaborate and we both focused on the cake we were eating for a moment. Then Katherine brought Sophie over and Craig traded his paper plate for his daughter. He hugged her gently, looked at Katherine, then looked back at me and said, "This is what it's all about, isn't it?" To which I could only respond, "It is."

Michele Patrick was also baptized at St. Mark's along with Craig. Raised Presbyterian, she has two daughters with her Catholic husband Dan, and has attended Mass with them for many years. Although not connected to the Presbyterian church, she still thought of herself "as a Presbyterian who was attending this Catholic church with my husband and then my family." As her children and then she started to become more involved in the parish school and community, she began to feel "a bit like a fraud . . . being in between being a Presbyterian and Catholic." She felt like she was being "selfish in not giving all of me to this family"—the extended family of the church. I approached Michele after the ceremony, and before I could say anything to her, she blurted out, "That wasn't so bad," like someone who has just returned from the dentist. "Did you expect it to be?" Chuckling, she said, "Gee, I don't know. I really didn't know what to expect." As with Craig, I asked Michele how she felt. She replied, "It's hard to say. Pretty special." "What's going to be different?" "Well, I'm Catholic now. Really. I can't wait to get back to the school with my girls. And Mass. I can't wait to go to Mass with the girls." And Dan? "Oh, yeah, and Dan." In this way, it may be appropriate in some cases to view the sacraments of initiation as both an incorporation into the church body and a family-based life course transition, not unlike marriage or childbirth. By becoming Catholic, the individual also becomes a "good husband" or "good mother"—a status transition from feeling "like more of a bum" or "a bit like a fraud."

Perhaps the most vivid example of the connection between church and family came not in something anyone said, but in something Katie and Sean O'Brien did. During the Easter Vigil at St. Marks, after Katie was baptized and confirmed, everyone in the RCIA group was invited to go downstairs to see the O'Briens have their marriage blessed. Katie and Sean had been married for over 20 years, but because she was unbaptized, their marriage was not officially recognized by the Church. Having now been baptized, the marriage can be "convalidated" using an abbreviated version of the church's "Rite for Celebrating Marriage Outside Mass." The service takes only about five minutes, but the group is downstairs for about twice that amount of time because they have to wait for Katie to get changed out of her wet clothes and to do her hair. Everyone can hear the blow drier running over the music from upstairs and the hum of conversation in the room. In addition to people involved in the RCIA, there are about a dozen of the O'Briens' friends and family present for the ceremony. It is touching. There are plenty of tears, and some good laughs, especially when they both have to struggle mightily to get their rings off—not surprisingly, after all those years. All of this is taking place during the Easter Vigil. When everyone gets back upstairs, the newly confirmed Catholics bring up the gifts for communion. Katie, a new Catholic along with her "new" husband Sean, is among the first in line to receive the Eucharist. The O'Briens' embrace of one another when they sit down speaks volumes about the incorporation of church and family in the initiation process.

Even those who drew on expressive individualist and utilitarian individualist cultural schemas in describing their motivation for becoming Catholic often sang a different tune after their initiation. For many of them, they experienced incorporation through the sacraments of initiation as a sort of homecoming—like Steinbeck bringing Rocinante back to Connecticut after his long sojourn. Forty-two-year-old mother Rachael Stroud described entering the RCIA process in expressive individualist language, realizing there "wasn't any time left for Rachael" in the wake of her work as a mother, wife, and nurse. She "found Rachael by getting closer to God . . . in the Catholic church." When I saw her after her Easter initiation, she spoke of feeling like she was "just wandering around" before becoming Catholic and of being "home" and "grounded" after. Bill Buxley drew on the utilitarian individualist language of having better things to do with his time than to attend a Lutheran church (his background) and a Catholic church (his wife's). "You know," he said, "I'm not really doing this because I want to turn Catholic." After his initiation, his language also shifted to focus more on coming home. Surveying the elaborate post-Vigil reception organized by St. Mark's Rosary Society, Bill compared what he saw to a family reunion. He saw the excitement and hugs shared with him freely and frequently, many with people he had never met before, as being "like meeting relatives you barely know, but you have a connection with them still. You don't really know them, but they're still family."

Not every RCIA process or Easter Vigil inspired the same sense of family, home, or community. Although everyone who received the sacraments of initiation was objectively incorporated in the church, not all of them were clearly subjectively incorporated. This seems most evident at St. Peter's. At the conclusion of the Easter Vigil, Father William stands and thanks RCIA director Sister Marie Smith and her one helper, Bill Symanski (who was actually not at the Vigil), for preparing the RCIA group. He then welcomes all the newly initiated Catholics—six adults in total—to the church again, and announces that there will be a reception in honor of them downstairs after Mass. He invites the entire assembly to stay for a while and share in fellowship with them. Surprisingly few people involved with the RCIA process accept Father William's invitation. As at St. Mark's, a generous collection of food is offered buffet-style by St. Peter's hospitality committee. Chris Short, who was received into full communion, makes her way through the buffet line with her husband and son. She briefly accepts the congratulations of a number of people at the reception, but focuses all of her attention on her son. She never has a conversation with anyone else. Philip Verace attended the Vigil with his sponsor, but his wife and two children are noticeably absent. He comes to the reception, grabs some food, and leaves before anyone can talk to him. The other four individuals who were initiated do not even attend the reception. Sheila Provencher, who had attended the Vigil with at least a dozen family and friends, is a no-show, as are Betsy Gonzalez, Doris Ford, and Cathy Appleby. This leaves the observer to wonder just how incorporated into the church these individuals really are. The lack of fellowship at the reception mirrors the group dynamic through the entire process at St. Peter's. After attending meetings together for months, people are still basically strangers to one another and are not well incorporated into the parish community. There is no sense of community generated in the RCIA. Unlike at St. Mark's, where everyone at the reception smells of chrism because of all the hugs given, at St. Peter's the newly initiated do not even congratulate one another. As at St. John Bosco, they just drift away into the Saturday night.

CONCLUSION

It is easy to mistakenly read Arnold van Gennep's three-stage model of initiation as placing equal emphasis on each stage. As noted in this book's introduction, however, a close reading reveals that he recognized that different rites of passage place greater or lesser emphasis on different moments in the process. As Grimes summarizes van Gennep, "Funerals emphasize separation; births and weddings, incorporation; and initiations, transition."[12] The association of initiations with transition here is no doubt due to the influence of Victor Turner, who did more to develop van Gennep's model than anyone. Turner placed his greatest emphasis on the middle stage, famously elaborating his concept of liminality and all that flows from it. In the contemporary Rite of Christian Initiation of Adults, the separation and transition stages of the initiation process are heavily shaped and constrained by the realities of modern society. Emphasis falls, therefore, on the third stage of incorporation. According to the ritual text, "In the celebration of the eucharist, as they take part for the first time and with full right, the newly baptized reach the culminating point in their Christian Initiation" (RCIA, no. 217). This brings me back to those who criticize the "ritual illusion" or "problem of dissonance" in studying initiation. In the end, these critics are only half right—or half wrong—at least with respect to adult initiation in the contemporary Catholic church.

Following La Fontaine's analysis of initiation rituals, I concur that many are "self-fulfilling in one sense."[13] From an objective perspective, they do in fact do what they say they do. Receiving the sacraments of initiation is a significant threshold for the individual becoming Catholic, after which the individual has a new status: full membership and the rights/responsibilities of full participation in the church. The sacraments—by virtue of being sacraments—have their power regardless of the subjective state of the individual receiving them. That said, while we can certainly analyze rites of initiation strictly in terms of their objective structure and function, the critics are right to highlight what we miss by not exploring the subjective dimension of incorporation. The subjective dimension calls our attention not to the universal outcome of initiation, but to the diversity of incorporation outcomes. This variation opens up to broader questions about the overall patterns of difference that the RCIA makes in the lives of those who complete the process and become Catholic. Do these individuals experience change in their religious beliefs and practices? If so, what is the nature of that change? And is that change systematically related to the way the RCIA is implemented in different parishes? These questions are taken up in the next chapter, which takes as its point of departure the final stage in the RCIA process: mystagogy.

MYSTAGOGY: THE END AND THE BEGINNING

Two weeks after their initiation at the Easter Vigil, new Catholics around the Diocese of Fort Wayne–South Bend return to their parishes to participate in the awkwardly named concluding period of the RCIA process: mystagogy. Or at least some of them do. At St. Peter's, very few cars are in the parking lot at 7:00 p.m. when the first mystagogy session is supposed to begin. Gathering in the meeting room, Sister Marie says that Sheila will be absent due to a new job on Monday nights and that Chris also called to say she will be absent. Cathy is not at the meeting either, but Sister Marie does not mention it. Though the room feels emptier than usual, the session proceeds as if nothing is different. Mystagogy is intended as a special time after Easter for the neophytes to deepen their understanding of the mysteries they experienced at their initiation and to put their new skills of Christian discipleship into practice. At St. Peter's, however, "mystagogy" is Greek for "more of the same."

The five RCIA meetings at St. Peter's following Easter are simply a continuation of the formal catechesis that came before it. Sister Marie tells the group that because Easter fell early this year, there was not enough time to discuss all of the necessary topics before the Vigil. So this week they will hear guest lecturers speak about the sacrament of marriage and natural family planning. Next week Sister Marie will present to the group on the sacrament of holy orders, then they will have a session on prayer and the Christian life, and she is trying to arrange for the diocesan director of Catholic Charities to give a guest lecture. She also says that in one of the following weeks they will look at "the topic of mystagogy." At St. Peter's even mystagogy itself is treated as another topic, another subject to be lectured on, another term to read about in the *Catechism*.

Sitting in the same meeting room listening to another lecture on another topic, one wonders if the Easter Vigil even happened at St. Peter's. Other than fewer people, this evening looks just like any other evening during the previous eight months. But the Vigil did happen. People were initiated. So perhaps the process has come full circle today. The sunny weather is reminiscent of the beginning of the program back in August. There has been a lot taught since then, many presentations have been made, and much information has been shared. Those who sought to become Catholic have all been fully initiated. Tonight some of them are back, again in shorts, back to learn more.

*   *   *

Across the diocese, the same night that St. Peter's is holding the first of its five mystagogy sessions, St. John Bosco is having its one and only post-initiation meeting. Of five people initiated at the Easter Vigil, only two are in attendance: Rick and Kris. Sara, Anna, and Cathy are all absent. (Debbie McWilliams is also at the meeting. She was initiated during Lent because her family had planned a trip to Disney World, which prevented her from being initiated at the Easter Vigil.) Deacon Zeke—now retired for some three to four weeks—looks rested and relaxed as he calls the meeting to order just after 7:00 p.m. He begins by asking people their impressions of the Vigil. "Well, Rick, what'd you think?" Rick remarks that "it was nice, real beautiful." Deacon Zeke suggests that perhaps it was "long," but Rick says he was expecting for it to be longer, adding, "I like Father Post. He just zoomed through everything. He picked really fast readers." Others offer more of the same sorts of sound bites: "really beautiful," "moving," "long," and so on. Deacon Zeke's question seems to carry the weight of asking a high school student about prom night. He does not press them to reflect more deeply on the sacramental mysteries, redirecting them instead by asking, "So how's everybody been doing since then? Do you have any questions about anything?" Everyone just nods with rather blank looks on their faces, so Deacon Zeke brings the group "back on task." He announces that the session will be "kinda short tonight. I don't have that much for you."

Deacon Zeke sits in his usual spot at the front of the room, at his usual table, and reads from his usual notebook for most of the evening. As a way of helping the new Catholics to better understand and become involved in the life of the church, he reads about parish and diocesan hierarchies, and on different parish programs like adult education and marriage preparation. Because his notebook is really the RCIA book *Making Disciples: A Comprehensive Catechesis for the RCIA Catechumenate,* written by Mary Jane Carew of the diocesan Office of Catechesis, the programs described do not reflect what St. John Bosco actually does. This leads Zeke to make apologetic disclaimers after a number of them. "We don't do this here, but we're supposed to. But look, we've got only one priest, you know." He throws up his arms at this, rather exasperated. He then lists some of the programs that the parish actually sponsors: St. Vincent de Paul, Rosary Society, lectoring, helping in liturgy, Scrip, youth ministry, child care in the nursery.

Deacon Zeke continues reading from his notebook, outlining some of the precepts of the church, such as the rules of fasting and abstinence during Lent. He jokingly confesses that he doesn't think that giving up meat on Friday means that much to him "cuz I just like seafood more." At this he lets out one more Deacon Zeke belly laugh and concludes unceremoniously by saying, "That's basically it. There's not much here. I just wanted us all to get together one last time. Do you have any questions about anything?" Silence. This is mystagogy at St. John Bosco. The session is done before 7:40 p.m. On the bright side, it is still light out when they emerge from the basement of the rectory. This is a nice symbol. For most of the year, by the time the class sessions ended at 8:00, the sun had set. Tonight it is still shining, giving hope that these new Catholics will continue to live in light rather than darkness well beyond their time in the RCIA process.

* * *

At Queen of Peace, Jill Turnock says they are all still trying to understand this time of mystagogy. They have a few meetings and events planned after the Vigil, and they also have activities for the neophytes in the fall and the following Lent. This is in response to an instruction in the United States bishops' *National Statutes for the Catechumenate* that reads: "After the immediate mystagogy or postbaptismal catechesis during the Easter season, the program for the neophytes should extend until the anniversary of Christian initiation, with at least monthly assemblies of the neophytes for their deeper Christian formation and incorporation into the full life of the Christian community" (no. 24). Jill also tries to get the neophytes involved in the parish on some level, though she says that this particular group is already doing things. Overall, her approach to mystagogy is casual. She does not require attendance, so people regularly trickle in late. Some attend rarely, if at all. For those who do attend, there is a sense that they are no longer students but are peers of those who were once their teachers.

For the last scheduled meeting during the Period of Mystagogy proper, the group gathers to prepare sack lunches for the Center for the Homeless. This is something that the parish does once a month as part of their social outreach. All but one of the new Catholics are in attendance. A sign-up sheet was passed around the previous week for the necessary supplies for the lunches: lunch meat, jelly and peanut butter, napkins, bananas, carrots and celery, bread. Everyone brought something. With a little explanation, the group gets started. A line forms for washing hands, and rubber gloves are donned. All year long this has been a fun group, joking with and kidding one another throughout presentations, throughout prayer. Tonight is no different. The rubber gloves are blow up and tossed around like balloons. They are used to snap each other. People criticize the amount of peanut butter or meat put on a sandwich by someone or another. The mood is very light. A genuine sense of community has been built throughout the year.

From the very first gathering in August, Jill encouraged members of the group to share information about themselves. Throughout the year, they learned more and more about each other. They watched Rick Commons get sick and miss many a class, only to welcome him back with great enthusiasm and thanksgiving for his recovery. They regularly talked about Steve Gallager's and his fiancée Amy's wedding plans, joking with Steve about how little planning he was actually doing. They embraced Les Burns, a baptized Protestant who had been attending the Catholic church with his wife Mary for 48 years prior to entering the RCIA process. Because they spend the winter months in Florida, Les went through the Rite of Reception into the Full Communion of the Catholic Church before the rest of the group in February. While he and Mary were in Florida, the rest of the group signed and sent cards to them, reminding them that they were in the group's thoughts even while away. Upon their return from Florida, they took their place in the sack lunch assembly line along with their fellow Catholics.

Prayer brought this group together, small group discussions helped them to know one another and the Catholic faith, and the celebration of the public rites moved them from being a group that gathers in the basement once a week to a part of the broader parish community. Friendships, as well as Catholics, are made at Queen of Peace. Many had attended Mass at Queen of Peace before beginning the RCIA process, but their formation over the course of the year made them feel more incorporated into the parish as the People of God. Les Burns is as fine an example of this as any. After 48 years of Mass attendance as a Protestant, this new Catholic talks about becoming more involved in church activities and furthering the goodness that the RCIA has brought to his life. He has come to see the church as a place for his growth and happiness in life, a place of meaning, a place to be with other people, a place to exercise his gifts. He speaks with a sense of being on a journey as well, of not having it all figured out yet. This last mystagogy meeting was not the end for Les, but the beginning.

As we will see in Chapter 6, for many the Period of Mystagogy is both an end to the RCIA process and a beginning of their new lives as full members of the church. But not all who complete the RCIA process grow or gain as much as Les. Steve Gallagher was baptized at Queen of Peace's Easter Vigil, and that was the last anyone saw of him. He took advantage of Jill's casual attitude toward attendance at mystagogy sessions and skipped every one. So, RCIA processes vary, but even within the same RCIA process, experiences vary. As the final stage in the RCIA process, therefore, the period of mystagogy represents an appropriate time to consider the difference that the RCIA process makes.

CHAPTER SIX

THE DIFFERENCE IT MAKES

Although the initiation of new members culminates with the celebration of the sacraments at the Easter Vigil, the Rite of Christian Initiation of Adults continues through the Period of Mystagogy, which normatively lasts for the 50 days of the Easter season. This is sometimes called the period of "post-baptismal catechesis," because it seeks to lead the newly initiated more deeply into reflection on the experience of the sacraments and membership in the church community. According to the ritual text, "This is a time for the community and the neophytes together to grow in deepening their grasp of the paschal mystery and in making it part of their lives through meditation on the Gospel, sharing in the eucharist, and doing the works of charity" (*RCIA*, no. 244). Practically speaking, in this final period neophytes are propelled out of the cocoon of their RCIA experience and into the life of the parish, sometimes.

If the Easter Vigil sacraments are the climax of the initiation process in the Catholic church, the Period of Mystagogy that follows it is without question anticlimactic. As one RCIA director put it, "So much attention is given to the Easter Vigil, and so much energy goes into it, that it's hard to keep going after that. It's like graduation from high school. No one goes back to school after they graduated. But that's like what we're asking people to do with this mystagogy stuff. They're graduated, but still in school." Although 87.5% of parishes I surveyed offer a period of mystagogy, only 12.5% of those parishes offer a full seven weeks (50 days). The average mystagogy period lasts only four weeks. Officially, mystagogy is intended as a special time after Easter for the neophytes to deepen their understanding of the mysteries they had experienced at their initiation and to put their new skills of Christian discipleship into practice. As the brief descriptions of St. Peter's, St. John Bosco, and Queen of Peace in the prelude to this chapter suggest, this intention is rarely fulfilled.

Indeed, the implementation of mystagogy is so sporadic and variable that it cannot be easily systematized. Therefore, rather than looking at the Period of Mystagogy per se, this chapter takes up issues related to its function as a point of transition out of the RCIA and into the everyday life of the church. Thinking about mystagogy as the final stage in the RCIA process naturally leads to some reflective questions. In particular, do the individuals who become Catholic through the RCIA change? If so, how? Ultimately, does the RCIA process itself make a difference? This chapter answers these questions by drawing on both qualitative interviews and quantitative data from surveys. It first examines the socialization of individuals into the Catholic tradition by considering their ways of thinking about what it means to be Catholic. It then examines their incorporation into the church by looking beyond the cognitive level of beliefs and understandings to their ecclesial involvement and spiritual practices. In the end, the RCIA process does make a difference for many, though its effects are not uniform. The RCIA process is most effective in those parishes that more closely follow the vision of the process as outlined in the normative text of the *Ordo* and the United States bishops' *National Statutes* that guides its implementation.

START TO FINISH: CHANGES IN UNDERSTANDING WHAT IT MEANS TO BE CATHOLIC

To establish how individuals change (or do not change) in the course of the RCIA process, I conducted open-ended interviews with individuals in the RCIA process, both when they were inquirers and when they were neophytes. In this analysis, I draw on the responses of the 39 individuals from 17 parishes for whom I have complete data.

In the initial interviews, I asked each individual, "What does it mean to be Catholic?" To be sure, there is not a single, universally agreed-upon understanding of what it means to be Catholic, but every RCIA process attempts to convey some sense of this, consciously or unconsciously. So, how individuals answer this question is of considerable interest in understanding the difference that the RCIA process makes. By asking this same question again after they completed their initiation, I am able to track systematically any changes that take place over the course of the RCIA process for these individuals.

The largest group of individuals in the first round interviews—38%—is those who could not articulate a clear understanding of what it means to be Catholic. This is not surprising. Although many were strongly motivated to become Catholic even before beginning the RCIA process, in most of these cases the motivation was personal rather than theological (see Chapter 2). Typical responses in this category are:

- I was afraid you were going to ask me that! You stumped me.
- I knew you were going to ask that! Uhhhhh. Well, I'm still, I'm still a little bit in the dark about it.
- Oh, my. . . . You know, I don't think I can answer that at the moment.
- I'm not sure that I really understand the Catholic faith yet to know to the full extent of what it means to be Catholic.

Some of these individuals reminded interviewers that it was a hard question to answer because they were just beginning the process of joining the church. Fred Jenkins, for example, is a 41-year-old unbaptized husband and father of three. Although he has been attending the Catholic church for 15 years with his wife, his response to the question is, "Well, I don't know if I have a good answer for that. I'm not even sure I have an answer for that. I think that's part of the reason I'm going through this." Similarly, Teri Mack is an unbaptized 60-year-old retired school teacher and widow who became attracted to the Catholic church as her husband of 24 years was dying. She highlights her ignorance and desire to learn more in the RCIA process. "At this point, I'm still investigating. I don't know. I'm still learning. You're never too old to learn, right? And I'm really not sure I can answer that question right at this point in time."

The second largest group of respondents—20%—is those who answered the question with specific ideas, but who ended up in one way or another concluding that being Catholic is no different from being Christian. James Adams is a 41-year-old inquirer who was baptized in the Church of God. He has been married for 17 years and has been attending St. Mark's with his wife and two children for the past 12 years. As he explains his understanding, "To be Catholic and to be Christian, I see not that much—I don't see a difference between the two. I think . . . Catholic is Christian. I don't know, I guess I don't. My understanding of a Catholic is that they, I don't know. I guess I really don't know. Because to me Catholic and Christian means the same." Sandy Glenn, baptized in a Baptist church but raised in nondenominational Christian churches, answered similarly: "My understanding is that to be a practicing Catholic is going to church, reading the Bible, following the commandments, and basically to me that's what a Catholic is. It's basically any Christian and that's what should be expected of anyone who actually believes in Christ." Like James and Sandy, all of the individuals in this category were already baptized in other Christian traditions and stressed the continuity between their current Christian faith and their future (potential) Catholic faith. Twenty-five-year-old Colleen Doe is a good example. She was baptized in the Church of the Brethren and attended a Brethren college, where she met her future husband. After graduation, she got a job teaching at a Catholic school and attended Catholic services with her fiancé. They had been married 18 months when she entered the RCIA process, also at St. Mark's. She answers the question, "Right now, I guess I feel like it's just a—to me, any kind of religion is just a label and it's your own personal life is what you have with Jesus or God. Right now I feel it's just a label and I don't feel like I'm, and even when I become Catholic, I'm not going to feel like I'm this new person. I just feel like it's just a name put to something."

Close behind this group are the 18% of respondents who also give specific ideas about what it means to be Catholic, but use the language of "they" or "them" in their descriptions. These individuals conveyed some sense of Catholicism, but clearly did not (yet) see themselves as fitting the description. For example, Ann Fischer is unbaptized and was not religious at the time she married her husband of nine years. She expresses a sense of what it means to be Catholic, but does not yet identify with the faith: "A lot of prayer, a lot of going to church and, um, really understanding Mass. Um, saying the rosary. That's what I see in them." Others answer similarly. Jennifer Smith imagines what she might be like if she were Catholic, answering, "I think myself if I was to be a Catholic I would [be] very devoted, like I know it's an obligation to be at church every Sunday . . . To be very um, generous. I don't think that I've ever seen as many generous people as I have in the Catholic church. They're so giving of their time and everything. I mean, I've never seen people be like that before." Emily Coulson says, "I mean they're at peace with themselves, they're at peace with what the world has to offer them and they're ready to take on anything." Like Ann, both Jennifer and Emily are unbaptized and come to the question of what it means to be Catholic without strong preconceptions of either Catholicism or Christianity. Their perspectives are definitely that of outsiders looking in.

Only 8% of the respondents—3 of 39 individuals—give answers that I consider to be relatively clear and articulate. Again, this is not surprising; after all, the entire point of the RCIA process is not to confirm what people already know about Catholicism but to develop their understanding of the Catholic faith and to form them into Catholics. As is commonly said by those involved in initiation ministry, Catholics are *made, not born.*[1] So, a crucial question is to what extent do individuals' understandings of what it means to be Catholic grow and develop over the course of the RCIA process? The short answer is, considerably. In comparing individuals' initial responses as inquirers to their later responses as neophytes, I find that nearly two-thirds (64%) of respondents show some development in their answers, while just over one-third (36%) gave answers that showed no development or were simply idiosyncratic.

Beginning with the smaller of these two groups, recall Teri Mack, who at the outset of the process said, "I'm really not sure I can answer that question right at this point in time." She also added at that time, "Ask me that question six months from now. I probably could answer it better than I can right now." Ten months later, after she received the sacraments of initiation at the Easter Vigil, I did ask her this question again, and her response had not changed: "Aw, that is a tough one. (Pause.) And I'm not sure I can answer that." Fred Jenkins initially said he did not have a good answer for the question and this is part of the reason he was in the RCIA process. After he is initiated, he is no more able to answer the question. He admits in response to the follow-up question, "I wouldn't say a lot of things really changed. I think [becoming Catholic] was just something I wanted to do. And just got up the nerve to do it." Brian Wilson came to the RCIA process with little understanding of religion in general, so not surprisingly he initially said, "I'm still a little bit in the dark about it. Um, you know, we've, you know, we still have quite a few classes to go. And I'm not really 100% sure what the difference between a Catholic and anyone else is." In fact, although Brian said initially he was baptized Methodist, he ended up not being able to document this, so he was baptized, confirmed, and received first communion at St. Catherine's. Upon completing his initiation, Brian's sense of what it means to be Catholic seems idiosyncratic. He says, "Well, I think it means that on a personal level for me I just need to be nicer to the people around me, I need to be more understanding of other's faults, and that I can't demand and expect everybody to do and think as I do. Because everybody's an individual, everybody does things different." Several others in this group gave answers like Brian's.

A number of individuals whom I classified as showing no development over the course of the RCIA process were very consistent between their initial responses and their post-initiation responses. After attending St. Mark's for 12 years with his family, James Adams was received into the full communion of the Catholic church. But his view that there is no specific difference between being Catholic and being a member of any Christian church (like the Church of God, the tradition in which he was raised) remained unchanged. "My understanding of what it means to be Catholic. (Pause) You know, I guess my understanding of Catholic would be to, um, I guess walk in the path of Jesus. Um, you know, live like Jesus-type situation and basically mirror what he did and so forth, would be my understanding of being Catholic." Sandy Glenn's view that to be a Catholic is just to be a Christian was extremely consistent across the two interviews. In her post-initiation interview she answers, "Um, Catholic to me is just a word, it just means 'universal.' So being a Catholic to me, how can I explain this? It is just being a Christian, and to do the will of God, and that's basically what it means to me. There's no real difference at all. I don't see any difference at all."

What of the 64% of individuals classified as showing growth and development in their responses to the question? Here I find three dominant patterns of change. The first is movement from no, vague, or inarticulate answers in the initial interview to clearer, more specific answers in the follow-up interview. Many of these are quite concise. Susan Smith went from not being able to answer the question as an inquirer to answering as a neophyte, "I suppose to live a Christian life, attend Mass, and take the sacraments, and you know, participate in reconciliation. I think receiving communion every week. It makes you feel closer [to God], like you have that spiritual renewal every week." Joanna Broderick went from a vague answer concluding in "I don't know how to explain it," to a clear, three-point answer: "To have a close relationship with God. To have a close relationship with the other members of the parish. And to help those in need. Catholics try to help people around them, whether they are Catholic or not. If people are in need, we do it. At least in our parish." George Smith gave a rambling, idiosyncratic response to the question initially.

After his initiation, he responds more clearly and succinctly, "The body and the blood of Christ. The Eucharist. I think that is the main, for me, that is the most important reason why I wanted to become Catholic."

The second pattern is movement from seeing Catholics as "they" or "them" to seeing oneself as and being a part of the church. Pat Kline, for example, initially spoke of Catholics as "they." "They still keep all of the old traditions. . . . They try to become closer to God. . . . They're more personable." After his initiation, his answer to this same question changes considerably. In the follow-up interview he says,

> Wow. I think probably the biggest thing is just understanding that it is the actual body and blood that you receive. That's the greatest thing I think of being something I didn't believe before taking classes. I think anyone can have a hard time with it. I think that is the greatest thing I learned, that I truly believe that, and that is the greatest thing that has hit me the most, is now that when I receive it just sends a different kind of chill every time it happens.

As previously noted, Emily Coulson also initially spoke of Catholics as "they": "They're at peace with themselves, they're at peace with what the world has to offer them." Nine months later, after completing the RCIA process, Emily focuses again in her response on peace, but places herself within rather than outside the church: "I'm much more at peace. More positive outlook on life. Don't worry quite as much. Though I do feel guilty if I don't make it to church. I feel like I'm missing something if I don't go." This pattern evidences the sort of incorporation discussed in the previous chapter. In fact, one respondent even used this specific language. Initially, Ann Fischer answered the question by talking about "what I see in them." After she became Catholic, her language shifts to "I" and "us," as in, "It means getting back to the Eucharist and knowing that Jesus died on the cross for us, to save us. That, you know, I'm still considered a sinner. It has more meaning to say I'm sorry for what I did now that I'm allowed to take the Eucharist." She added, "You feel, I want to say, incorporated. Like you're Catholic, OK, and I don't feel like an outsider like I did before when I would go to church with my husband and I couldn't take communion and I felt really left out."

The third pattern is evident among many of those who became Catholic from other Christian traditions. These individuals tended to emphasize specific doctrinal beliefs in the follow-up interviews, beliefs that are different from the traditions in which they were raised. Raised in the Brethren Church and attending St. Mark's with her Catholic husband, Colleen Doe initially said she did not expect to feel like a "new person" when she became Catholic. Although she falls short of saying she is a new person since her initiation, in her follow-up interview Colleen does seem to think that Catholic is more than "just a label" or "just a name to put to something." Post-initiation she says what it means to be Catholic "for me now, it's attending church regularly and how important that is. And the renewal that I get from going to church. If I've missed a Sunday and then we go a week later I feel, you know, rejuvinized. And I don't know, that's just important for me now, attending Mass and growing that way." Other Protestants showed this pattern as well, but none more so than Rory Friend.

Rory is a 35-year-old handyman and father of three children under seven years old. His wife May is Catholic, and they have attended her church for the seven years they have been married. He had been thinking about becoming Catholic for a couple of years, but he was raised in a fundamentalist Baptist family. As he said, "A lot of the things that Catholics do, as far as their traditions and things, are extremely unknown to us. I mean, we have no idea." Motivated by the desire to "get a little closer to my wife" and recognizing that they were raising their children Catholic, he entered the RCIA process. When he was first asked about what it means to be Catholic, he responded, "Oh boy, I'm just starting to really learn, um, I would say, um, that it means to be a very opened, um, universal type faith, where everyone is drawn in, in that it's the belief in God as the Creator and Christ as the Savior. And really nothing major more than that." When he was interviewed again 10 months later, after having been receiving into the full communion of the Catholic church, his answer to this question is much more specific and elaborate:

> I guess the biggest change for me now would be in the belief of Mary being the Mother of God and the Trinity. In thinking of those kinds of things it's almost mind boggling because it's almost too hard for the human mind to fathom, to grasp that concept. But I think I understand it more. Before I was really adamant about not giving Mary a whole lot of hoopla. She's just part of the plan. But I see now that it took someone very special to take on that role in our faith. So I think I understand a lot more in that way. And in the belief that the Holy Spirit transcends and turns the Eucharist into the actual body and blood of Christ. It's not just a representation. But in my faith, in knowing what God is capable of doing, it's not out of the realm of possibility.

As the interviewer begins to move to the next question, thinking Rory had completed his response, Rory continues beyond ideas about Mary and the Eucharist to ideas about service:

> I think acceptance and compassion for me. . . . In the faith that I was raised in it wasn't, you really weren't considering yourself the hands and feet of Christ. Whereas that is pretty much, at least at [our parish] what our whole belief is, our whole establishment is. That we are carrying on the work. And so we're not just a mouthpiece, but we're actually doing, getting out there and getting our hands dirty, marching the miles. Doing what Jesus would have done if his ministry hadn't ended. So I think that's really what being Catholic means to me. Being really open and accepting of everyone. And that you're not passing judgment, but you're leading by example.

The before and after responses here exemplify growth and development in understanding what it means to be Catholic. Clearly, Rory got something out of the RCIA process in his parish.

Not everyone was able to articulate their ideas to the extent that Rory was, though. Whether they were classified as showing growth and development or not, across both groups some people definitely struggled to put into words their experiences and understandings. Listening to these struggles on the audio recordings of the interviews made me wonder about the fairness of expecting coherent answers to a question like "What does it mean to be Catholic?" Wondering whether I could even give a reasonable answer to this question, I recall the e. e. cummings poem from 1926 that begins, "Since feeling is first / who pays any attention / to the syntax of things."[2] Unable to put into words specific doctrinal beliefs, a few individuals simply fall back on their feelings about being Catholic. Stella and Nick Jones are a married couple who both went through the RCIA process the same year. Although they were interviewed separately, their post-initiation responses are remarkably similar. Stella struggles to answer at first. "Um. (Pause.) I just feel, um, ah, I guess it's hard for me to define. Um. (Pause)." She then says, "Well, I'm glad I'm a part of it. I'm glad I'm Catholic." Nick gets to his identical response more quickly. "Um (pause), I'm um glad that I did join the Catholic church. I didn't really have a lot of religion before that. And I feel good about it."

During the heat of the battles between liberals and conservatives over what the Catholic church is, Michael Leach and Therese Borchard edited a collection of reflections by famous and ordinary Catholics called *I Like Being Catholic*. The title comes from a famous quip by Catholic priest and author Andrew Greeley on the Phil Donohue television show in response to a member of the audience who asked him, "If you don't like the Catholic church, why don't you stop being a priest and leave the church?"[3] The book shows how, doctrinal disputes aside, there is a common ground of positive feelings that people have for the church and their involvement in it. This sentiment is echoed by Steve Johnson, a 46-year-old who was not raised in a religious tradition, but whose eight- and six-year-old children were attending Catholic school. "What is my understanding?

Uh, I don't know," Steve begins falteringly. Then without prompting he continues, "I like being Catholic. I like the church we joined. And I'm glad I got baptized finally."

As Thomas Landy has suggested, "Religious traditions as commonly lived and experienced might best be understood, in Clifford Geertz's terms, as 'collections of notions' rather than internally fully-consistent sets of beliefs." In Michael Polanyi's famous phrase, "*we know more than we can tell*" (italics in original). But in sociology generally there is often an Enlightenment rationalist bias. As Robert Wuthnow has argued, "The fully functioning [research] subject is expected to have a view of the world that is accurate and internally consistent."[4] In the sociology of religion, this becomes—in what some might see as a Protestant Christian bias[5]—an expectation that our respondents can function as amateur theologians. This overemphasis on the cognitive over the sentimental, emotional, or behavioral can lead to erroneous conclusions about how well incorporated people like the Joneses or Steve Johnson are into the Catholic church. By focusing strictly on beliefs or doctrine, some individuals may appear to be unorthodox, uninformed, or unbelieving. By focusing instead on practices, we can see the integrity of religious purpose that transcends doctrinal beliefs. Quoting the poet Wallace Stevens, Robert Bellah says of the modern orientation to religion, especially in America: "We believe without belief, beyond belief."[6]

RELIGIOUS PRACTICES: THE DIFFERENCE IMPLEMENTATION MAKES

Instead of changes in religious beliefs and understandings over the course of the RCIA process, this section focuses on religious *practices*. This draws our attention to the issue of how well the RCIA process prepares individuals to make the post-initiation transition into the everyday life of being Catholic and how well new Catholics are incorporated into the body of the church. In this section I draw on a unique set of data that links information on individuals who completed their

initiation with information about the characteristics of the RCIA processes they went through. These data allow me to say concretely how
individuals' religious practices changed in the course of the RCIA process, and to connect that change to the RCIA process itself.[7] Thus,
I can truly speak to the question many people ask about the RCIA
process: What difference does it make?

To begin, Table 6.1 compares the average responses to a number of
questions about religious practices asked of those becoming Catholic
at the beginning of the RCIA process and after the conclusion. Specifically, I look at two areas, what I call *ecclesial involvement*—the extent
to which individuals are actively involved in their parishes—and *spiritual practice*—the extent of involvement in more individualized religious practices that are related to the development of the respondent's
interior, spiritual life.

I explore ecclesial involvement through three specific questions:
"How often, if ever, do you attend Mass in the Catholic church?"
"Other than the RCIA, how often, if ever, do you participate in any
spiritual group in the parish, such as Bible study, a prayer group, a
faith sharing group, or any others?" And, "Are you currently participating in any ministry or committee in the parish, such as the ushers,
the school committee, youth ministry, outreach ministry, or any
others?" As column 2 in Table 6.1 shows, the average response to the
Mass attendance question is very high, even at the start of the RCIA
process, falling between "two or three times a month" (= 5) and "once
a week" (= 6). This makes sense given that we know those beginning
the RCIA process (called "inquirers") are often already connected to
the Catholic church, especially through Mass attendance with their
nuclear families. The average response to the spiritual group participation question is much lower, falling very close to "almost never" (= 2).
This suggests that although the inquirers have some connection to
their parishes, they are not highly integrated. Finally, regarding participation in ministries or committees, 14% of inquirers responded yes.
Follow-up questions revealed that many of these are people involved
in work with the parish school and youth, which again corresponds to

Table 6.1. Change in Various Aspects of Religious Practice during the RCIA Process

Question/Description	(1) Range of Individual Change from Start to Conclusion	(2) Mean at Start of RCIA Process (Std. Dev.)	(3) Mean After RCIA Process (Std. Dev.)	(4) Mean Change (Std. Dev.)	(5) % Change
Ecclesial Involvement Items					
How often, if ever, do you attend Mass in the Catholic church? (1 = never; 7 = more than once a week)	−3 to 4	5.49 (0.86)	5.52 (1.08)	0.314 (1.22)	+ 0.5
How often, if ever, do you participate in any spiritual group in the parish, such as Bible study, a prayer group, a faith sharing group, or any others? (1 = never; 7 = more than once a week)	−5 to 6	1.92 (1.62)	2.98 (2.07)	1.063 (2.21)	+ 55.2*

Are you currently participating in any ministry or committee in the parish, such as the ushers, the school committee, youth ministry, outreach ministry, or any others? (0 = no; 1 = yes)	−1 to 1	0.14 (0.35)	0.34 (0.48)	0.201 (0.56)	+ 142.9*
Spiritual Practice Items					
How often, if ever, do you pray privately? (1 = never; 7 = more than once a week)	−5 to 5	6.66 (0.99)	6.57 (0.99)	−0.088 (1.17)	−1.4
How often, if ever, do you read the Bible? (1 = never; 7 = more than once a week)	−5 to 5	4.82 (2.04)	4.29 (2.02)	−0.529 (1.76)	−11.0*

* Indicates that the change is statistically significant at the 0.001 level (using 2-tailed paired samples t-test).

185

the importance of children for many in their motivation for entering the process of becoming Catholic.

How does ecclesial involvement change from the beginning of the RCIA process to the end? The results in columns 3, 4, and 5 in Table 6.1 tell the story. Mass attendance increases, but only very slightly. The very high levels of Mass attendance at the outset did not leave much room for improvement. Participation in spiritual groups, however, increased significantly. Although the absolute level is still somewhat low—increasing from "almost never" to "less than once a month"—the percentage increase in the average level was 55.2%. The most dramatic increase in ecclesial involvement came in terms of participation in parish ministries or committees. By the end of the RCIA process, more than one-third of individuals—brand new Catholics—were already participating, a 143% increase over the 14% participating at the outset. Taken together, these data indicate that over the course of the RCIA process, initiates do become more involved in the life of their parishes—a key indicator of successful incorporation.

Turning now to the second set of religious behaviors, which I call spiritual practice, the data show an interesting and different pattern. The two questions explored here are: "How often, if ever, do you pray privately?" and "How often, if ever, do you read the Bible?" The response categories are the same as for Mass attendance and spiritual group participation, a seven-point scale where 1 = never and 7 = more than once a week. As column 2 of Table 6.1 shows, inquirers have very strong spiritual practices from the start. With respect to prayer, the average (6.67) is nearly at the maximum possible. Although not as high, the extent of Bible reading is also quite high, at nearly 5 ("two or three times a month") on the seven-point scale. With these high levels already reported at the start, it is not altogether surprising that by the end of the RCIA process the new Catholics have not increased their level of spiritual practice. What is surprising, looking at columns 3, 4, and 5, is that in both cases we see a *decline*. The 11% decline in Bible reading is not as large as the increases in ecclesial involvement, however, and the change in private prayer (1.4% decline) is not statistically significant. Still, compared to the development in individuals' spiritual lives that is normatively expected in the RCIA process, the lack of growth in spiritual practice is notable.[8]

Averages are useful in providing a summary of a large number of cases, but they can also obscure important dynamics taking place below the surface of central tendencies. Column 1 in Table 6.1 highlights the range of individual change from start to finish for each of the five practices being considered here. In terms of Mass attendance, the largest decline in attendance was three categories, and the largest increase was four categories. This translates, for example, to a decline from "once a week" to "less than once a month" or an increase from "almost never to once a week." And the range of individual change on the other questions with a seven-point response scale is even greater. For participation in spiritual groups, private prayer, and Bible reading, the greatest decline is five categories—for example, from "once a week" to "never"—and the largest increases are the same or higher. So, even where the averages at the beginning of the RCIA process and at the end are fairly close, there is a great deal of individual variation that begs to be explained. How is it that one person can go from participating in a spiritual group "once a week" to participating "never," while another person goes from participating "never" to participating "more than once a week"? Is it possible that these are not simply individual idiosyncrasies but are systematic patterns that can be explained (in part) by the RCIA process itself?

In explaining this individual variation in changes in ecclesial involvement and spiritual practice, I do in fact examine the effect of the level of implementation of the RCIA in different parishes. By "level of implementation," I mean the extent to which the full normative vision of the *Rite of Christian Initiation of Adults* is implemented in a given parish. As we have seen throughout this book, the basic elements of the RCIA process—depicted in Table 1.1 in Chapter 1—are universal. But like most universal rituals in the church, the RCIA process is variably implemented in practice.[9]

This variation provides an opportunity to understand the relationship between levels of RCIA implementation and individual outcomes. Michael McCallion and David Maines, for example, distinguish between RCIA processes led by coordinators who are "text adherers," "moderate text adherers," and "text adapters"—each implementing the RCIA with different levels of fidelity to the ritual text.[10] Rather than placing parishes in categories, I look at parish RCIA processes along a continuum from *more fully* to *less fully* implemented. When the RCIA process is more fully implemented, according to the normative vision specified in the ritual text itself and the United States bishops' *National Statutes*, the initiation of adults is an always ongoing process that unfolds differently and at different rates for different individuals. When the RCIA process is less fully implemented, those seeking initiation are treated more uniformly, as a "class" that begins the process in the fall and "graduates" in the spring. For this reason, I refer to this as a "school year" model of initiation. Analysis of pastoral works like Thomas Morris's *The RCIA: Transforming the Church*[11] and sociological studies such as those by McCallion and Maines suggests five major elements. When taken together, these elements operationalize the continuum of "levels of implementation" in this analysis.

(1) *Ongoing Inquiry*: The guiding texts of the RCIA process do not specify when during the year the Period of Evangelization and Precatechumenate (for brevity, "inquiry") should begin. The idea that the church should welcome those interested in becoming Catholic on an ongoing basis, whenever they are ready, is strongly held by many. This ongoing approach to inquiry contrasts with the "school year" model wherein individuals can only begin the RCIA process when "classes" start in the fall. Among the parishes in this study, 72% have an ongoing Precatechumenate, and 28% begin their RCIA classes once per year.

(2) *Multiple Rites of Acceptance*: The Rite of Acceptance into the Order of Catechumens is the ritual transition from inquiry to the catechumenate. If not everyone enters the RCIA process at the same time, not everyone will be ready to commit to entering the catechumenate at the same time.[12] Parishes that more fully implement the RCIA process accommodate to this reality by celebrating the Rite of Acceptance more than once during the year. This contrasts with parishes using more of a "school year" model in which everyone must celebrate the rite at the same time in order to keep on track for "graduation." Among the parishes in this study, 66% celebrate this rite just once per year, and 34% celebrate this rite more than once per year.

(3) *One-Year Minimum of Instruction*: The catechumenate is the main time of instruction for those seeking initiation. Modeling the lengthy process seen in the early church, the ritual text specifies that the catechumenate "may last several years" (*RCIA*, no. 7.2), and the United States bishops' *National Statutes* maintain that the catechumenate "should extend for at least one year of formation, instruction, and probation" (no. 6). One rationale for this is that it exposes the catechumen to instruction for a full liturgical year, in contrast to the "school year" model, which lasts only nine months. Among the parishes in this study, only 34% follow the normative vision of the rite and require a minimum of one year of formation.

(4) *Rite of Dismissal Year-Round*: The Roman Catholic church practices closed communion, restricting reception of the Eucharist to full members in good standing. Because they are not baptized members of the church, catechumens cannot partake of the Eucharist, though they are expected to attend Mass on Sundays. Therefore, as part of their formation during the catechumenate, the ritual text suggests that catechumens be sent forth by the assembly in a Rite of Dismissal just prior to the Liturgy of the Eucharist. They are dismissed from the Mass in order to "reflect more deeply upon the word of God which you have shared with us today" (*RCIA*, no. 67). According to the ritual text, as long as individuals are in the period of the catechumenate, they should participate in these dismissal sessions. However,

among the parishes in this study, only 31% celebrate dismissals year-round. The remaining 69% do so only part of the year, or not at all.

(5) *Full Period of Mystagogy*: As noted in the introduction to this chapter, this period of the RCIA process is supposed to last for the 50 days of the Easter season, but many parishes offer far less. In the pure "school year" model, Easter represents graduation, after which "school's out." In most cases, however, parish RCIA processes offer some mystagogy. In this study, 87.5% of parishes offer a Period of Mystagogy, averaging four weeks. Only 12.5% offer the full seven weeks specified in the ritual text.

Focusing on these five elements of the RCIA process highlights key points of divergence in the ways in which different parishes implement the RCIA process. Taken together, these elements measure implementation of the RCIA process in different parishes along a continuum from more fully to less fully implemented. On one end of the continuum are parishes that offer an RCIA process that is "always ongoing." They have inquiry sessions whenever during the year people want to enter the RCIA process, celebrate multiple Rites of Acceptance, require a year minimum of instruction in the catechumenate, celebrate the Rite of Dismissal of catechumens from Mass year-round, and offer a full seven-week Period of Mystagogy. On the other end of the continuum are parishes that offer an RCIA process that operates according to a "school year" model. They begin their inquiry process once per year (in the fall), celebrate the Rite of Acceptance once per year, require less than a full year of time in the catechumenate (so that people can "graduate" by spring), celebrate the Rite of Dismissal not at all or only part of the year (school's out in the summertime), and offer something less than seven weeks of mystagogy (because people don't want to go back to school after "graduation").

That the RCIA is universally scripted but variably implemented in parishes allows us to ask and answer the question: Does the extent of implementation of the RCIA process make a difference in the lives of the individuals who are initiated through it? In order to isolate implementation as an explanatory variable, I use statistical models that allow me to "control" for other variables that could affect individuals' religious formation and incorporation—such as parish size, respondent's gender and education, respondent's effort and subjective evaluation of the RCIA process. Net of these other factors—*ceteris paribus*, all other things being equal—my statistical models show that the level of implementation of the RCIA process is the key factor that explains individual change. *In terms of ecclesial involvement—Mass attendance, participation in spiritual groups, and participation in ministries—the effect of RCIA implementation on individual change is statistically significant and positive.* In fact, the effect of this explanatory variable on changes in ecclesial involvement is three times that of the next most influential variable.

With respect to spiritual practice, we see that for the entire sample there is a slight decrease from the start of the RCIA process to the conclusion—against what those involved in RCIA ministry would hope for—but also underlying that average is some individual variation. The question is: Does the extent of implementation of the RCIA process itself have an effect on this change, positively or negatively? Using the same statistical models to control for other possible factors, *I find that the level of implementation of the RCIA has a statistically significant and positive effect on changes in individuals' spiritual practice. Although the effect on spiritual practice is not as large as the effect on ecclesial involvement, RCIA implementation is again the strongest predictor of changes in spiritual practice by a wide margin.*

These multivariate statistical models support the idea that the RCIA process *can* make a positive difference in the formation and incorporation of individuals in the church. It makes more of a difference the more it is implemented in accordance with the normative vision of the rite embodied in the *Ordo* and United States bishops' *National Statutes for the Catechumenate*. In the end, those who are initiated through RCIA processes that are more "fully implemented" are not only more actively engaged with their parishes (ecclesial involvement), but also grow more in their level of spiritual practice.

CONCLUSION

The Period of Mystagogy is supposed to be a time of reflection on the mysteries experienced by the newly initiated. But practically speaking, it becomes a time in which individuals transition from the cocoon of the RCIA into the wider life of the parish. From the perspective of the analyst, it is an appropriate point in the process at which to stand back and address the question: What difference does the RCIA process make? In this chapter, I have addressed this question from two different angles, looking both at changes in understandings of what it means to be Catholic and changes in religious practices. In both cases, I use data collected on individuals when they were inquirers first beginning the RCIA process and when they were neophytes having just completed their initiation. And in both cases, individuals going through the RCIA process often do experience change in the direction of greater understanding and better incorporation—especially when the RCIA process is more fully implemented.

Although looking at people immediately following their initiation and assessing whether the RCIA process made any difference in their lives is important, it is also just a moment in time. Most of those involved in RCIA ministry do not see themselves as having the discrete task of taking inquirers and seeing them through the sacraments of initiation, any more than parents see themselves as only responsible for making sure that their children graduate from high school. One RCIA director from Fort Wayne explained that her ideal "is always to have them grow in their understanding of their faith and especially in their relationship with Christ. We try to meet their immediate needs, and try to give them an awareness of what it means to be Catholic. But also I never, never want them to leave the RCIA process with a sense of, 'Now I've got everything.' But rather, they've begun a journey that's lifelong. It keeps going forever." Similarly, one of her colleagues from a different parish in Fort Wayne said this was a question that her RCIA team asked itself all the time. "They're new Christians, what is it that you would like to leave them with?" At some point, the team came to "the realization that the new Catholic's journeys are just beginning. And we go over and over and over that. This isn't the culmination. This isn't the end of their journey, that this is really just the beginning. That you can always grow and learn. That their hearts and their souls have been stirred. That the seeds of faith have been sown. And, I think that's what we came up with."

Although a lofty goal, it can be and is sometimes realized. Consider the story in the prelude of Les Burns at Queen of Peace. For Les, the last mystagogy meeting was an end to the RCIA process but the beginning of his new life in the church. Others interviewed after their initiation expressed similar senses of the implications of becoming Catholic. After she received the sacraments of initiation at the Easter Vigil, 50-year-old Christina Elfman realized that her process of becoming is ongoing. "I'm sure that I'll feel even more deeply in the future," she says. "There is still this process of figuring out the church and drawing my own conclusions to a certain extent that I'm going through. You know the church is a mystery to a certain extent that I will continually seek to have a full understanding of." Philip Cat, the 51-year-old engineer from St. Mary's in Fort Wayne, spoke even in his initial interview of the process of becoming Catholic as "a continuing journey." Weeks after receiving the sacraments of initiation at St. Mary's Easter Vigil, Philip reflected, "You know, RCIA is the first step basically. And initiation into the church is a stepping stone along the way."

CONCLUSION: CATHOLIC INITIATION AS . . .

The historical development of Christianity, particularly Roman Catholicism, has been profoundly shaped by conversion. Without the conversion of the first apostles, there would be no Jesus Movement. Saul's being knocked down by a flash of light while on the road to Damascus is now an archetype of the dramatic conversion experience. The Roman Emperor Constantine's conversion and endorsement of one branch of the Christian faith paved the way for the growth of Christianity and the consolidation of the Roman church around a particular apostolic succession. Skipping forward several hundred years, as noted in this book's introduction, some of the most prominent Roman Catholics of the modern age have been converts, including John Henry Newman, St. Elizabeth Ann Seton, Dorothy Day, J. R. R. Tolkien, and Thomas Merton. The stories of these converts have been told and retold by scholars recounting the remarkable "rise of Christianity" and its transformation over the past two millennia.[1] *Becoming Catholic* also tells the story of Christian conversion, specifically to Roman Catholicism in America, but from a different perspective. Rather than examining the lives of historic figures, intellectuals, and religious virtuosi, I focus on what may be called "everyday conversion." This is a book about some of the hundreds of thousands of individuals who became Catholic in America at the beginning the twenty-first century, the formal process of initiation they went through, and what this tells us about Catholicism and religion more generally in a late-modern society like that of the United States.

Within these broader concerns has been a focus on bringing the idea of *initiation* back into the sociological study of religion.

Initiation has been a long-standing concern of anthropologists and folklorists studying smaller, preindustrial societies, but as religious historian Mircea Eliade observed, "in the modern Western world significant initiation is practically nonexistent."[2] Consequently, work on initiation by sociologists—who have tended to focus on Western industrial societies—has been practically nonexistent as well. This is unfortunate because, as Ronald Grimes notes, there has been a resurgence of popular interest in rites of passage in the modern West in the past two to three decades. Lacking existing rites that are "explicit and compelling" and adequate to the complexity of modern society, many individuals and groups are trying their hand at reinvention.[3] Among them is the Roman Catholic church. Shortly after Eliade but long before Grimes, the church leaders from around the world who met at the Second Vatican Council called for a restoration of the "catechumenate"—an ancient ritual process for initiating adults. As recounted in Chapter 1, this call gradually became a reality, known in the United States as the Rite of Christian Initiation of Adults (RCIA). By the new millennium, over 8 in 10 American parishes had implemented some version of the RCIA process; consequently, most of the over 1.5 million individuals who have become Catholic in the United States in the past 10 years have done so through the RCIA process.[4] In recognition of its significance as a concept for the sociological study of religion and as a social reality embodied in the contemporary RCIA process, in this conclusion I elaborate some of the many insights to be gained from looking at initiation as . . .

TRADITION AND MODERNITY

"Simply equating modernity with an inexorable 'detraditionalization,'" suggests Jerome Baggett, "is overwrought and underappreciative of just how tradtioned modern people, Catholics included, truly are."[5] There is no better evidence of this than the Rite of Christian Initiation of Adults that was reinvented by the Catholic church after the Second

Vatican Council. As noted in Chapter 1, the *Ordo* reflects two of the major theological emphases at Vatican II. It was born from a "return to the sources" of the ancient church (*ressourcement*). In this respect, it is evidence of tradition being brought into modernity. At the same time, the church in the modern world must "recognize and understand the world in which we live, its explanations, its longings, and its often dramatic characteristics."[6] To thrive, tradition must be open to the realities of modern society and renew itself in light of them (*aggiornamento*). In a word, tradition must be living,[7] and we see evidence of this in the reinvention of adult initiation in the Catholic church as well.

As outlined in this book's introduction, the ancient practice of adult initiation on which the *Ordo Initiationis Christianae Adultorum* was based maps closely onto Arnold van Gennep's model of rites of initiation having three phases: separation, transition, and incorporation. In examining the contemporary RCIA process in light of the ancient practice of adult initiation and van Gennep's model, however, we see a number of ways in which tradition is adapted so as to live more comfortably in modernity. In the first place, radical physical and geographic *separation*—the first stage in van Gennep's model—does not exist in the contemporary RCIA process. Throughout the process individuals remain a part of their families, work, neighborhoods, and even the church community itself. Beyond physical separation, as individuals go through the various rites that demarcate points of passage along the way, there are no markers that symbolically separate the individual from the rest of the church community (e.g., different clothing) either. To be sure, individuals are encouraged to develop their "selves" as they deepen their commitment to becoming Catholic, but no great rupture between the old and new self is experienced by most people along the way. A memorable example of continuity over separation was given to me by the subject of the prelude to Chapter 2, Diane Gall. With an attitude of horror, Diane revealed that when David Roberts, the RCIA director at St. Paul's, found out she was living with her fiancé Jack at the time she entered the RCIA process, he asked if one of them could move in with relatives until

Diane completed the RCIA process and they could be married. Or, if that was not possible, could they at least sleep in separate beds until they were married? Diane's shocked response, the fact that she did not comply, and that David did not follow up on the request are all telling. Not only could no radical separation be required, but the idea of it alone was received with incredulity.

Van Gennep's second stage is *transition*—the time of teaching and learning, cleansing and testing that follows separation. As we have seen, in the contemporary RCIA process, the catechumenate is the transitional time designated for catechesis (Chapter 3) and the Period of Purification and Enlightenment is the time of cleansing and testing (Chapter 4). Compared to the ancient practice, however, most would not recognize the characterization of the catechumenate given by Cyril of Jerusalem (313–386) as "doing battle with the 'dragon of the sea.'" Although pedagogies differ between parishes, the teaching and learning that take place in the contemporary RCIA are very much bounded by the classroom walls and modern understandings of education. Similarly, unlike in the ancient church, Lent is certainly not a time of significant asceticism anymore (in the RCIA process and the broader church). Prayer and fasting is suggested, sometimes, but not required. The significance of the scrutinies in the contemporary RCIA is too often lost on those becoming Catholic because those leading them do not know how to capitalize on the experiences and emotions they generate as formational opportunities. And ideas of sin and sacrifice are downplayed to the point of invisibility.

Still, there are aspects of these two periods that resonate with earlier practices. Upon entering the catechumenate, the "catechumen" is not statusless, per se, but has a sort of probationary status in the church. Not fully an outsider any longer, but not fully an insider either, the catechumen cannot receive the Eucharist but is entitled to a Christian burial if she dies during the catechumenate (*RCIA*, no. 47). Similarly, in those parishes that have dismissal sessions during the Mass, catechumens attend the Liturgy of the Word, but not the Liturgy of the Eucharist. I am reminded that this liminality is noticed by people in the church by one priest's exasperated question to me: "Why are we kicking them out of church?" In the Period of Purification and Enlightenment, the individuals preparing for initiation are "elect"— chosen by God to become members of the church—but must still go through a process of purification prior to receiving the sacraments. In many parishes this is accomplished in part by having the elect take a "retreat" from the everyday reality of home and parish life.

In van Gennep's third stage, *incorporation,* we see the most commonality between the practices of the ancient and contemporary church. As noted in the introduction, van Gennep allows for differing emphases on his three stages in different rites of passage. In the contemporary RCIA process, the separation and transition stages are heavily shaped and constrained by the realities of modern society. Emphasis falls, therefore, on the third stage in which the rites of initiation—baptism, confirmation, and Eucharist, celebrated at the Easter Vigil—mark the incorporation of the new Catholic into the body (*corpus*) of the church. Historical theologian Edward Yarnold calls his book on the origins of the RCIA in the fourth-century rite *The Awe-Inspiring Rites of Initiation.* Chapter 5 of this book shows that the contemporary rites of initiation can be, but are not always, awe inspiring. This raises the possibility also of differences in the extent and quality of incorporation through the contemporary RCIA process.

Of course, without variation in outcomes, there is nothing for the sociologist to explain. Looking at initiation as tradition and modernity through van Gennep's framework of rites of passage opens a window onto other differences to be explained in studying the contemporary RCIA process. As the following sections make clear, this study offers insights into the initiation process as objective and subjective, individual and collective, universal and local, and as an end and a beginning.

OBJECTIVE AND SUBJECTIVE

Examining incorporation as the final stage in van Gennep's model of rites of passage raises questions about the effectiveness of initiation rites. Some ritual scholars are critical of studies of initiation that simply examine the formal properties of initiation rites and draw conclusions from them. The underlying question they raise is: Do rites of initiation do what they say they do? As I argue at length in Chapter 5, at least for the Rite of Christian Initiation of Adults in the contemporary Catholic church, there are two answers to this question: Yes, when viewed objectively, and sometimes, when viewed subjectively. Rather than making a forced choice between the two, scholars ought to consider both dimensions of incorporation when studying initiation rites.

In an objective sense, once they cross the threshold of incorporation by receiving the sacraments of initiation, individuals are no longer *becoming* Catholic; they *are* Catholic. They are insiders in the worldwide Roman Catholic church's closed system of communion. They can be married in the church, even while their hair is still wet from baptism, as we saw in the case of the convalidation of Katie and Sean O'Brien's marriage at St. Mark's (Chapter 5). They can receive member discounts at Catholic schools, they can serve as Eucharistic ministers, and so on. Objective incorporation is therefore universal and suggests that, in one sense, the RCIA does what it says it does.

But objective incorporation without any subjective sense of attachment to the Catholic church is not likely to be sufficient to maintain the kind of active involvement in the church that the normative vision of the rite expects and that those who labor in initiation ministry hope for. Here the universality of objective incorporation gives way to a diversity of outcomes in terms of subjective incorporation, which I explore in Chapters 5 and 6. Subjectively, the RCIA *sometimes* does what it says it does. This diversity of outcomes itself can be looked at from different perspectives, such as examining what sociologists call "within-group variation" and "between-group variation." On the one hand, we see differences in outcomes between individuals within the same group, the same RCIA process. This suggests that what individuals bring to the process matters. For example, despite the very rich sense of the church as the "People of God" into which those becoming Catholic at Queen of Peace parish are initiated, not everyone is subjectively incorporated to the same extent. As noted in the prelude to Chapter 6, Les Burns is a model of post-initiation engagement, while Steve Gallagher completed the RCIA process and was never heard from again. On the other hand, we see differences in outcomes between different groups, such as the differences in the collective sentiments seen at and after the Easter Vigil at St. Innocent and St. Mark's compared to St. John Bosco and St. Peter's (Chapter 5). These between-group differences are also apparent in the statistical analysis in Chapter 6 that shows individuals who are initiated in parishes that more fully implement the normative vision of the rite experience more positive change in ecclesial involvement (Mass attendance, participation in spiritual groups, and volunteering in the parish) and spiritual practices (prayer and Bible reading).

INDIVIDUAL AND COLLECTIVE

Although it is perhaps most evident in the final stage—where the newly initiated is made part of the body of the church—every stage of van Gennep's model of rites of passage highlights activity that takes place at the *intersection* of the individual and collectivity in the initiation process. Religious communities initiate; individuals are initiated. You cannot understand one without the other. Theoretically and methodologically, understanding individuals in their organizational environments is fundamental to the sociological enterprise. In the sociology of religion, qualitative studies like those of Nancy Ammerman and her colleagues, as well as larger scale quantitative studies like the US Congregational Life Survey and its international affiliates, highlight the importance of understanding religious individuals in their congregational contexts.[8]

This suggests a very different approach to religious change from those that combine conceptual and methodological individualism and drive attention to what is happening *within* the individual.

The periods and ritual transitions of the Rite of Christian Initiation of Adults are designed to lead people gradually into a deeper of understanding of faith and higher levels of practice in the church, culminating in crossing a final threshold of incorporation. This process, occurring at the nexus of the individual and collectivity, can be studied both qualitatively and quantitatively. Using qualitative data from fieldwork and interviews in Chapter 4, I highlight the connection between liturgical practices and personal experience, as well as the relationship between personal experience and what it is (or is not) made into in the process of formation. Taking experiences generated in the RCIA process's liturgical rites and helping individuals make sense of them by bringing them into dialogue with the Catholic tradition is essential to the process of becoming Catholic, in the sense of being able to "walk the Catholic walk." But where there is a disconnect between personal experience and formational practices—either because teacher-mentors do not give shape to the individuals' experiences or because the experiential base is missing—the formational opportunities are lost.

The changes that individuals experience over the course of the RCIA process can also be approached quantitatively. Asking the same set of questions of individuals through a closed-ended survey at the beginning of the RCIA process and after its conclusion, then comparing individuals' responses at these two points in time, gives a clear (albeit somewhat superficial) picture of change. The change that can be quantified in this way is interesting, as far as it goes, but it does not go far enough. Because initiation is an organizationally embedded process undergone by individuals, we need to assess the changes that individuals experience over this period of time in relation to different characteristics of the organizations in which they are involved. Here information about the characteristics of the RCIA process itself is important, especially the extent to which the process in different parishes is implemented according to the normative vision of the rite specified in the *Ordo* and the United States bishops' *National Statutes for the Catechumenate*. Technically speaking, connecting before-and-after data on individuals to organizational-level data constitutes a type of nonequivalent group, pre-test/post-test design. As discussed in Chapter 6, employing this type of quasi-experimental research design strengthens my ability to make causal inferences about the effect of different levels of implementation of the RCIA process on individual outcomes. It allows me to say with some specificity the difference that the RCIA process makes.[9]

UNIVERSAL AND LOCAL

Throughout this book I have distinguished between the *Rite of Christian Initiation of Adults* and the Rite of Christian Initiation of Adults. The italics are used to denote the ritual text, translated from the Latin *editio typica* published in 1972 under the title *Ordo Initiationis Adultorum Christianae,* and mandated for use in the United States since 1988 by the National Conference of Catholic Bishops. Without italics, the title refers to the actual process of adult initiation as it is practiced in those American parishes that implement some version of the *Rite.* The distinction between these two uses of the same words suggests the need to understand initiation as universal and local.[10]

Transforming Catholicism: Liturgical Change in the Vatican II Church is a definitive study of the process by which universal ideals emanating from Rome become variably implemented on the local level in Catholic parishes. In it, sociologists David Maines and Michael McCallion view the various constitutions promulgated by the Second Vatican Council—including *Sacrosanctum Concilium,* the Constitution on the Sacred Liturgy—"as policy statements insofar as each identifies a set of problems pertaining to various areas of church life and then proposes lines of action to be taken as solutions to those problems." Their question, then, is, "How are the intentions of policy makers translated into action, and to what extent is the resulting action in accordance with the policy intentions?"[11] Empirically, they analyze three liturgical changes originating in Vatican II: first communion, the (re-)location of the tabernacle, and the restoration of the catechumenal process of initiation. They focus their explanation of the universal to local transformation on the various liturgists—and indeed, the new class of professional liturgists that arose in the wake of the Council—who take the lead in implementing change in dioceses and parishes. In the case of the RCIA process, their analysis looks at urban versus suburban RCIA coordinators and, as noted in Chapter 6, their different orientations of adhering to or adapting the ritual text in the implementation process.

Although Maines and McCallion have already (literally) "written the book" on the subject of the universal and local in liturgy, I offer a few reflections of my own based on this study. The observable differences in the RCIA process in different parishes—evident throughout this book but crystalized in the "tale of two parishes" that introduces Chapter 3—recalls one of the major conclusions of the Notre Dame Study of Catholic Parish Life in the 1980s: "Relative to the life of the rest of the church, parishes seem to have a life of their own." In his survey of Catholicism in America, theologian Chester Gillis observed that "differences in composition of the parish community, leadership, interests, preaching, programs, worship, and organization can make one parish, even in the same diocese or city, very different from another." From this observation he concludes, "To this extent, all Catholicism is local." This is so everywhere, but it may be even more true in the United States. As Stephen Warner has famously argued, religion in America—regardless of formal denominational polity structure—is characterized by *de facto congregationalism*. In a congregational polity, the authority of the local congregation is supreme.[12]

Unfortunately, there is a temptation to slide too easily from recognizing the importance of the local to ignoring the universal. For the Catholic church, at least, Warner's de facto congregationalism does not tell the whole story. The Catholic church's polity structure is "episcopal," which means that it places ultimate authority over local churches in the centralized hands of bishops (the Greek word is *episcopos*). Each of the church's nearly 20,000 congregations in the United States are geographically defined and clustered into a "diocese," which is under the authority of the local bishop, and so on up the organization, ultimately all falling under the authority of the bishop of Rome (i.e., the Pope). This is not just a *de jure* organization chart on paper, either, but a reality that can be seen in many ways. The Pope appoints bishops to lead local dioceses. Bishops appoint priests to lead the parishes under their authority. In the same fashion, liturgical changes mandated by the church hierarchy find their way into local parishes. When the Mass was changed from Latin to the vernacular as a result of Vatican II, it happened. Indeed, as many have recounted, it happened startlingly fast. It is, therefore, important to understand both the universal and the local and how they relate to one another. In the case of adult initiation in the Catholic church, there are multiple levels of translation taking place from the universal to the local. As explained in Chapter 1, *Sacrosanctum Concilium* led to the *Ordo*, which led to the *Rite*, which is implemented in parishes. Understanding this movement is important. I think of this as being like the image on the cover of Pink Floyd's album *Dark Side of the Moon*. The album cover shows a beam of white light hitting a triangular prism, which refracts it to create a rainbow of colors. The culture and resources of local parishes do act as prisms, but without the light, you have no rainbow.

An End and a Beginning

I started this book with John Steinbeck and so it seems only appropriate to return to him to conclude. Steinbeck's journey, like most, had a beginning and an end. He began caught up in the centrifugal forces of modernity, embarking on a road trip adventure that inspired envy. He ended being drawn into the countervailing centripetal force created by his desire for home. Faith is a journey as well, one that in many of the cases examined here begins in restlessness that subsequently gives way to a desire for rootedness and ends in a homecoming in the church. It is easy to think of the RCIA process as having a beginning and an end, as well. As chronicled in this study, the journey of initiation begins with the individual's decision to consider becoming Catholic and enter into the inquiry period. After many stops along the way, it ends with the period of post-baptismal catechesis known as mystagogy.

Some involved in initiation ministry worry that for many new Catholics, mystagogy is not just the end of the RCIA process but the end of their active involvement in the church—or at least the beginning of the end. If receiving the sacraments of initiation at the Easter Vigil is the climax of the process, then mystagogy is the anti-climax and sets the stage for the anti-climactic nature of simply being a member of the Catholic church on a day-to-day basis. Receiving the sacraments of initiation, like a school graduation, is important, but what follows is arguably even more important. A friend who has worked in initiation ministry for a number of years and worries about what becomes of individuals once they leave the friendly confines of the RCIA process recalled the bittersweet song by Bruce Springsteen, "Glory Days." "There is nothing worse," she said, "than seeing these new Catholics who every time you see them after the RCIA is over, all they can talk about are the 'glory days' of the RCIA. How great things were in the RCIA, how everyone cared about them, and they had a personal team of instructors and coaches and sponsors to look out for them. But that's not the reality of church."

What happens to these individuals one, five, or ten years down the road? Does their journey end? Do they settle into a routine of life in the church? Do they continue to grow in faith and involvement? No one really knows, including me. In Chapter 6 of this book, I highlight ways in which individuals who become Catholic actually change over the course of the RCIA process, and how the RCIA process itself makes a difference. But my second wave of data collection came immediately following the individuals' initiations. More scholarship is needed in this area, to determine the levels of long-term incorporation and whether the RCIA process influences it.[13]

In the end, these reflections remind us that there are two meanings of the word *initiation*. Throughout this book I have treated initiation as a process that culminates in the individual's incorporation in the Catholic church. In this sense, initiation is the end of the RCIA process—its goal, its climax, its conclusion. But initiation also has another meaning—"to begin." At the same time that initiation ends, it also begins. As Mark Searle writes, upon receiving the sacraments of initiation, "The journey of initiation is complete. Yet, for Christian pilgrims, baptism is the first stage in a longer journey."[14] As we saw in the conclusion to Chapter 6, some RCIA directors and people who complete the Rite of Christian Initiation of Adults recognize the ongoing, lifelong process of becoming Catholic. As St. Innocent RCIA team members Phil and Deanna Koehler were fond of saying at many of their sessions, "This is only just the beginning."

NOTES

ACKNOWLEDGMENTS

1. Jerome P. Baggett, *Sense of the Faithful: How American Catholics Live Their Faith* (New York: Oxford University Press, 2009), p. 56.

INTRODUCTION

1. John Steinbeck, *Travels with Charley in Search of America* (New York: Viking, 1962), p. 24.
2. James Jasper, *Restless Nation: Starting Over in America* (Chicago: University of Chicago Press, 2000); David Brooks, *On Paradise Drive: How We Live Now (and Always Have) in the Future Tense* (New York: Simon & Schuster, 2004). This restlessness is evident in the high levels of mobility in America. Brooks notes that Americans "don't perceive where they live as a destination" but rather see it "merely as a dot on the flowing plane of multidimensional movement" (p. 4). He later observes, "The simple fact is that Americans move around more than any other people on earth. In any given year, 16 percent of Americans move, compared with about 4 percent of the Dutch and Germans, 8 percent of the Brits, and about 3 percent of the Thais" (p. 67).
3. R. Stephen Warner, "Work in Progress toward a New Paradigm for the Sociological Study of Religion in the United States." *American Journal of Sociology* 98 (1993):1044–1093; Roger Finke and Rodney Stark, *The Churching of America: Winners and Losers in Our Religious Economy* (New Brunswick, NJ: Rutgers University Press, 2005); Phillip Hammond, *Religion and Personal Autonomy: The*

Third Disestablishment in America (Columbia: University of South Carolina Press, 1992), pp. 9–10, drawing on Robert Handy, *A Christian America* (New York: Oxford University Press, 1984); Will Herberg, *Protestant-Catholic-Jew: An Essay in American Religious Sociology* (New York: Doubleday, 1955).

4. On personal autonomy and the "third disestablishment," see Hammond, *Religion and Personal Autonomy*, pp. 10–11. See also Roof and McKinney, *American Mainline Religion: Its Changing Shape and Future*, (Rutgers, NJ: Rutgers University Press, 1987), pp. 33–39. Robert Wuthnow distinguishes between a "spirituality of dwelling" grounded in the connection between place, family, and faith, and a contemporary "spirituality of seeking" which arises in a society in which place, family, and faith have been disrupted. See *After Heaven: Spirituality in American since the 1950s* (Berkeley: University of California Press, 1998).

5. Robert Bellah, "Religious Evolution," in *Beyond Belief: Essays on Religion in a Post-Traditional World* (San Francisco: Harper & Row, 1970), p. 40; Robert Bellah, Richard Madsen, William Sullivan, Ann Swidler, and Steven Tipton, *Habits of the Heart: Individualism and Commitment in American Life* (Berkeley: University of California Press, 1985), p. 221.

6. Peter Berger, *The Heretical Imperative: Contemporary Possibilities of Religious Affirmation* (Garden City, NY: Anchor Books, 1980), pp. 14, 25. Berger notes that the word *heresy* "comes from the Greek verb *hairein*, which means 'to choose.' A *hairesis* originally meant, quite simply, the taking of a choice" (pp. 24–25). At the same time, we should recognize, with Sean McCloud, that "not all groups and classes of people are equally affected by late modernity" and not all have equal access to the same range of resources upon which to make choices. See Sean McCloud, "Liminal Subjectivities and Religious Change: Circumscribing Giddens for the Study of Contemporary American Religion," *Journal of Contemporary Religion* 22 (October 2007):295–309, p. 303.

7. Anthony Giddens, *Modernity and Self-Identity: Self and Society in the Late Modern Age* (Cambridge, MA: Polity Press, 1991), p. 20; Karl Marx, "Manifesto of the Communist Party," pp. 469–500 in Robert C. Tucker, ed., *The Marx-Engels Reader* (New York: W. W. Norton,

1978), p. 476; Marshall Berman, *All That Is Solid Melts into Air: The Experience of Modernity* (New York: Penguin Books, 1988); Jerome P. Baggett, *Sense of the Faithful: How American Catholics Live Their Faith* (New York: Oxford University Press, 2009), p. 19.

8. Jasper, *Restless Nation*, p. 213.

9. Steinbeck, *Travels with Charley*, pp. 243–244.

10. Wade Clark Roof quoting Walter Lippman quoting Aristophanes in *Spiritual Marketplace: Baby Boomers and the Remaking of American Religion* (Princeton, NJ: Princeton University Press, 1999), p. 294.

11. This argument is slightly different from that presented by Baggett in *Sense of the Faithful*, which focuses on the rootlessness of the self and the "generalized concern for individual authenticity" that grows from it (p. 65). The difference is perhaps due to Baggett's focus on currently active Catholics who are already attached to parishes, in contrast to my focus on individuals who are in the process of becoming Catholics.

12. Roof, *Spiritual Marketplace*, p. 178; Christian Smith, *Soul Searching: The Religious and Spiritual Lives of American Teenagers* (New York: Oxford University Press, 2005), p. 120. In explaining the vitality of American evangelicalism, Smith goes so far as to argue that choice in fact is the key to greater religious commitment: "Moderns authenticate themselves through personal choice. Therefore, modern religious believers are capable of establishing stronger religious identities and commitments on the basis of individual choice than through ascription." See *American Evangelicalism: Embattled and Thriving* (Chicago: University of Chicago Press, 1998), p. 104.

13. The phrase appears several times in Walter Lippman's *A Preface to Morals* (New York: Macmillan, 1929). This idea is captured in Max Weber's famous observation that the modern world is "disenchanted." See Max Weber, "Science as a Vocation," pp. 129–156 in *From Max Weber: Essays in Sociology* (New York: Oxford University Press, 1958), p. 139.

14. Baggett, *Sense of the Faithful*, p. 211.

15. Baggett, *Sense of the Faithful*.

16. John Seidler and Katherine Meyer, *Conflict and Change in the Catholic Church* (New Brunswick, NJ: Rutgers University Press, 1989).

17. Andrew Greeley, *The Catholic Revolution: New Wine, Old Wineskins, and the Second Vatican Council* (Berkeley: University of California Press, 2004), p. 13. See also Michele Dillon, *Catholic Identity: Balancing Reason, Faith, and Power* (Cambridge: Cambridge University Press, 1999).

18. Jose Casanova, *Public Religion in the Modern World* (Chicago: University of Chicago Press, 1994), pp. 72–73.

19. Greeley, *The Catholic Revolution*, chapter 1. Melissa Wilde, *Vatican II: A Sociological Analysis of Religious Change* (Princeton, NJ: Princeton University Press, 2007), chapter 1. *Lumen Gentium* was approved by a 2,151 to 5 vote of the bishops and promulgated by Pope Paul VI on November 21, 1964. *Dignitatis Humanae* was approved by a vote of 2,308 to 70 and promulgated by Pope Paul VI on December 7, 1965. *Gaudium et Spes* was approved by a vote of 2,307 to 75 and promulgated by Pope Paul VI on December 8, 1965. These and other conciliar documents are available on the Vatican website (http://www.vatican.va/archive/hist_councils/ii_vatican_council/index.htm) or in Austin Flannery, ed., *Vatican Council II: The Conciliar and Post Conciliar Documents* (Northport, NY: Costello Publishing, 1975).

20. David R. Maines and Michael McCallion, *Transforming Catholicism: Liturgical Change in the Vatican II Church* (Lanham, MD: Lexington Books, 2007); Mark S. Massa, *The American Catholic Revolution: How the Sixties Changed the Church Forever* (New York: Oxford University Press, 2010).

21. Richard Erickson, *Late Have I Loved Thee: Stories of Religious Conversion and Commitment in Later Life* (New York: Paulist Press, 1995).

22. Out of the 100+ denominations in the United States that reported membership data to the *Yearbook of American and Canadian Churches, 2010*, ed. Eileen Lindner (Nashville, TN: Abingdon Press, 2010). Data on Catholic converts is from the Pew Forum on Religion & Public Life's *U.S. Religious Landscape Survey* (Washington, DC: Pew Research Center, 2008). The number of

Catholic converts in America is based on an estimated adult population of 225 million in the year of the survey.

23. Aidan Kavanagh, *The Shape of Baptism: The Rite of Christian Initiation* (Collegeville, MN: Liturgical Press, 1991), p. 145.

24. Mircea Eliade, *Rites and Symbols of Initiation: The Mysteries of Birth and Rebirth* (Putnam, CT: Spring Publications, 1994 [1958]), p. ix.

25. Ronald L. Grimes, *Deeply into the Bone: Re-Inventing Rites of Passage* (Berkeley: University of California Press, 2000), pp. 89, 100, 90–94, 3. Moreover, as society changes, so too do the social statuses that people occupy. Communal rites of passage simply do not exist for status transitions such as "emptynesting," divorce, or retirement on one's own. Thus, individuals are left to cope with these life transitions on their own. They might redecorate their departed child's room, burn pictures of their ex-, or take up a new hobby to occupy their time. But these individual coping mechanisms differ considerably from a communal celebration. See Barbara G. Myerhoff, Linda A. Camino, and Edith Turner, "Rites of Passage," pp. 380–386 in Mircea Eliade, ed., *Encyclopedia of Religion*, vol. 12 (New York: Macmillan, 1987), p. 385.

26. Arnold van Gennep, *The Rites of Passage* (Chicago: University of Chicago Press, 1960 [1909]).

27. Victor Turner, *The Forest of Symbols: Aspects of Ndembu Ritual* (Ithaca, NY: Cornell University Press, 1967), p. 93; also Victor Turner, *The Ritual Process: Structure and Anti-Structure* (Baltimore, MD: Penguin Books, 1969), chapter 3.

28. van Gennep, *The Rites of Passage*, p. 109; Victor Turner, *The Ritual Process: Structure and Anti-Structure* (Chicago: University of Chicago Press, 1969); Thomas V. Peterson, "Initiation Rite as Riddle," *Journal of Ritual Studies* 1/1 (1987):73–84, quotes from pp. 74–75, citing John (Fire) Lame Deer and Richard Erdoes, *Lame Deer: Seeker of Visions* (New York: Washington Square, 1972).

29. Myerhoff, Camino, and Turner, "Rites of Passage," p. 385.

30. Thomas E. Ricks, *Making the Corps*, 10th anniversary edition (New York: Scribner, 2007). Thanks to Simon Hallberg for this and other references to the USMC not listed.

31. Erving Goffman, *Asylums: Essays on the Social Situation of Mental Patients and Other Inmates* (Garden City, NY: Anchor Books, 1961).

32. Max Weber, *The Methodology of the Social Sciences* (New York: Free Press, 1997 [1903–1917]), p. 90.

33. Van Gennep, *The Rites of Passage,* pp. 10–11.

34. Although it has been the dominant framework for understanding initiation cross-culturally, some specialists in ritual studies have questioned the universality of van Gennep's three stage schema. Bruce Lincoln, for example, has proposed that separation-transition-incorporation is the dominant model for men, but for women the pattern is butterfly-like: enclosure-metamorphosis-emergence (*Emerging from the Chrysalis: Rituals of Women's Initiation* [New York: Oxford University Press, 1991]). Nikki Bado-Fralick has suggested that Wiccan initiation rituals depart from van Gennep's model because there is no geographic or physical separation of the candidates for initiation and the process is more circular than linear (*Coming to the Edge of the Circle: A Wiccan Initiation Ritual* [New York: Oxford University Press, 2005]). Ronald Grimes observes that scholars have proposed processes of initiation involving eight steps or ten steps rather than three phases, and argues that even a ten-step schema has the potential to reduce the complexity of real-life initiation rituals (*Deeply into the Bone,* pp. 106–107). These challenges and modifications are points well taken, but do not fundamentally undermine the van Gennep model understood as an ideal type.

35. Mark Searle, "The Rites of Christian Initiation," pp. 457–470 in Louise Carus Mahdi, Steven Foster, and Meredith Little, eds., *Betwixt and Between: Patterns of Masculine and Feminine Initiation* (LaSalle, IL: Open Court, 1987), p. 458.

36. Mark Searle, "The Rites of Christian Initiation," pp. 460–462. Also see Edward Yarnold, S.J., *The Awe-Inspiring Rites of Initiation: The Origins of the RCIA,* 2nd ed. (Edinburgh: T&T Clark, 1994).

37. Rodney Stark and Roger Finke, *Acts of Faith: Explaining the Human Side of Religion* (Berkeley: University of California Press, 2000), p. 114.

38. David Snow and Richard Machalek, "The Sociology of Conversion," *Annual Review of Sociology* 10 (1984):167–190, quote from p. 171.

39. Maxwell Johnson, *The Rites of Christian Initiation: Their Evolution and Interpretation* (Collegeville, MN: Liturgical Press, 1999), p. 296.

40. Dean R. Hoge, *Converts, Dropouts, Returnees: A Study of Religious Change among Catholics* (New York: Pilgrim Press, 1981).

41. The best existing sociological study of the RCIA process is that of David R. Maines and Michael McCallion, reported in various articles and in the previously cited book *Transforming Catholicism*. In October 2000, the National Conference of Catholic Bishops (NCCB) released *Journey to the Fullness of Life: A Report on the Implementation of the Rite of Christian Initiation of Adults in the United States* (Washington, DC: United States Catholic Conference, 2000), based on a three-year study overseen by Dean Hoge and Rev. Dr. Robert O'Donnell. Like most good research, the study raises as many questions as it answers. By collecting diocesan-level data on the implementation of the RCIA process—reporting the percentage of parishes in the dioceses that had implemented various aspects of the process—the study reveals the RCIA process to be widely but unevenly implemented. Unfortunately, by neglecting the parish as a unit of analysis, the study does not allow for a systematic investigation of the relationship between the implementation of the RCIA process in different parishes (the organizational level) and the experiences of those becoming Catholic in those parishes (the individual level). Moreover, by relying exclusively on survey data, the NCCB study neglects what is arguably the central aspect of this new model of adult formation and initiation: its *liturgical* dimension (see Chapter 1). Understanding the process of becoming Catholic through the RCIA process requires understanding its ritual dimension.

42. Together, the three of us published a book for pastors, lay ministers, catechists, and directors of religious education, as well as those in seminaries and dioceses responsible for training them, based on five of our six case studies. See David Yamane and Sarah MacMillen,

with Kelly Culver, *Real Stories of Christian Initiation: Lessons for and from the RCIA* (Collegeville, MN: The Liturgical Press, 2006).

43. Patrick Allitt, *Catholic Converts: British and American Intellectuals Turn to Rome* (Ithaca, NY: Cornell University Press, 1997); Lorene Hanley Duquin, *A Century of Catholic Converts* (Huntington, IN: Our Sunday Visitor Publishing, 2003).

    Had our fieldwork sites included a Catholic Church on or near a college campus (e.g., a Newman Center), we might have found more intellectual conversions among our "circumstantial converts." Speaking just from my own experience, however, when I became Catholic at the St. Paul University Catholic Center on the campus of the University of Wisconsin-Madison, I was recruited by the same mundane factors and motivated by the same moral factors discussed in Chapter 2. Although I appreciated the intellectual approach to the faith I found there, this was neither the recruitment mechanism nor the motivation for my being there. Others who were in the process with me at that time, as well as individuals I later sponsored or taught in the RCIA process, were similar. This reinforces my sense that intellectual conversions are rare.

44. Rodney Stark and William Sims Bainbridge, "Networks of Faith: Interpersonal Bonds and Recruitment to Cults and Sects," pp. 307–324 in *The Future of Religion: Secularization, Revival, and Cult Formation* (Berkeley: University of California Press, 1985).

45. Christian Smith, *Moral, Believing Animals: Human Personhood and Culture* (New York: Oxford University Press, 2003).

46. Maines and McCallion, *Transforming Catholicism*.

47. Margaret Mohrmann, "On Being True to Form," pp. 90–102 in Carol Taylor and Roberto Dell'Oro, eds., *Health and Human Flourishing: Religion, Medicine, and Moral Anthropology* (Washington, DC: Georgetown University Press, 2006).

48. Baggett, *Sense of the Faithful*, p. 66.

49. Grimes, *Deeply into the Bone*, p. 100; Catherine Bell, *Ritual: Perspectives and Dimensions* (New York: Oxford University Press, 1997), p. 57, quoting Vincent Crapanzano, "Rite of Return: Circumcision in Morocco," pp. 15–36 in Werner Muensterberger and L. Bryce Boyer, eds. *The Psychoanalytic Study of Society* 9 (1981), p. 32.

50. Baggett, *Sense of the Faithful*; Tricia Colleen Bruce, *Faithful Revolution: How Voice of the Faithful Is Changing the Church* (New York: Oxford University Press, 2011); Michele Dillon, *Catholic Identity*; Andrew Greeley, *The Catholic Imagination* (Berkeley: University of California Press, 2000).

51. Matthew Loveland, "Religious Switching: Preference Development, Maintenance, and Change," *Journal for the Scientific Study of Religion* 42 (2003):147–157; Darren E. Sherkat and John Wilson, "Preferences, Constraints, and Choices in Religious Markets: An Examination of Religious Switching and Apostasy," *Social Forces* 73 (March 1995):993–1026; Mark C. Suchman, "Analyzing the Determinants of Everyday Conversion," *Sociological Analysis* 53S (1992):15–33.

CHAPTER 1

1. David R. Maines and Michael McCallion, *Transforming Catholicism: Liturgical Change in the Vatican II Church* (Lanham, MD: Lexington Books, 2007).

2. *Sacrosanctum Concilium* and other conciliar documents are available on the Vatican website (http://www.vatican.va/archive/hist _councils/ii_vatican_council/index.htm) or in Austin Flannery, ed., *Vatican Council II: The Conciliar and Post Conciliar Documents* (Northport, NY: Costello Publishing Company, 1975).

3. Michael McCallion and David Maines, "The Liturgical Social Movement in the Vatican II Catholic Church," *Research in Social Movements, Conflicts, and Change* 21 (1999):125–149, quote from p. 129.

4. Melissa Wilde, *Vatican II: A Sociological Analysis of Religious Change* (Princeton, NJ: Princeton University Press, 2007), p. 1. Wilde also notes, "Though it was fifth in the bound copies of the preparatory documents the bishops received prior to the Council, progressives quickly set about making sure that it became the first issue addressed by the Council" (p. 20).

5. Peter Steinfels, *A People Adrift: The Crisis of the Roman Catholic Church in America* (New York: Simon and Shuster, 2003), p. 168.

Michael McCallion notes that the environmental changes are seen by some as a "Protestantization of Catholic church buildings" ("Lay and Professional Views on Tabernacle Location in Catholic Parishes," *Journal of Contemporary Ethnography* 29 [December 2000]:717–746, p. 740). One priest we interviewed characterized his newly built church as a "nondenominational chapel in a retirement home." Notable criticisms of these developments are Thomas Day, *Why Catholics Can't Sing: The Culture of Catholicism and the Triumph of Bad Taste* (New York: Crossroad Publishing, 1990) and Michael Rose, *Ugly as Sin: Why They Changed Our Churches from Sacred Places to Meeting Spaces and How We Can Change Them Back Again* (Manchester, NH: Sophia Institute Press, 2001).

6. The Eucharist is also considered a sacrament of initiation, though it differs from these other two in being repeatable.

7. The *National Statutes* are published as Appendix III to the *Rite of Christian Initiation of Adults,* have the status of a "complementary norm" in accord with Canon 788§3 of the *Code of Canon Law* on the catechumenate, and thereby officially govern the RCIA process in the United States.

8. Marcellino D'Ambrosio, "*Ressourcement* Theology, *Aggiornamento,* and the Hermeneutics of Tradition," *Communio* 18 (Winter 1991), www.crossroadsinitiative.com/library_article/54/Ressourcement_ Theology__Aggiornamento_and_the_Hermeneutics_of_Tradition. html, accessed January 8, 2013. D'Ambrosio concludes, "*Ressourcement* theology was, in essence, a deft exercise in the hermeneutics of tradition that successfully navigated between the Scylla of archaism and the Charybdis of modernism."

9. Although some view *aggiornamento* and *ressourcement* as competing liberal/progressive and conservative/traditionalist visions at the Council of how to invigorate the church, George Lindbeck (the distinguished Yale University theologian and delegated observer of the Council from the Lutheran church), recalled in 1994, "The *ressourcement* and *aggiornamento* people at the Council thought of themselves as collaborators. *Ressourcement* and *aggiornamento* were understood to be two dimensions of the same reality. But the dimension labeled '*aggiornamento*' could be used in a program of *accommodation* to the

modern world, rather than one of an opening to the modern world; and when that happened, *aggiornamento* fell into opposition to *ressourcement*. But in my memory of the Council, there was absolutely no tension between the two, with the exception of the debate over what became the Pastoral Constitution on the Church in the Modern World." See "Re-Viewing Vatican II: An Interview with George A. Lindbeck," *First Things* 48 (December 1994):44–50, www.firstthings.com/article/2007/01/re-viewing-vatican-iian-interview-with-george-a-lindbeck-2, accessed January 8, 2013.

Indeed, mid-twentieth-century French advocates of *la nouvelle théologie* saw *ressourcement* as an essential precondition for *aggiornamento*. Post-conciliar struggles to define the meaning of the Council, as noted in the conclusion to this chapter, have tended to drive these two complementary positions apart. See Matthew L. Lamb and Matthew Levering, eds., *Vatican II: Renewal within Tradition* (New York: Oxford University Press, 2008) and John W. O'Malley, *What Happened at Vatican II* (Cambridge, MA: Harvard/Belknap, 2008).

10. As compared to traditionalism, which is "the dead faith of the living." Jaroslav Pelikan, *The Melody of Theology: A Philosophical Dictionary* (Cambridge, MA: Harvard University Press, 1988), p. 252.

11. See Paul Turner, *The Hallelujah Highway: A History of the Catechumenate* (Chicago: Liturgy Training Publications, 2000), p. 37.

12. The word "catechumen" comes from the Greek *katēkhoumenos* (one receiving verbal instruction). It appears, among other places, in Galatians 6:6, "One who is being instructed in the word should share all good things with his instructor." See Aidan Kavanagh, *The Shape of Baptism: The Rite of Christian Initiation* (Collegeville, MN: Liturgical Press, 1991) and Maxwell Johnson, *The Rites of Christian Initiation: Their Evolution and Interpretation* (Collegeville, MN: Liturgical Press, 1999).

13. Johnson, *The Rites of Christian Initiation*, p. 154.

14. Turner, *The Hallelujah Highway*, chapters 29–30.

15. Michael McCallion, David Maines, and Steven Wolfel, "Policy as Practice: First Holy Communion as a Contested Situation," *Journal*

of Contemporary Ethnography 25 (October 1996):300–326, quote from p. 302.

16. James Dunning, *Echoing God's Word* (Arlington, VA: North American Forum on the Catechumenate, 1993), p. xix; "The Rite Leadership," *Church* 16 (Winter 2000):4; and information provided to me in 2004 by James Schellman, who was executive director of the North American Forum on the Catechumenate at the time.

17. For a similar table that breaks the process down by baptismal status and whether or not the candidate is catechized, see Thomas Morris, *The RCIA: Transforming the Church* (New York: Paulist Press, 1997), p. 59. The RCIA process can also be used to initiate children of catechetical age. See Robert Duggan and Maureen Kelly, *The Christian Initiation of Children: Hope for the Future* (New York: Paulist Press, 1991).

18. David Yamane and Sarah MacMillen, with Kelly Culver, *Real Stories of Christian Initiation: Lessons for and from the RCIA* (Collegeville, MN: Liturgical Press, 2006).

19. Yamane and MacMillen, *Real Stories of Christian Initiation*, pp. 132–133; Maxwell Johnson, "Let's Stop Making 'Converts' at Easter," *Catechumenate: A Journal of Christian Initiation* 21 (1999):10–20; National Conference of Catholic Bishops, *Journey to the Fullness of Life: A Report on the Implementation of the Rite of Christian Initiation of Adults in the United States* (Washington, DC: United States Catholic Conference, 2000).

20. Mary Jo Weaver, ed., *What's Left? Liberal American Catholics* (Bloomington: Indiana University Press, 1999), and Mary Jo Weaver and R. Scott Appleby, eds., *Being Right: Conservative Catholics in America* (Bloomington: Indiana University Press, 1995). Philibert includes himself in the fundamentalist category (personal conversation); Ralph McInerny, *What Went Wrong with Vatican II: The Catholic Crisis Explained* (Manchester, NH: Sophia Institute Press, 1998).

21. Duggan and Kelly, *The Christian Initiation of Children*, p. 6.

22. Home page of the North American Association for the Catechumenate, www.catechumenate.org, accessed December 15, 2012. See also Johnson, *The Rites of Christian Initiation*.

CHAPTER 2

1. Phil Zuckerman, *Invitation to the Sociology of Religion* (New York: Routledge, 2003), p. 51; Robert Wuthnow, *Growing Up Religious: Christians and Jews and Their Journeys of Faith* (Boston: Beacon Press, 1999), p. 5.
2. Pew Forum on Religion & Public Life, *U.S. Religious Landscape Survey* (Washington, DC: Pew Research Center, 2008), p. 5.
3. Pew Forum on Religion & Public Life, *U.S. Religious Landscape Survey.*
4. Joseph H. Fichter, *Social Relations in an Urban Parish* (Chicago: University of Chicago Press, 1954); Ruth A. Wallace, "A Model of Change of Religious Affiliation," *Journal for the Scientific Study of Religion* 14 (1975):345–355; Dean Hoge, *Converts, Dropouts, Returnees: A Study of Religious Change among Catholics* (New York: The Pilgrim Press, 1981); Matthew Loveland, "Religious Switching: Preference Development, Maintenance, and Change," *Journal for the Scientific Study of Religion* 42 (2003):147–157; Mark Musick and John Wilson, "Religious Switching for Marriage Reasons," *Sociology of Religion* 56 (1995):257–270; Mark C. Suchman, "Analyzing the Determinants of Everyday Conversion," *Sociological Analysis* 53 (1992): S15–S33.
5. Rodney Stark and Roger Finke, *Acts of Faith: Explaining the Human Side of Religion* (Berkeley: University of California Press, 2000), pp. 122, 117, 118.
6. Hoge, *Converts, Dropouts, Returnees,* p. 32.
7. Theories of action have deep roots in the discipline of sociology, from Max Weber, Talcott Parsons, and George Herbert Mead, through Jürgen Habermas, Anthony Giddens, and Alain Touraine, though their influence on empirical research projects is not always evident. See Hans Joas, *The Creativity of Action* (Chicago: University of Chicago Press, 1996).
8. Rodney Stark and William Sims Bainbridge, *A Theory of Religion* (New Brunswick, NJ: Rutgers University Press, 1996), p. 325.
9. Laurence R. Iannaccone, "Rational Choice: Framework for the Scientific Study of Religion," pp. 25–42 in Lawrence A. Young, ed.,

Rational Choice Theory and Religion: Summary and Assessment (New York: Routledge, 1997), p. 26.

10. Laurence R. Iannaccone, "Religious Practice: A Human Capital Approach," *Journal for the Scientific Study of Religion* 29 (1990):297–314.

11. Iannaccone, "Rational Choice," p. 32.

12. As a side note, this may help explain the increasing popularity of nondenominational churches—churches in which people do not have to forgo their accumulated religious capital and that do not cost the individual much to learn specifics of the new tradition.

13. Nonetheless, it is the case that those who maintain religious intermarriage have lower rates of religious participation than those who marry within the faith.

14. Stark and Finke, *Acts of Faith*, p. 125.

15. Robert D. Putnam and David E. Campbell, *American Grace: How Religion Divides and Unites Us* (New York: Simon & Schuster, 2010), p. 151.

16. Michael J. Rosenfeld, "Racial, Educational and Religious Endogamy in the United States: A Comparative Historical Perspective," *Social Forces* 87 (September 2008):1–32.

17. Putnam and Campbell, *American Grace*, Figure 5.3, pp. 145, 149, 152.

18. Here some rational choice theorists of religion have begun to add additional assumptions to their analyses (about cultural influences on the formations of preferences, for example) to make their analyses more "sociological." Stark and Finke want to make room in their rational choice theory for "religious emotions, and for ritual, prayer, sacrifice, miracle, mystical experiences, for bargaining with the gods, and even for religious procrastination." As they put it, "Our aim is to construct a theory in which both phenomenologists and rational choice theorists can take comfort" (*Acts of Faith*, p. 84).

19. Stark and Finke, *Acts of Faith*, p. 38.

20. Iannaccone, "Rational Choice," p. 26.

21. Indeed, Coleman recognizes that the assumption is a methodological convenience: "The assumption of utility maximization is necessary only for the quantitative development of the theory . . . both for mathematical modeling and for the quantitative research which

makes use of those models." James S. Coleman, *Foundations of Social Theory* (Cambridge, MA: Harvard/Belknap Press, 1994), p. 18.

22. Christian Smith, *Moral, Believing Animals: Human Personhood and Culture* (New York: Oxford University Press, 2003), p. 3.

23. Smith, *Moral, Believing Animals*, p. 4.

24. Smith, *Moral, Believing Animals,* p. 8. Smith makes the contrast to rational choice approaches explicitly: "The moral also involves a sense of normative duty to express or perform obligations that are intrinsically motivated—because they are right, good, worthy, just, and so on—rather than motivated by the means/ends–orientated desire to obtain the benefit of consuming a good or service" (*Moral, Believing Animals,* p. 11). Here Smith is referencing Amitai Etzioni's *The Moral Dimension* (New York: Free Press, 1988).

25. Smith, *Moral, Believing Animals*, pp. 18, 11.

26. Smith writes, "As moral animals, humans are inescapably interested in and guided by normative cultural orders that specify what is good, right, true, beautiful, worthy, noble, and just in life, and what is not. To be a human person, to possess an identity, to act with agency requires locating one's life within a larger moral order by which to know who one is and how one ought to live" (*Moral, Believing Animals,* p. 118).

27. Smith, *Moral, Believing Animals*, p. 15.

28. I say *dominant* rather than *exclusive* in recognition of the fact that there are in American culture what Smith calls "many competing and blended moral orders" (*Moral, Believing Animals,* p. 27), so the cultural schemas upon which people draw may be blended or overlapping.

29. Penny Edgell, *Religion and Family in a Changing Society* (Princeton, NJ: Princeton University Press, 2006), pp. 77, 70.

30. Robert N. Bellah, Richard Madsen, William M. Sullivan, Ann Swidler, and Steven M. Tipton, *Habits of the Heart: Individualism and Commitment in American Life* (Berkeley: University of California Press, 1985), pp. 221, 334. Although this language has only come into full flower in recent decades, it has deep roots in American culture. It can be seen in Walt Whitman's Americanization of

Romanticism and Ralph Waldo Emerson's Transcendentalism in the nineteenth century, as well as psychotherapy, Jungian psychology, and the embrace of Eastern spiritualties in the twentieth century.

31. Richard Cimino and Don Lattin, *Shopping for Faith: American Religion in the New Millennium* (San Francisco: Jossey-Bass, 2002).

32. Given the historical connection between traditional religion and spirituality, it may be better to use the term Eva Hamberg suggests— "unchurched spirituality"—to refer to religious beliefs and practices that exist outside traditional religious institutions. See "Unchurched Spirituality," pp. 742–757 in Peter Clarke, ed., *Oxford Handbook of the Sociology of Religion* (Oxford: Oxford University Press, 2009).

33. Expressive individualism as a cultural schema is thus associated with emotivism as an ethical perspective. See Alasdair Macintyre's critique in *After Virtue: A Study in Moral Theory*, 3rd ed. (South Bend, IN: University of Notre Dame Press, 2007).

34. Bellah et al., *Habits of the Heart*, p. 336. Like expressive individualism, this schema also has deep roots in American culture. The quintessential eighteenth-century exponent was Benjamin Franklin, whose ideas have become part of American common sense: "A penny saved is a penny earned," "Lost time is never found again," "Early to bed and early to rise" (Bellah et al., *Habits of the Heart*, p. 32). Today's rational choice theorists are modern-day Franklins.

35. Smith, *Moral, Believing Animals*, pp. 32, 33.

36. David Yamane and Sarah MacMillen, with Kelly Culver, *Real Stories of Christian Initiation: Lessons for and from the RCIA* (Collegeville, MN: Liturgical Press, 2006).

CHAPTER 3

1. Jerome P. Baggett, *Sense of the Faithful: How American Catholics Live Their Faith* (New York: Oxford University Press, 2009), p. 215.

2. The *Rite of Christian Initiation of Adults* clearly distinguishes between the goals of the Period of Evangelization and Precatechumenate and the Period of the Catechumenate, and there is a transitional Rite of Acceptance into the Order of Catechumens, which is supposed to demarcate the periods and effect a change

in the individual's status from "inquirer" to "catechumen." From the perspective of those becoming Catholic, however, there is not a significant difference between what they experience in these two periods. They both involve teaching and learning about the core beliefs and practices of the Catholic tradition in a classroom setting. In some cases, like St. Mark's, the need to cover the entire "Sacramental Plan of Salvation" from September to Easter requires beginning the series of topics during inquiry and continuing them through the catechumenate (see David Yamane and Sarah MacMillen, with Kelly Culver, *Real Stories of Christian Initiation: Lessons for and from the RCIA* [Collegeville, MN: Liturgical Press, 2006], chapter 3). For these reasons, this chapter covers the catechesis that takes places *both* during the inquiry period and the catechumenate.

3. David R. Maines and Michael J. McCallion, *Transforming Catholicism: Liturgical Change in the Vatican II Church* (Lanham, MD: Lexington Books, 2007).

4. For more on the "school year" model, see Chapter 6, which draws on my article, "Ritual Initiation in the Contemporary Catholic Church: What Difference Does It Make?" *Review of Religious Research* 54 (December 2012):401–420. The levels of implementation in this study are higher than nationally in large part because I have complete data only for the more advanced RCIA processes in the Diocese of Fort Wayne–South Bend. Those parishes with less developed RCIA processes were less likely to respond to my survey. National data are from *Journey to the Fullness of Life: A Report on the Implementation of the Rite of Christian Initiation of Adults in the United States* (Washington, DC: United States Catholic Conference, 2000), and online methodological appendices to the study ("Amazing Growth: The RCIA Story") are available at the United States Catholic bishops' legacy website (http://old.usccb.org/evangelization/data.shtml, accessed February 1, 2012).

5. Dorothy Bass, "Congregations and the Bearing of Traditions," pp. 169–191 in James P. Wind and James W. Lewis, eds., *American Congregations*, vol. 2 (Chicago: University of Chicago Press, 1994), p. 178.

6. Max Weber, *The Protestant Ethic and the Spirit of Capitalism* (New York: Scribner's, 1958 [1904–1905]); James D. Davison and Ralph E. Pyle, *Ranking Faiths: Religious Stratification in America* (Lanham, MD: Rowman & Littlefield Publishers, 2011); Alfred Darnell and Darren E. Sherkat, "The Impact of Protestant Fundamentalism on Educational Attainment," *American Sociological Review* 62 (1997):306–316; David Sikkink, "The Social Sources of Alienation from Public Schools," *Social Forces* 78 (1999):51–86; Darren E. Sherkat, "Religion and Verbal Ability," *Social Science Research* 39 (2010):2–13; Keith Roberts and David Yamane, *Religion in Sociological Perspective,* 5th ed. (Thousand Oaks, CA: Sage/Pine Forge Press, 2012), chapter 9.

7. Baggett, *Sense of the Faithful,* p. 20. Prominent overviews of American Catholic history include Jay P. Dolan, *The American Catholic Experience: A History from Colonial Times to the Present* (Garden City, NY: Doubleday, 1985); James T. Fisher, *Communion of Immigrants: A History of Catholics in America* (New York: Oxford, 2008); James J. Hennesey, *American Catholics: A History of the Roman Catholic Community in the United States* (New York: Oxford University Press, 1981); Charles R. Morris, *American Catholic: The Saints and Sinners Who Built America's Most Powerful Church* (New York: Times Books, 1997); James M. O'Toole, *The Faithful: A History of Catholics in America* (Cambridge, MA: Harvard University Press, 2008).

    Andrew M. Greeley's work across the decades includes *The Catholic Experience: A Sociologist's Interpretation of the History of American Catholicism* (New York: Doubleday, 1967); *The American Catholic: A Social Portrait* (New York: Basic Books, 1977); *The Catholic Myth: The Behavior and Beliefs of American Catholics* (New York: Scribner's, 1990); *The Catholic Imagination* (Berkeley: University of California Press, 2000).

8. Timothy Matovina, *Latino Catholicism: Transformation in America's Largest Church* (Princeton, NJ: Princeton University Press, 2012). See also, for example, Margarita A. Mooney, *Faith Makes Us Live: Surviving and Thriving in the Haitian Diaspora* (Berkeley: University of California Press, 2009) and Peter C. Phan, *Vietnamese-American Catholics* (Mahwah, NJ: Paulist Press, 2005).

9. Aidan Kavanagh, *The Shape of Baptism: The Rite of Christian Initiation* (Collegeville, MN: Liturgical Press, 1991), p. 145.

10. Gerald Graff and William Cain, "Peace Plan for the Canon Wars," *The Nation* (March 6, 1989), p. 310.

11. James Davison Hunter, *Culture Wars: The Struggle to Define America* (New York: Basic Books, 1991); David Yamane, *Student Movements for Multiculturalism: Challenging the Curricular Color Line in Higher Education* (Baltimore, MD: Johns Hopkins University Press, 2001).

12. A. V. Kelly, *The Curriculum: Theory and Practice*, 6th ed. (London: Sage Publications, 2009), p. 10. The term "hidden curriculum" was coined by Philip W. Jackson in *Life in Classrooms* (New York: Holt, Rinehart & Winston, 1968), in which he focused on classrooms as loci of socialization processes beyond formal learning. It was taken up especially by critical education scholars like Michael Apple in "The Hidden Curriculum and the Nature of Conflict," *Interchange* 2 (1971):27–40, and Henry Giroux in *The Hidden Curriculum and Moral Education* (Berkeley, CA: McCutcheon Publishing, 1983).

13. E. D. Hirsch, *Cultural Literacy, What Every American Needs to Know* (Boston: Houghton Mifflin, 1987).

14. Cardinal Joseph Bernardin, *Consistent Ethic of Life* (Kansas City, MO: Sheed & Ward, 1988).

15. Alex Moore, *Teaching and Learning: Pedagogy, Curriculum, and Culture*, 2nd ed. (New York: Routledge, 2012).

16. Paulo Freire, *Pedagogy of the Oppressed* (New York: Continuum, 1970).

17. Stephen D. Brookfield and Stephen Preskill, *Discussion as a Way of Teaching: Tools and Techniques for Democratic Classrooms* (San Francisco: Jossey-Bass, 1999), pp. xv, 4. Adam Gamoran and Martin Nystrand also focus on the centrality of negotiation and reciprocity to discussion in "Background and Instructional Effects on Achievement in Eighth-Grade English and Social Studies," *Journal of Research in Adolescence* 1: 3 (1991):277–300.

18. Pope Paul VI, "Address at the Close of the Second Session of the Vatican Council," December 4, 1963, in Austin Flannery, ed. *Vatican II: The Liturgy Constitution* (Dublin: Scepter Books, 1964), p. 9, on

promulgating the document *Sacrosanctum Concilium* (Constitution on the Sacred Liturgy).

19. The foundational work here is Melvin Kohn's *Class and Conformity: A Study in Values* (Chicago: University of Chicago Press, 1977). Among the most important of the many who have pursued this line of thinking recently are Annette Lareau and her collaborators. See, for example, Laureau, *Unequal Childhoods: Class, Race, and Family Life,* 2nd ed. (Berkeley: University of California Press, 2011); Elliot B. Weininger and Annette Lareau, "Paradoxical Pathways: An Ethnographic Extension on Kohn's Findings on Class and Childrearing," *Journal of Marriage and Family* 71 (2009):680–695; Jessica McCrory Calarco, "'I Need Help!' Social Class and Children's Help-Seeking in Elementary School," *American Sociological Review* 76 (2011):862–882.

20. Amid much fanfare and controversy, this catechism was promulgated by Pope John Paul II on October 11, 1992, the 30th anniversary of the opening of the Second Vatican Council. A revised Latin typical edition was published in 1997 and is the basis for official translations like those available on the Vatican website (http://www.vatican.va/archive/ENG0015/_INDEX.HTM). See also Michael J. Walsh, ed., *Commentary on the Catechism of the Catholic Church* (Collegeville, MN: Liturgical Press, 1993) and Msgr. Michael J. Wrenn and Kenneth D. Whitehead, *Flawed Expectations: The Reception of the Catechism of the Catholic Church* (San Francisco: Ignatius Press, 1996).

21. Second Vatican Council, *Lumen Gentium* (Dogmatic Constitution on the Church), no. 40.

22. Second Vatican Council, *Lumen Gentium* (Dogmatic Constitution on the Church), nos. 40, 7–8, 32.

23. A fifteenth-century prayer made popular in the seventeenth century by Father Claude Bernard: "Remember, O most gracious Virgin Mary, that never was it known that anyone who fled to thy protection, implored thy help, or sought thine intercession was left unaided. Inspired by this confidence, I fly unto thee, O Virgin of virgins, my mother; to thee do I come, before thee I stand, sinful and sorrowful. O Mother of the Word Incarnate, despise not my petitions, but in thy mercy hear and answer me. Amen."

24. The text of the *Salve Regina* is:

> Hail, holy Queen, Mother of Mercy!
> Our life, our sweetness, and our hope!
> To thee do we cry, poor banished children of Eve;
> to thee do we send up our sighs,
>> mourning and weeping in this valley of tears.
> Turn, then, most gracious Advocate,
>> thine eyes of mercy toward us;
> and after this our exile show unto us
>> the blessed fruit of thy womb, Jesus.
> O clement, O loving, O sweet Virgin Mary.

25. Sean McCloud, *Divine Hierarchies: Class in American Religion and Religious Studies* (Chapel Hill: University of North Carolina Press), p. 14.
26. Baggett, *Sense of the Faithful,* p. 35.
27. Dorothy Bass, "Congregations and the Bearing of Traditions," p. 178.
28. Janet Eyler and Dwight E. Giles, Jr., *Where's the Learning in Service-Learning* (San Francisco: Jossey-Bass, 1999).

CHAPTER 4

1. Michele Dillon, "What Is Core to American Catholics in 2011," *National Catholic Reporter On-Line* (October 24, 2011), ncronline. org/news/catholics-america/what-core-american-catholics-2011, retrieved on September 17, 2012.
2. For some comments along these lines by a sociologist who learned to dance the Lindy Hop, see Black Hawk Hancock, "Learning How to Make Life Swing," *Qualitative Sociology* 30 (2007):113–133.
3. More than that, the lived experiences of Catholics and the understandings of the Catholic faith that grow from them constitute a *sensus fidei*—a "sense of faith" that "should be taken seriously as a source of theological insight by the whole church." Jerome

P. Baggett, *Sense of the Faithful: How American Catholics Live Their Faith* (New York: Oxford University Press, 2009), pp. 66, 233.

4. Michele Dillon, *Catholic Identity: Balancing Reason, Faith, and Power* (New York: Cambridge University Press, 1999), p. 207.

5. Dillon, "What Is Core to American Catholics in 2011."

6. Dillon, *Catholic Identity*, p. 211.

7. Margaret Mohrmann, "On Being True to Form," pp. 90–102 in Carol Taylor and Roberto Dell'Oro, eds., *Health and Human Flourishing: Religion, Medicine, and Moral Anthropology* (Washington, DC: Georgetown University Press, 2006), pp. 93, 95. I am grateful to Sandy Stroud for pointing me to the literature on formation in the medical field, which applies so well to formation in any field.

8. David Yamane and Sarah MacMillen, with Kelly Culver, *Real Stories of Christian Initiation: Lessons for and from the RCIA* (Collegeville, MN: Liturgical Press, 2006).

9. Pope Paul VI, "Address at the Close of the Second Session of the Vatican Council," December 4, 1963, in Austin Flannery, ed. *Vatican II: The Liturgy Constitution* (Dublin: Scepter Books, 1964), p. 9, on promulgating the document *Sacrosanctum Concilium* (Constitution on the Sacred Liturgy).

10. Pope Benedict XVI, *Sacramentum Caritatis*, Post-Synodal Apostolic Exhortation on the Eucharist as the Source and Summit of the Church's Life and Mission, February 27, 2007, no. 64. http://www.vatican.va/holy_father/benedict_xvi/apost_exhortations/documents/hf_ben-xvi_exh_20070222_sacramentum-caritatis_en.html, Accessed September 19, 2012.

11. Susan Ridgely Bales, *When I Was a Child: Children's Interpretations of First Communion* (Chapel Hill: University of North Carolina Press, 2005).

12. Mark Searle, "The Rites of Christian Initiation," pp. 457–470 in Louise Carus Mahdi, Steven Foster, and Meredith Little, eds., *Betwixt and Between: Patterns of Masculine and Feminine Initiation* (LaSalle, IL: Open Court, 1987), p. 462.

13. Baggett, *Sense of the Faithful*, p. 21.

14. David Wells, *God in the Wasteland: The Realities of Truth in a World of Fading Dreams* (Grand Rapids, MI: Eerdmans, 1994), p. 90.

15. Thomas Landy, "A Place for Sacrifice: American Catholics and the Religious Value of Sacrifice" (unpublished doctoral dissertation, Department of Sociology, Boston University, August 2000), p. 1, 60, 213. *Baltimore Catechism,* no. 3 (New York: Benziger Bros., 1952), number 357, quoted in Landy, "A Place for Sacrifice," p. 62.

16. Landy, "A Place for Sacrifice," p. 1.

17. Alan Wolfe, *The Transformation of American Religion: How We Actually Live Our Faith* (New York: Free Press, 2003).

18. Landy, "A Place for Sacrifice," p. 64.

19. Landy, "A Place for Sacrifice," pp. 13, 212, 213, 218.

20. Landy, "A Place for Sacrifice," pp. 124–125, 213.

21. Father Seraphim Michalenko, *The Divine Mercy Message and Devotion,* rev. ed. (Stockbridge, MA: Marian Press, 2001) pp. 13–15, 48–51.

22. Patricia Benner, "Formation in Professional Education: An Examination of the Relationship between Theories of Meaning and Theories of the Self," *Journal of Medicine and Philosophy* 36: 4 (2011):342–353.

23. Patricia Benner, Molly Sutphen, and Victoria Leonard, *Educating Nurses: A Call for Radical Transformation* (San Francisco, CA: Jossey-Bass, 2009), p. 89.

CHAPTER 5

1. Ronald Grimes, *Deeply into the Bone: Re-Inventing Rites of Passage* (Berkeley: University of California Press, 2000), pp. 98, 100. I am sympathetic to this point of view. As the title suggests—highlighting the *real* over the ideal—my book with Sarah MacMillen and Kelly Culver, *Real Stories of Christian Initiation: Lessons for and from the RCIA* (Collegeville, MN: Liturgical Press, 2006), is a more general response to this challenge.

2. Quoted in Mark Searle, "The Rites of Christian Initiation," pp. 457–470 in *Betwixt and Between: Patterns of Masculine and Feminine Initiation,* eds. Louise Carus Mahdi, Stephen Foster, and Meredith Little (LaSalle, IL: Open Court, 1987), p. 465.

3. Edward Yarnold, *The Awe-Inspiring Rites of Initiation: The Origins of the RCIA*, 2nd ed. (Collegeville, MN: Liturgical Press, 1994).

4. Yamane and MacMillen, *Real Stories of Christian Initiation*, chapter 4. As we recount in the epilogue to that chapter, to his credit in the year following our observation, Deacon Zeke implemented changes, including a two-day Lenten retreat, celebration of the scrutinies in the context of the Mass, and participation in the Rite of Election with the bishop at the cathedral.

5. Catherine Bell, *Ritual: Perspectives and Dimensions* (New York: Oxford University Press, 1997), p. 57, quoting Vincent Crapanzano, "Rite of Return: Circumcision in Morocco," pp. 15–36 in Werner Muensterberger and L. Bryce Boyer, eds. *The Psychoanalytic Study of Society* 9 (1981), (New York: Psychohistory Press, 1981) p. 32.

6. M. E. F. Bloch, "Symbols, Song, Dance and Features of Articulation," *European Journal of Sociology* 15/1 (1974):4.

7. J. S. La Fontaine, *Initiation* (Manchester, UK: Manchester University Press, 1986), pp. 184–185.

8. Susan Ridgely Bales, *When I Was a Child: Children's Interpretations of First Communion* (Chapel Hill: University of North Carolina Press, 2005), p. 5.

9. David Yamane, "Narrative and Religious Experience," *Sociology of Religion* 61 (2000):171–189.

10. Bales, *When I Was a Child*, p. 172.

11. Bales, *When I Was a Child*, pp. 123, 124, 146.

12. Grimes, *Deeply into the Bone*, p. 104.

13. La Fontaine, *Initiation*, p. 185.

CHAPTER 6

1. James D. Shaughnessy, ed., *Made, Not Born: New Perspectives on Christian Initiation and the Catechumenate* (Notre Dame, IN: University of Notre Dame Press, 1985).

2. e. e. cummings, *100 Selected Poems* (New York: Grove Press, 1954), p. 35.

3. Michael Leach and Therese J. Borchard, eds., *I Like Being Catholic: Treasured Traditions, Rituals, and Stories* (New York: Doubleday,

2000); Andrew Greeley, *The Catholic Revolution: New Wine, Old Wineskins, and the Second Vatican Council* (Berkeley: University of California Press, 2004), chapter 9.

4. Thomas Landy, "A Place for Sacrifice: American Catholics and the Religious Value of Sacrifice," unpublished doctoral dissertation, Boston University, August 2000, p. 22, citing Clifford Geertz, *Islam Observed: Religious Development in Morocco and Indonesia* (Chicago: University of Chicago Press, 1968), p. 97; Michael Polanyi, *The Tacit Dimension* (Chicago: University of Chicago Press, 2009 [1966]) p. 4; Robert Wuthnow, *Meaning and Moral Order: Explorations in Cultural Analysis* (Berkeley: University of California Press, 1987), p. 46, quoted in Landy, "A Place for Sacrifice," p. 21.

5. Meredith B. McGuire, "What Really Matters," *Spiritus: A Journal of Christian Spirituality* 6 (Spring 2006):107–112.

6. Robert Bellah, *Beyond Beliefs: Essays on Religion in a Post-Traditional World* (New York: Harper & Row, 1970), p. 203. I make some arguments along these same lines in David Yamane, "Beyond Beliefs: Religion and the Sociology of Religion in America," *Social Compass* 54(1):33–48.

7. This section is based on statistical models that are fully reported in David Yamane, "Initiation Rites in the Contemporary Catholic Church: What Difference Do They Make?" *Review of Religious Research* 54 (December 2012):401–20. Technically speaking, I employ a quasi-experimental (nonequivalent group, pre-test/post-test) design—collecting data on individuals at the beginning of their involvement in the RCIA process and after their initiation at the Easter Vigil (N = 159)—to identify the extent of change in different domains of religiosity over the course of the RCIA process. I use organizational-level data on characteristics of the RCIA process in 32 different parishes to explain differences in the extent of individual change. I am, therefore, in the unique position of being able to assess directly the effect of differences in the implementation of the RCIA on the quality of initiation into the Catholic Church.

8. An anonymous reviewer of this research correctly observed that "a lower level of [Bible] reading might not necessarily mean a low level." It is the case that at the end of the process the average level

of Bible reading was 4.29—above the category "once a month" (= 4)—compared to 4.82 at the start.

9. Michael J. McCallion, David R. Maines, and Steven Wolfel, "Policy as Practice: Holy Communion as a Contested Situation," *Journal of Contemporary Ethnography* 25 (2006):300–326; David R. Maines and Michael J. McCallion, *Transforming Catholicism: Liturgical Change in the Vatican II Church* (Lanham, MD: Lexington Books, 2007).

10. Michael J. McCallion and David R. Maines, "Spiritual Gatekeepers: Time and the Rite of Christian Initiation of Adults," *Symbolic Interaction* 25 (2002):289–302.

11. Thomas Morris, *The RCIA: Transforming the Church, A Resource for Pastoral Implementation* (New York: Paulist Press, 1997).

12. Although ideally ongoing inquiry corresponds with multiple Rites of Acceptance, many of the parishes that have ongoing inquiry simply hold over their inquirers so that multiple groups of inquirers come together into a common celebration of the Rite of Acceptance.

CONCLUSION

1. For example, Rodney Stark, *The Rise of Christianity: How the Obscure, Marginal Jesus Movement Became the Dominant Religious Force in the Western World in a Few Centuries* (San Francisco: HarperCollins, 1997). The Wikipedia entry "List of Converts to Catholicism" includes other interesting and well-known figures such as actors Gary Cooper and Faye Dunaway, politicians Tony Blair and Sam Brownback, theologians Jacques Maritain and Avery Dulles, musician Dave Brubeck, tenor Andrea Bocelli, and Oglala Sioux medicine-man Black Elk. en.wikipedia.org/wiki/List_of_converts_to_Catholicism, accessed January 3, 2013. Sociologist Christian Smith, on whose work I build in Chapter 2 of this book, recounts his own "shift" from evangelical Protestantism to Roman Catholicism in *How to Go from Being a Good Evangelical to a Committed Catholic in Ninety-Five Difficult Steps* (Eugene, OR: Cascade Books, 2011).

2. Mircea Eliade, *Rites and Symbols of Initiation: The Mysteries of Birth and Rebirth* (Putnam, CT: Spring Publications, 1994 [1958]), p. ix.

3. Ronald L. Grimes, *Deeply into the Bone: Re-Inventing Rites of Passage* (Berkeley: University of California Press, 2000), p. 100.

4. National Conference of Catholic Bishops, *Journey to the Fullness of Life: A Report on the Implementation of the Rite of Christian Initiation of Adults in the United States* (Washington, DC: United States Catholic Conference, 2000). But see David Yamane and Sarah MacMillen, with Kelly Culver, *Real Stories of Christian Initiation: Lessons for and from the RCIA* (Collegeville, MN: Liturgical Press, 2006), Table 2, for data from the bishops' study on the unevenness of implementation of various components of the RCIA process.

5. Jerome Baggett, *Sense of the Faithful: How American Catholics Live Their Faith* (New York: Oxford University Press, 2009), p. 215.

6. *Gaudium et Spes* (Pastoral Constitution on the Church in the Modern World), no. 4, www.vatican.va/archive/hist_councils/ii_vatican_council/documents/vat-ii_cons_19651207_gaudium-et-spes_en.html, accessed January 1, 2013.

7. Of course, as Baggett observes, "The expression 'living tradition' is commonly used, but, because traditions are organic, ongoing conversations with the past, it is actually redundant" (*Sense of the Faithful*, p. 212).

8. Nancy T. Ammerman, Jackson W. Carroll, Carl S. Dudley, and William McKinney, *Studying Congregations: A New Handbook* (Nashville, TN: Abingdon Press, 1998); Nancy T. Ammerman, "Congregations: Local, Social, and Religious," pp. 562–580 in Peter B. Clarke, ed., *Oxford Handbook of the Sociology of Religion* (New York: Oxford University Press, 2009); Cynthia Woolever and Deborah Bruce, *A Field Guide to U.S. Congregations: Who's Going Where and Why*, 2nd ed. (Louisville, KY: Westminster John Knox Press, 2010). See also "The U.S. Congregational Life Survey," www.uscongregations.org, accessed June 10, 2012.

9. Melvin M. Mark and Jennifer Mills, "Experiments and Quasi-Experiments for Decision Making: Why, How, and How Good?," pp. 459–482 in Goktug Morcol, ed. *Handbook of Decision Making*

(New York: CRC Press, 2007). As previously noted, the complete statistical models presented briefly in Chapter 6 are available in David Yamane, "Initiation Rites in the Contemporary Catholic Church: What Difference Do They Make?" *Review of Religious Research* 54 (December 2012):401–420.

10. The *Rite of Christian Initiation of Adults* itself, as the vernacular typical edition of the *Ordo Initiationis Adultorum Christianae,* represents an adaptation of the universal rite to the American context, a power delegated to the conferences of bishops in the Congregation for Divine Worship's "Christian Initiation, General Introduction" (no. 30). The most notable adaptations made by the American bishops are the inclusion of "additional (combined) rites" for situations in which both unbaptized and baptized individuals are present, which I discuss in the caveat in Chapter 1. Also by this authority, the American bishops issued their *National Statutes for the Catechumenate* (published as Appendix III in the *Rite*), which govern the adult initiation process specifically in the United States, but nowhere else in the (Catholic) world.

11. David R. Maines and Michael McCallion, *Transforming Catholicism: Liturgical Change in the Vatican II Church* (Lanham, MD: Lexington Books, 2007), p. x.

12. Joseph Gremillion and Jim Castelli, *The Emerging Parish: The Notre Dame Study of Catholic Life since Vatican II* (San Francisco: Harper & Row, 1987), p. 47; Chester Gillis, *Roman Catholicism in America* (New York: Columbia University Press, 1999), p. 32; R. Stephen Warner, "Work in Progress Toward a New Paradigm for the Sociological Study of Religion in the United States," *American Journal of Sociology* 98 (March 1993): pp. 1044–1093.

13. To attempt to bring some empirical evidence to bear on this question, in 2006 I attempted a four-to-five-year follow-up survey, one page in length, of the 167 individuals for whom I had two complete waves of data (including 159 who completed the initiation process). The results were disappointing, to say the least. Of the 167 mail surveys I sent out, I received just 8 responses. But just over half of the letters were returned to me as undeliverable because the individuals had moved and their forwarding orders had expired. This led me to

wonder whether a large segment of the "disappearing" RCIA initiates are not in the parishes they were initiated at because they had
moved. I cannot answer this definitively, but it is worth some further
investigation.

Another large segment probably have lowered or discontinued
their involvement five years after their initiation. Certainly not all,
but probably a large proportion of the 43% who received but did not
return their surveys fall into this category. The survey was just six
questions long, so I read the failure to respond as indicating a disengagement from the church (perhaps this is just hubris on my part,
though). Among the eight surveys that were returned, one individual
was still in his same parish but was attending Mass less than once a
month, and one was no longer involved in any church, Catholic or
other.

With a response rate of 10% of the 80 surveys that were delivered,
it is impossible to say anything generalizable about the eight respondents to my follow-up survey. But we do well sometimes to focus
on individuals and not just averages. Six of the individuals who responded to my follow-up survey continued to be actively involved in
their parishes, attending Mass weekly or nearly weekly and praying regularly. Half of these are even more involved in the life of
their parishes, including "Coach K," who serves as a Sunday school
teacher and middle school youth ministry volunteer at St. Mary's,
and Mary Miller who volunteers with St. Mark's ministry to the
sick. Rachel Dowdell, who was initiated at St. Innocent, has gone so
far as to become the director of youth ministry there.

14. Mark Searle, "The Rites of Christian Initiation," pp. 457–470 in
    Louise Carus Mahdi, Steven Foster, and Meredith Little, eds., *Be-
    twixt and Between: Patterns of Masculine and Feminine Initiation*
    (LaSalle, IL: Open Court, 1987), p. 469.

INDEX

action, theories of, 52–53, 58, 221n7
  See also moral actor theory, rational
    choice theory
authority, orientations to, 19, 91,
  100–102, 104, 107, 109, 112
  See also Catholicism—visions of, cur-
    riculum, social class
American Catholics Today surveys, 121,
  137

Baggett, Jerome, vi, 5, 21, 83, 111–12,
  122–23, 135, 196
Bales, Susan Ridgely, 130, 157–59
baptized adults. *See* Candidates for Full
  Communion with the Catholic Church
beliefs. *See* Catholicism—core beliefs
Bell, Catherine, 155
Bellah, Robert, x, 3, 65–66, 68, 182
bible reading. *See* spiritual practice
Bruce, Tricia, 23
Brusselmans, Christiane, 31

Call to Continuing Conversion. *See* Rite
  of Election
Candidates for Full Communion with the
  Catholic Church, 39
catechesis, 16, 19, 23, 30, 38, 40, 83–114,
  198, 225n2
  See also curriculum, formation
Catechism of the Catholic Church, 105,
  122, 158

Catechumenate, Period of the, xi, 17, 33,
  34, 84–85, 189, 190, 198
catechumenate
  as model of faith formation, 40
  in ancient church, xi, 12–13, 28–29,
    198
  restoration of the, 27, 28–29, 196
catechumens, xi, 12, 29, 33, 36, 38, 84,
  189
Catholic, meaning of being, 19, 23, 85,
  90, 92, 102, 121, 125, 172–81, 192
  See also formation
Catholicism
  as living tradition, 83, 113, 122, 235n7
  core beliefs, 83, 90–94, 121, 179–80,
    182
  universal and local, 19, 159, 187–88,
    203–5
  visions of, 19–20, 83, 85, 90, 92, 112
  See also authority—orientations to,
    catechesis, curriculum, formation
class. *See* social class
Coleman, James, 57–58, 222n21
congregationalism, de facto, 204
Constitution on the Sacred Liturgy (*Sacrosanctum Concilium*), 7, 18, 25–27,
  203, 205
conversion, 13–14, 17–18, 49–50, 51, 195
  "everyday conversion," 50–51, 195
  mechanisms of, 51, 71
  motivations for, 52, 71